MINING COUNTRY

A HISTORY OF CANADA'S MINES AND MINERS

JOHN SANDLOS AND ARN KEELING

JAMES LORIMER & COMPANY LTD., PUBLIS

TORONTO

For our families, and for the mining communities who
have generously shared their knowledge with us.

James Lorimer & Company Ltd., Publishers acknowledges funding support from the Ontario Arts Council (OAC), an agency of the Government of Ontario. We acknowledge the support of the Canada Council for the Arts, which last year invested $153 million to bring the arts to Canadians throughout the country. This project has been made possible in part by the Government of Canada and with the support of the Ontario Media Development Corporation.

Cover design: Tyler Cleroux

Front cover: Flickr/Murray Foubister (top), BC Archives (bottom left, B-05286), Northwest Territories Archives (bottom centre, N-1979-052-7798), Library and Archives Canada (bottom right, C-023983)

Back cover: Wikimedia/Diego Delso (top left), Royal BC Museum and Archives (top right, E-02631), Library and Archives Canada (centre left, 4086000), Thunder Bay Museum (centre), Nunavut Archives (centre right, N-1979-051: 2316S), University of Washington Libraries (bottom left)

Library and Archives Canada Cataloguing in Publication

Title: Mining country : a history of Canada's mines and miners / John Sandlos and Arn Keeling.
Names: Sandlos, John, 1970- author. | Keeling, Arn, author.
Description: Includes bibliographical references and index.
Identifiers: Canadiana 20200312294 | ISBN 9781459413535 (softcover)
Subjects: LCSH: Mines and mineral resources—Canada—History. | LCSH: Mineral industries—Canada—History. | LCSH: Mining corporations—Canada—History. | LCSH: Miners—Canada—History.
Classification: LCC TN26 .S26 2021 | DDC 622.0971—dc23

James Lorimer & Company Ltd., Publishers
117 Peter Street, Suite 304
Toronto, ON, Canada
M5V 0M3
www.lorimer.ca

Printed and bound in Korea.

Contents

Dredge No. 4 National Historic Site at Bonanza Creek near Dawson City, Yukon. Part of the Klondike National Historic Sites complex, the site symbolizes the enduring popularity of Canada's mining history and heritage.

Introduction

Mining consolidated the Canadian Provinces — East and West; fostered the construction of railways and the demand for highways and airways. Mining transformed the Wilderness; established new frontiers; extended urban centres; encouraged civilisation and stimulated prosperity in critical periods.
— B.F. Townsley, *Mine-Finders: The History and Romance of Canadian Mineral Discoveries* (1935)

Mine: blast: dump: crush: extract: exhaust — there was indeed something devilish and sinister about the whole business.

— Lewis Mumford, *Technics and Civilization* (1934)

Among the multitude of human economic activities, few inspire such romantic and nostalgic accounts as the discovery and development of mines. From legends of El Dorado to the prospectors of the Klondike, mining (especially, but not exclusively, for gold) has long fired the imagination with tales of instant riches dug from the earth. Exploration for minerals, in this positive view, lured humans to far reaches of Earth, expanding geographical knowledge and driving the expansion of the European powers. Many still celebrate the industry as a nation-building enterprise, promoting frontier mining as the best opportunity for development in otherwise "empty" territories. In older mining towns, many of which have suffered the shock of mine closure, residents still look longingly to the excitement of the early boom days and the esprit de corps among the families who inhabited frontier mining communities. For its boosters, mining is not only a source of considerable local wealth, but has provided the lion's share of the critical materials that sustain cities and enable our modern, technology-driven lifestyles.

Mining also inspires intense feelings from a largely opposing viewpoint. The industry's detractors have long linked mining with the unbridled exploitation of both people and the environment. According to this darker view of mining history, prospectors and geologists did not merely conduct a courageous search for valuable minerals, but served as agents of empire who laid the groundwork for the violent conquest and dispossession of distant lands. Even the most legendary mines of the "New World" (such as Potosí in Bolivia, sources of Spanish imperial wealth beginning in the sixteenth century) are sullied by their association with slavery and death. Throughout much of the industry's long history, critics have noted that mining work is notoriously dangerous, workers have been subject

to low wages and other forms of exploitation, and boom–bust mining economies have become synonymous with resource exhaustion and community collapse

From the earliest days of the industry, observers have condemned the environmental impacts of mining, such as the construction of massive tailings ponds, the production of waste-rock piles, the pollution of waterways, and the emission of toxic smelter smoke.

Much popular mining history reflects the boosterish side of these polarized views. In North America especially, mining history has tended to be of the "sourdoughs and gold pans" variety: stories that are intensely local and generally celebratory. These histories often provide valuable records of the communities founded by mining and the colourful people associated with developing the mining frontier. Yet rarely do such accounts look beyond local developments to consider how these communities fit into the wider pattern of mining as an industry. Nor do they reckon with the products (and byproducts) of mining — what historian William Cronon called the "paths out of town" — that connected remote mines and settlements to industrial technologies and consumers in distant cities, and that linked mining activities to their "downstream" ecological impacts.

In this book, we explore both sides of the historical debate over Canadian mining history without embracing either extreme. Our work acknowledges that mineral products are undoubtedly central to the economies and lifestyles of our contemporary world, and mining holds a prominent — if curiously neglected — place in the history of Canadian colonization and development. At the same time, we acknowledge that these benefits (if

The Horne smelter at Rouyn-Noranda, Quebec was opened in 1927 to process ore from the nearby Horne mine. Although the mine closed in 1976 the smelter continues to process metals from other sources.

indeed they are seen as such) have also come with great costs: the dispossession of Indigenous groups from their land base, the maiming and death of mine labourers, and the degradation of the environment. The multiple mining stories included in this book do not add up to a simple homage or denunciation of mining, but they do indicate the industry's generally neglected importance to the history of Canada and the legacies of this history for mining communities and regions today.

Mining Country introduces readers to major themes and developments in the history of Canadian mining, from Indigenous trade in minerals to the large-scale, integrated industrial developments of the late twentieth century. The search for valuable minerals, we argue, played a key role in the expansion of European settlement and economic activity in northern North America, and the interactions between colonists and Indigenous peoples. By the early twentieth century, mining emerged as the sole resource industry with a significant presence in every region of Canada, from east to west coasts to the northern territories. Over the century since, mining became a significant contributor to Canada's resource economy, and Canadian companies rose to become some of the world's most prominent mining firms. Yet aside from a lively body of locally focused popular histories and some scholarly case studies, there is no general synthesis of mining history in Canada. Although some (largely celebratory) chronicles of mineral discoveries and major developments appeared in the mid-twentieth century, a general narrative of Canadian mining history remained, until now, unwritten.

Our approach to this history reflects themes and issues we have encountered in our own research into the twentieth-century history and geography of mining in northern Canada. In this, it departs from the heroic narratives of prominent "mine-finders" or social histories of mining settlements (although these themes are not totally absent). Nor do we focus intently on mineral geology or the development of specific mining technologies (except in passing). Instead, we focus on the broad pattern of Canada's mining history, highlighting significant episodes and developments in each period. In doing so, we illuminate five key themes in the history of Canadian mining.

The first of these is the industry's fraught relationship with Indigenous peoples. From its earliest days in Canada, mineral exploration and development engendered conflict with Indigenous peoples over land and access to resources. Popular narratives of mineral "discoveries" have tended to obscure the role of Indigenous knowledge of minerals, elevating instead the role of the hardy (white) prospector. The mineral rushes that followed such discoveries often led to the invasion of Indigenous territories and pressure on Indigenous communities to sign treaties granting access to mineral lands. As our account shows, Euro-Canadian and Indigenous interactions on the mining frontier have long been a mixture of conflict, resistance, and accommodation, often to the detriment of Indigenous sovereignty, land use, and economies. Complicating this story of conflict, however, is the fact that there is also a long history of Indigenous mining, from extensive pre-contact mineral trades, through the colonial and national periods when Indigenous people prospected and worked for mines. This history provides a foundation for the extensive engagement of Indigenous communities with the mining industry today.

A second major theme is the experiences of workers who made their livelihoods in the industry. Mining has long been one of the most dangerous industrial occupations, particularly for underground miners. For much of its history, the industry paid very poor wages and often imposed close company control of working conditions — all fuel for the potent clashes between labour and mining capital that characterize the industry's history in Canada and beyond. While not solely a labour history, our story highlights the often brutal and exploitative conditions faced by workers and the frequent tragedies that rocked mining communities. From the deadly coal fields of Cape Breton and Vancouver Island to the radiological hazards of radium

Diamond drilling at Pine Point, Northwest Territories, 1964. Mining often attracted workers and technology to previously remote regions of Canada in search of valuable minerals.

and uranium mines to the lung-destroying environment of asbestos workers, miners suffered from long-term health issues as much as they did the immediate dangers of the underground environment. In many cases these workers resisted the negligence and outright hostility of management, often engaging in strikes and other organized resistance that reflected the intense camaraderie and solidarity forged through their shared daily experience of the hazards of the job.

Of course, no history of mine labour would be complete without considering the places in which the workers lived. As with other resource industries, mining was often characterized by the creation of that classic Canadian settlement form: the single-industry town. This was a community whose economy and reason for being originated with and remained reliant on the mine (and thus the company). Though our story focuses closely on the industrial work of mineral production, it also touches on the dynamics of mining communities — from the company-controlled townsites clustered around the pithead of colonial coal mines, to the chaotic boomtowns of the country's many mineral rushes, to the carefully planned modern mining settlements of Canada's mid-twentieth-century northern resource frontier. Mining communities were frequently polyglot and transient places, attracting workers and their families from across the country and around the world to often remote, hardscrabble locations. As our history shows, however, rather than forming the basis for permanent, stable communities, their singular reliance on a finite resource supplying volatile markets often left mining towns subject to economic busts that could turn even the best-planned community into a virtual ghost town.

The decline of human communities is mirrored in the book's fourth major theme: the destructive environmental impacts of mining. With a few exceptions (notably placer mining), mineral extraction entails the breaking up of rock formations so as to extract the typically tiny percentage that is valuable ore. Because waste rock and mine tailings can carry a veritable laundry list of toxic material (lead, cadmium, mercury, arsenic, etc.), mining and mineral processing has been associated with waste, pollution, and environmental degradation since at least Roman times. Canada's experience is no different, and this book reckons with the often dramatic and destructive environmental changes associated with mineral development. Key to understanding these changes, we show, is the scale of mining activity and the technologies of extraction and processing employed. While small-scale, high-grade mining (such as Indigenous copper-quarrying or pioneer gold-panning) may create some localized disturbances, the advent of large-scale, capital-intensive mining technologies beginning in the late nineteenth century magnified and extended these impacts through the comprehensive disassembly of local landscapes. These processes not only enabled the extraction of ever-smaller fractions of target minerals, but also destroyed surface environments and liberated formerly inert substances, from sulphur to heavy metals and other toxic contaminants. Industry actors often resisted environmental regulation, claiming that mining affected only a small portion of Canada's vast land base. But by the late twentieth century many in Canada had concluded that the environmental cost of mining exceeded its benefits, and demanded tighter rules and the cleanup of degraded lands.

The book's final theme assesses these environmental legacies and the competing interpretations applied to post-mining sites. For people associated with the mining industry — from companies to workers to exploration geologists — old mines represent a living record of a way of life, a source of pride and identity etched into the landscape. Such sentiments are amply displayed in the many heritage museums, interpretive sites, and web pages dedicated to mining history. These commemorations often emphasize nostalgic stories from early exploration rushes, the "good old days" of a mine's (and mining community's) early history, and the development of new mining technologies. Mining heritage sites may also embrace the less salutary aspects of the industry, serving as poignant memorials to the lives lost and communities shattered by mining tragedies or health impacts. It is far less common, however, for heritage sites to acknowledge the long-term legacies of physical and environmental hazards from mining. From hidden mine shafts to abandoned open pits and massive toxic sites, the landscape scars left behind are often slow to heal and may leave behind long-term hazards threatening the environment and human health. While federal, provincial, and territorial governments (and to some extent the mining industry) have begun to address some of these sites through mine cleanup and remediation, environmental problems at many other sites remain unaddressed or difficult to resolve, saddling future generations with the long-term legacy costs of intensive mining development.

While our coverage of Canada's mining history is comprehensive, it is not complete. We address many of the country's most significant historical mines and, where possible, follow them through time. Although we aim for broad regional coverage, due to source and space limitations prominent mines in some parts of the country may receive scant mention. In addition, our focus is mainly confined to metal mining (hard-rock and placer) and coal. The extraction for quarrying and construction are not addressed because the industry is organized around a vast number of smaller extractive operations. A history of every gravel pit by the highway is simply not possible, though the accumulated impact of such quarrying has caused considerable controversy in some regions (i.e., the Niagara Escarpment) and even inspired a protest song by singer Sarah Harmer. Nor do we address, except briefly, the country's oil and gas industry, including the oil sands. Although there are similarities with some forms of surface mining (especially for coal), the boom in oil sands extraction is of relatively recent vintage and tied more to unique global energy markets than "traditional" mining.

One goal of this book is to highlight the importance of mining history for all Canadians, not just those who work in the industry or live in mining towns. The predominantly rural and remote location of most mineral developments means that most Canadians have little direct experience of mining — even as they remain deeply entangled with mining through the consumption of minerals. We are all "mineral people" (as historian Timothy LeCain argues), whose daily lives are intertwined with and shaped by mineral-based technologies, economies, and infrastructures. From the remotest northern mine sites to the canyons of Toronto's Bay Street (a global centre of mining capital), Canada itself is very much a mining nation, a country shaped by the extraction, trade, and consumption of minerals. A richer, critical understanding of the industry's history in Canada, we hope, will contribute to contemporary debates around the costs, benefits, and practices of mining, both in this country and beyond.

Ramah Bay on the northeast coast of Labrador, site of an ancient quarry for chert, a silica rock Maritime Archaic Indigenous peoples used and traded as raw material for toolmaking beginning at least 7500 years ago.

CHAPTER 1
Deep Roots

The origins of mineral extraction in the territories we now call North America lie not with the arrival of Europeans, but stretch back into the ancient worlds of the continent's Indigenous peoples. Nobody knows exactly when mining began in North America, but the continent's first people likely gathered all manner of rocks for useful purposes — chert, slate, or quartzite for tools and weapons, or in some areas soapstone for the carving of symbolic crafts — since their arrival at least 13,000 to 15,000 years ago. The Plano culture in Ontario built the oldest known mine in what is now Canada, a quartzite quarry at Sheguiandah on Manitoulin Island dated to 10,000 years ago. Approximately 7,500 years ago the Maritime Archaic people who inhabited the Labrador coast mined Ramah Bay chert (a prized tool-making silica rock) and traded it extensively in the Atlantic region. From very early in the human history of North America, geological material travelled along extensive networks as valued trade goods, connecting cultural groups across vast regional systems of exchange.

Undoubtedly the most extensive Indigenous mining activity in ancient North America was the copper mining

Stone hammer found at Ramah Bay, Labrador, used to extract and process chert.

Pictograph of Mishipeshu on the rocks of Agawa Bay on the east shore of Lake Superior in Ontario's Lake Superior Provincial Park. The Anishinaabe and other Indigenous groups depicted this mythological creature as a water lynx or panther, sometimes with horns made of pure copper. One of the creature's main roles was guardian of copper in the Great Lakes region.

Ancient mine in a copper-bearing vein on the east side of Isle Royale, an island in Lake Superior near the modern boundary between Michigan and Ontario.

and trading complex in the eastern part of the continent. At some point during the Archaic period (ca. 7900 BCE to the start of the Common Era), certainly by 4800–5000 BCE and possibly as far back as 6800 BCE, Indigenous people in the Eastern Woodland region of North America began to extract copper from surface deposits and work the malleable metal into a wide array of tools, projectile points, and finely crafted decorative objects. Although Indigenous people mined other metals such as gold, silver, lead (in its galena form), and meteoric iron, the much larger deposits of native (i.e., mostly pure) copper in the Eastern Woodlands and the western sub-Arctic provided a much more reliable and easier-to-exploit source of raw material. By far the largest producing area was the Lake Superior region, where archaeologist Kathleen Ehrhardt has estimated that Indigenous people excavated five thousand mines, mostly in the form of shallow pits and trenches that are still visible in some places.

There is no precise accounting of how much copper may have been extracted in the region, though Ehrhardt has ventured five thousand tons as a plausible estimate,

a significant contribution to the material wealth of Indigenous communities who engaged in mining. Most of the metal was extracted on the American side of the lake, in Michigan's Keweenaw Peninsula and on Isle Royale, but sources of accessible copper also existed on Superior's north shore. Some archaeologists have suggested that local areas of Indigenous production arose around the "float" or "drift" copper that the glaciers carried south and east from the Keweenaw as far as Illinois and New York. Indigenous people also mined copper in New England, the Mid-Atlantic States, the Appalachians, and on the shores of the Bay of Fundy in Nova Scotia. By 1000 CE, Indigenous people in Yukon and Alaska developed an important northern production area in the rich native copper deposits of the Wrangell–St. Elias region. Although Indigenous miners were far from dependent on copper for their survival, it became an economically important trade item in regions where it was extracted, a commodity that offered immediate practical utility but which also became culturally significant, woven into the stories, mortuary rituals, and spiritual life of those who mined it. The spiritual and practical significance of copper to Anishinaabe (Ojibway) people of the Superior Region is reflected in the figure of Mishipeshu, a fierce lynx-like creature living in the Great Lakes said to possess horns and scales of copper and who is the guardian of the sacred metal.

The Indigenous copper economy relied entirely on native copper deposits rather than the low-grade copper sulphide ores that were so important to development of industrial mining in nineteenth century North America. Copper is one of the few metallic minerals that can be extracted in relatively pure form. In the Keweenaw, the geological forces that produced so much native copper are complex, and played out over almost unimaginable spans of deep time. In brief, an increase in volcanic activity approximately 1.1 billion years ago resulted in repeated layering of magma and volcanic rock. The upward movement of the Earth's mantle produced a long rift that stretches from present-day Kansas to Lake Superior. Immense forces of compression pushed the edges of the rift upwards into a syncline with reverse faults on either side. As subsequent lava flows filled the fault lines and cooled, additional openings formed in the rock due to cracking, further faulting, and the rapid cooling of gas bubbles. Twenty to thirty million years after the layering of volcanic rock began, dissolved copper, occasional silver, and many other economically insignificant minerals began to flow into these empty spaces, carried along by thermally heated water from below and remaining as precipitate when cooling occurred. While forces of erosion carried large quantities of these minerals away with other sediment to form lower-grade copper ores, large deposits of native copper remained at, or just below the surface in erosion-resistant rock, settling as small pebbles, fine sheets, or large (at times boulder-sized) chunks of pure copper that formed the material base of the Indigenous copper economy.

As with prospectors and miners today, Indigenous methods of locating and exploiting these copper deposits likely involved a mixture of ingenuity and luck. Within the broader copper region, Indigenous miners inevitably stumbled on copper deposits exposed by water erosion or glacial scouring, the green hue of partially oxidized copper providing a dead giveaway that often led to additional deposits beneath the surface. When deposits remained wholly below the surface, Indigenous miners likely looked for telltale signs such as stunted vegetation, depressions in the soil indicating a fissure deposit, or exposed veins of companion minerals associated with copper. In the Keweenaw, it is possible that miners realized over time that the richest native copper deposits sat within a narrow band three to six kilometres wide that ran along the peninsula from present-day Wisconsin to the Indigenous copper mining complex on Isle Royale. Depending on the type of deposit, Indigenous miners engaged in two types of mining: fissure mining involved the construction of shafts that followed a vertical vein to depths of more than six metres, and lode mining consisted of uncovering copper veins in shallow pits of roughly two metres depth.

Indigenous miners began the extraction process with the removal of overburden (vegetation, soil, gravel), then proceeded to fracture the rock surrounding the deposit with stone hammers. The miners then hammered more precisely to cut the copper deposit away from the surrounding rock. Archaeological evidence suggests that Indigenous miners may have also used wooden paddles and flat rocks for digging and stripping away waste rock. They may have ignited and then rapidly extinguished fires to aid in the process of rock fracturing, but the scattered evidence of ancient burning is inconclusive. In some limited cases they may have used logs as wooden scaffolding to secure deeper shafts or trenches, but there is no evidence of underground tunnelling. This basic approach to copper mining remained remarkably consistent over thousands of years, even as the practical and cultural objects produced from the material changed. At the same time, centuries of Indigenous mining caused significant environmental changes in copper-rich areas, producing large areas where abandoned pits and trenches, many still visible centuries later, dominated the landscape. Recent studies have attributed ancient increases of lead deposition in the smaller lakes of the Superior region to surges in copper-mining activity. Though not on the scale of water issues associated

Archaeologists working in the Drier Copper Pit, McCargo Cove, Isle Royale, 1953.

Depiction of ancient copper mining on Lake Superior created by J.C. Tidball, originally published in *The History of the Indian Tribes of the United States*, by Henry R. Schoolcraft, 1855.

with modern mining, Indigenous copper miners in the Lake Superior region did pollute local lakes as their excavation process released toxic material from the rock surrounding the native copper deposits.

Once the copper was extracted there remained the task of processing it into a workable form. Copper is a malleable substance that could be shaped simply through repeated hammering. As the material thinned it became vulnerable to stress fracturing, splitting, and breakage. In response, Indigenous copper workers employed the technique of annealing, heating the copper to over two hundred degrees Celsius so that it recrystallized into a form that was both tougher and more malleable. There is no evidence that Indigenous copper workers smelted the metal, but of course they were blessed with so much easily accessible pure copper there was little need to develop this technology. Once the annealing process was completed and the copper ready to be worked, Indigenous copper workers used a wide array of techniques beyond hammering to shape the metal. At times they used wooden moulds to shape copper sheets into complex ornaments or specially designed wooden tools to produce particular shapes such as round beads. They ground the copper to produce sharp edges on axes and projectile points, folded or rolled thin sheets together to make larger objects, and cut the material into representational shapes. They manufactured copper rivets that allowed them to attach handles to tools and hunting weapons. Over a century and a half of archaeological research (and plundering in too many cases) has revealed an astounding array of artifacts: adzes, fish hooks, knives, cooking tools, awls, chisels, ornamental jewellery, and complex cut-outs of animals and other shapes. In the view of Ehrhardt, Indigenous copper workers produced "some of the most technologically sophisticated, symbolically powerful, and artistically breathtaking objects ever found in prehistoric North America."

Such a flattering assessment stands in stark contrast to the earliest historical and scientific treatments of Indigenous copper mining in the Eastern Woodlands. Since the discovery of the Lake Superior mining complex in 1847, commentators ranging from archaeologists to popular writers have made every effort to diminish the achievements of Lake Superior's Indigenous miners. One strand of thought, deeply imbued with social Darwinian evolutionary models of societal development, suggested that the ancient hunter-gathering cultures of the Lake Superior region were not sophisticated enough to engage in copper mining (and in any case had no need for the metal). Reflecting on his survey of the ancient mines in 1856, the geologist Charles Whittlesey argued, for instance, there were was no evidence of any historical linkage between the contemporary Indigenous people in the Lake Superior region and those who constructed the mines. Whittlesey went further, inferring that because Indigenous miners left no trace of habitation, then perhaps it was the old mound-building cultures of the Mississippi who moved north seasonally to exploit the copper, citing as evidence Lake Superior copper found as part on his earlier investigation of the mounds. Somewhat bizarrely, however, Whittlesey retreated from the mound-builder theory later in the article, concluding that local people were the primary miners in the region, and "they must have been numerous, industrious, and persevering, and have occupied the country a long time." Writing in 1865 for the Atlantic Monthly, A.D. Hagar was far less circumspect with his opinions on the cultural origins of Lake Superior copper: "we cannot consistently attribute the Herculean labor expended on these mines to the ancestors of the indolent race of North American Indians. We incline, rather, to the opinion that the miners were the mound-builders who lived south of the mines." Other nineteenth-century theorists (and at least one relatively recent popular book, Roger Jewell's *Ancient Mines of Kitchi-Guman*) postulated Lake Superior copper as a vector for early contact with Europeans, attributing the development of the mining complex to helpful interventions from technologically superior ancient Egyptians, Cypriots, or Minoans!

It took almost a century to dispel these unlikely theories, but the archaeologist James Griffin finally settled the debates about the cultural origins of ancient Lake Superior copper mining with intensive studies in the 1950s that identified the age of many artifacts as predating the zenith of the mound-builders and the relevant historical periods in Europe. Subsequent dating and provenance studies, primarily those of archaeologist Mary Ann Levine, debunked a parallel myth that all ancient North American copper came from the Lake Superior region. The weight of archaeological evidence clearly shows that, for at least seven millennia, the ancient Indigenous people of the Eastern Woodlands (and not casual interlopers from other places) engineered and developed a complex copper trade that exploited multiple sources of native copper, with the largest quantity (but not the sum total) originating with the massive deposits of the Lake Superior region.

The scattered and fragmentary evidence that constitutes the archaeological remains of the copper culture makes it very difficult to determine exactly the precise historical development of the copper trade, including the social, cultural, and economic context in which it occurred. There are nevertheless enough material remains to suggest at least a general historical narrative of the copper trade from the deep past up to the contact period. By 7500 BCE glacial-period ice and permafrost had finally retreated from the Lake Superior basin, allowing people to inhabit the region. Although there is evidence of copper in artifacts from the very earliest periods of human occupation, its presence is incidental within other materials (i.e., sandstone, quartzite) used to make tools and projectile points. The first clear evidence for copper use and manufacturing in the Lake Superior region comes from an archaeological site at South Fowl Lake that has been dated to 4800 BCE, though the technology to work the material had to have been developed earlier. Recent dating of charcoal associated with copper production and the aforementioned lead-deposition studies suggest copper mining occurred as far back as 6800 BCE at the Lake Manganese and Copper Falls Lake study sites in Michigan. Very little is known about the Early Archaic (ca. 7900–3000 BCE) people who first exploited Lake Superior copper, but the beginning of the period is

Burial goods from the Woodland Period made of antler, quartz, and copper, Cherry Island in the state of Michigan.

produce mostly practical objects (fishhooks, crescent knives, needles, awls, etc.), though some ornamental objects such as bracelets, rings, and beads have been found at key sites. The distinguishing feature of OCC artifacts is that they have mostly been found buried with the dead. Archaeologists can only speculate on the reasons for these burial practices. They have found both ornamental and well-used copper objects in the burial sites, in association with children, women, and men. The presence of copper may have indicated (or conferred) high social status in individuals, even in the relatively egalitarian hunting and gathering societies that inhabited the Great Lakes regions. It may also have reflected deeply held spiritual beliefs that associated copper with the supernatural power of manitous (spirits). Why copper was often buried with children remains a vexing question, but it could simply have been a reflection of material goods possessed by those families that engaged in the copper trade. In the latter stages of the Archaic Period, the OCC began to slowly merge with the newer Red Ochre Culture, which placed far greater emphasis on copper ornamentals and the demarcation of social differentiation through burial with prestige goods (often imported from elsewhere) made from copper.

The Old Copper Culture faded as the development of pottery (and over time agriculture and permanent settlements in some areas) ushered in the Woodland cultures that emerged in eastern Northern America roughly three thousand years ago. Copper production remained important for practical purposes among Early Woodland cultures in the Lake Superior region

marked by a general warming trend that allowed Indigenous groups to focus on local wildlife, fish, and other resources rather than pursue the large migratory animals that had dominated the faunal assemblages of the previous glacial period. The very few archaeological sites that date to this early period have contained projectile points and other small pieces of handcrafted copper. We can surmise that these people used copper to support and supplement a subsistence economy based on local hunting, fishing, and gathering, but the material evidence leaves only the grainiest picture of early copper use in the Lake Superior region.

The picture comes into much sharper focus with the archaeological remains of the so-called Old Copper Culture (OCC). This somewhat loose amalgam of distinct cultural groups, united by shared technological and cultural practices surrounding copper use, reached its zenith during the Lake Superior region's Middle Archaic (ca. 4000–1000 BCE) and Late Archaic (1000 BCE to the start of the Common Era) periods, spreading east from Wisconsin through trade networks to encompass much of the Great Lakes region. During the early stages of this period, copper workers used cold hammering and annealing techniques to (and often it is difficult to place a firm boundary between Archaic and Woodland cultural practices during transitional phases). Beginning around 100 CE however, the epicentre of copper processing shifted south to the so-called Hopewell cultures that inhabited much of what is now the Eastern and Southern United States. As with the "Archaic" designation, the cultures within the Hopewell complex are diverse, united mainly by their complex social structures, the development of expansive trade networks, and extravagant mortuary ceremonialism centred around burial mounds that often included valuable copper goods. Archaeologists have ranked copper as one of the most important materials circulating within the Hopewell complex, distinguished by the dominance of high-quality ornamentals over practical objects. Hopewellian copper workers produced intricate cut-outs of animal or geometrical shapes, finely worked earspools, bracelets, and beads. As with the Archaic cultures, the possession and distribution of copper goods (in life and in death) may have inferred leadership roles or high social status among those who controlled the trade. Hopewellian copper workers were important enough, and their works of such intricacy, that they may have been employed full time at their craft. As hinted at previously, it is not clear if the Hopewellians engaged in trade for raw copper from the Lake Superior region, or accessed enough sources of drift copper closer to home. Whether or not they depended on a distant area for raw material, the Hopewellians undoubtedly dominated the manufacture and trade of copper in eastern North America during the early centuries of the first millennium.

The dominance of southern manufacturers persisted at the later stages of the Woodland Period as a newer Mississippian cultural complex further developed the craft techniques and cultural importance of copper goods from roughly 900 CE to European contact. During this period, the Mississippians developed and refined new manufacturing techniques, most notably the production of ultra-thin copper foil that could be used to cover carved wooden objects such as animal and human likenesses. They created copper masks, decorated plates, badges and headdresses that were thoroughly integrated with the ceremonial and ritual life of their communities. In economic and political terms, the Mississippian cultures are characterized

Four Middle Woodland Period copper earl spools and copper celt from Snyders Mound, Calhoun County, in the state of Illinois.

by the growing importance of corn-based agriculture, the development of integrated networks of settlements (including ritual centres of mound-building and larger urban areas), the extension of trade networks, and the establishment of centralized political and religious authority. Within the Mississippians' hierarchical religious structure, copper artifacts became even more important as prestige goods, meant to emphasize the wealth and political power of those in authority in both life and death. Although the mound-building cultures went into severe decline with the introduction of European diseases beginning in the sixteenth century, their craft represents the pinnacle of copper art among Americans.

In the Great Lakes region, the copper economy was also changing in tandem with social and cultural transformations during Late Woodland Period. Where soils and climate permitted, the cultivation of corn, beans, and squash allowed for the development of more concentrated settlements, particularly the palisaded longhouse villages adopted by the Iroquoian (Wendat, Neutral, Haudenosaunee Confederacy) cultures of the lower Great Lakes and St. Lawrence River region. At Lake Superior, archaeological evidence suggests an increase in trade items from afar, including corn grown in

Hopewell copper artifact representing a bird of prey, Hopewell Culture National Historical Park in the southern part of the state of Ohio. Copper was prized for ceremonial and decorative uses.

more fertile areas, while the presence of traded copper goods among agricultural Iroquoians (and hunter-gathering Algonquians further east) at the time of contact is well documented. The discovery of a 700-year-old longhouse at the Juntunen archaeological site (on Bois Blanc Island in the Straits of Mackinac) suggests intimate contact and cultural diffusion among the hunter-gathers and copper producers of the northeast and the agricultural communities spread throughout the lower Great Lakes. Pottery fragments at Isle Royale strongly suggest that the copper-rich island had become an important trade and gathering place for diverse First Nations (possibly from as far afield as present-day eastern Ontario) eight hundred years ago. Copper remained an important item of manufacture and trade in northeastern North America until the arrival of European metal goods rapidly displaced copper items by the sixteenth century. One of the lesser-known impacts of early European colonialism, then, is the rapid decline of a copper

manufacturing economy and culture that had survived for possibly ten thousand years in eastern North America.

Northern Copper

Despite its prominence and longevity, the eastern North American centre of copper production was not the only one in the pre-contact world. In present-day Alaska and the Yukon, a rich copper manufacturing and trading complex arose between 1000 and 1700 CE among northwestern First Nations such as the Chugach, Dena'ina, Tutchone, Tanana, Gwich'in, Eyak, and Tlingit (with latter often forming kinship bonds with the Ahtna and acting as a middle agent for copper distribution to the Haida farther to the south). Although many of these groups exploited small local sources of copper, control of the trade largely rested with the Ahtna who inhabited the copper-rich Chitina River and Copper River valleys in the Wrangell–St. Elias mountain ranges. Among the three major Ahtna groups, the "Lower Ahtna" who lived near the coast (as opposed to the Upper and Middle Ahtna who lived farther up the Chitina River valley) directed much of the copper trade. Roughly a thousand years ago, the Ahtna began to collect and dig

Inuit copper knife with sheath. In the Central and Western Arctic, Inuit and Athapaskan peoples engaged in an extensive copper trade that included both finished products and raw material.

ABOVE: Copper tools from an archaeological dig at the Juntunen site in 1962.

LEFT: Archaeological dig at Juntunen National Historic Site in 1959 on Bois Blanc Island in the northwest corner of Lake Huron, part of the state Michigan. Here the discovery of remains of a longhouse confirmed Juntunen as a site as a cultural meeting point between woodland copper producers and agricultural peoples of the lower Great Lakes.

for native copper nuggets from these river beds and process it using the same hammering and annealing techniques as in eastern North America. As raw copper was traded throughout the Alaska-Yukon region, First Nations began to produce practical goods (i.e., needles, awls, projectile points, knives, and drills) and ornamentals (ear and nose decorations, neck bands, and rings). In return for raw copper and finished goods, other First Nations exchanged food items (berries, seaweed, etc.) and prestige goods (e.g., slaves, Haida canoes).

Copper was not merely a trade commodity for the Ahtna. Within Ahtna society it played a profoundly important role determining social class and influencing spiritual practices. According to archaeologist H. Kory Cooper, the Ahtna and other Dene linguistic groups did not themselves produce prestige goods from copper in the same manner as Indigenous people in eastern North America. Instead, the ability to establish effective control and ownership over the copper trade demarcated the social status of individual chiefs and kinship group. Ahtna

and Tlingit stories about the discovery of copper often included accounts of poorer individuals or slaves who moved rapidly up the ladder of social prestige after finding the metal. Cooper also suggests that copper wealth was often associated with luck, which was in turn derived from good relationships with the spiritual realm. The Ahtna thus attributed great spiritual power to copper weapons and hunting implements, undertaking spiritual preparation before crafting these items, associating the metal with powerful predatory animals such as the wolverine or the bear, or using copper knives as part of ceremonies celebrating the arrival of salmon in local rivers. Even though copper tools, weapons, and decorative objects were only one part of a complex array of material goods among the Ahtna, the metal was woven into the core of their economic, social, and spiritual lives.

Copper manufacturing and trade among the First Nations of the Alaska-Yukon region did not disappear as rapidly with the arrival of Europeans as it did in northeastern North America. From the beginning of

Haida copper art, circa 1870, with source material likely from the Yukon-Alaska copper production and trading complex that dates back at least 1000 years.

Russian commercial incursions in the 1780s through the period of U.S. exploration beginning in 1867, the Lower Ahtna managed to retain control of their copper resource, relinquishing control only when the advent of the Yukon Gold Rush in 1898 ushered in an intensive period of prospecting, and ultimately the development of the large-scale Kennecott copper mining complex in the heart of their traditional territory. The Ahtna recognized the trading opportunities that arrived with the newcomers, actively seeking out Russian trading posts to exchange copper and fur for European commodities. Aided by their remote location in a relatively inaccessible mountain valley, however, the Ahtna discouraged the establishment of Russian trading posts on their own land, controlled access to the accessible mountain passes leading into the Chitina Valley, and guarded jealously their knowledge of valuable copper deposits. The anthropologist Kenneth Pratt has nevertheless argued against a prevailing myth that the Lower Ahtna were a particularly violent people. In 1803 the Ahtna did murder Konstantine Galaktionov, leader of an expedition to search for copper in their territory, and in 1850 ransacked and killed the residents of a Russian trading post near their settlement of Taral, ending Russian attempts to directly explore and settle in the copper-rich area. But Pratt cites ample evidence that trading relations between the Lower Ahtna and the Russians were generally cordial, so long as the latter respected the authority of the Ahtna chiefs over the copper resource.

Ahtna relationships with American prospectors were even more gracious than with the Russians. Pratt suggests that Nicolai of Taral, a chief of the Lower Ahtna who controlled the copper trade between 1884 and 1900, often assisted American mineral prospectors as a means of reinforcing his prestige through acts of hospitality. In 1885, Chief Nicolai described the general character and location of the Chitina valley's copper deposits to the leader of an American expedition, Lieutenant Henry Allen.

In 1899 Chief Nicolai revealed to a group of American prospectors the exact location of his "Nikolai Mine," knowledge that quickly produced additional paydirt in

Copper Inuit, or Kugluktukmiut, digging for copper samples in 1929 at Husky Creek near Kugluktuk, on the Central Arctic coast in the territory of Nunavut (formerly the Northwest Territories.)

the form of the Bonanza copper deposits and the eventual development of the Kennecott Mine, a major copper producer (600,000 tons of the metal) between 1911 and 1938. Despite these good relations, Pratt argues that it was only the power vacuum left by the death of Chief Nicolai around 1900, the outbreak of smallpox among the Ahtna in 1899, and the Ahtna's subsequent abandonment of the Nizina basin (a tributary of the Chitina) that allowed American mining interests to advance into the region without resistance from the Indigenous miners. Very quickly after Ahtna control collapsed, ton after ton of copper began to flow south from the region, mainly to electrify U.S. cities; just as suddenly, the mining economy died in the 1930s as high-grade deposits became depleted and commodity markets collapsed during the Great Depression. Today it is mainly the more recent copper mining history, and less so centuries of Ahtna mining, that

are commemorated at the largely abandoned mining towns of Kennecott and McCarthy in Wrangell–St. Elias National Park, a popular tourism adventure off the beaten track of Alaska's main highways.

The second major centre of Indigenous copper production in the pre-contact Far North was the Coronation Gulf and southern Victoria Island region of the Central Arctic Coast. The Inuit who inhabited this region, Kugluktukmiut, were among the last Indigenous people in North America to experience sustained contact with Europeans. In 1914 Vilhjalmur Stefansson, one of the first European explorers to interact directly with the group, dubbed them the "Copper Eskimos" due to their manufacture of tools and weapons from the ubiquitous copper nuggets, rocks, and boulders found in Coppermine River Valley. Perhaps because the Kugluktukmiut were becoming more reliant on European metals at the time of contact, outside commentators have tended to underestimate the historical depth and importance of Indigenous copper production in the region. The anthropologist Diamond Jenness conducted ethnographic studies of the Kugluktukmiut during the Canadian Arctic Expedition (1913–18) and suggested that copper use

ABOVE: "Copper Inuit" [Kitlinermiut or Kugluktukmiut] fishing behind a stone weir in creek, Northwest Territories (now Nunavut). Kugluktukmiut manufactured tools and weapons, as well as trading copper found in the Coppermine River valley.

RIGHT: Image of "Copper Inuit" hunter drawing a bow, taken during Canadian Arctic Expedition, 1916.

had been confined to the past three centuries. In a 1972 publication, the archaeologist Robert McGhee argued that copper production among the Kugluktukmiut reached its zenith during the nineteenth century in tandem with the introduction of new trade markets in European metals. In 1984 the archaeologist Clifford Hickey argued that the abandonment of the ice-bound British ship HMS *Investigator* (sent to find Sir John Franklin's missing ships) in 1853, replete with its copper sheathing and iron material, resulted in an influx of metals among the Kugluktukmiut, producing increasing demand and trade values for native copper.

More recent archaeological work has questioned the idea of a nineteenth-century renaissance for copper production among the Kugluktukmiut. The archaeologist David Morrison's work revealed a greater abundance of copper artifacts among the Thule culture that spread to the Central Arctic between 1100 and 1400 CE than in

Kugluktukmiut sites. Indeed, copper production in the North American Arctic dates back at least to the Dorset people who inhabited the region from 2500 BCE to roughly 1000 CE, and possibly as far back as the so-called Arctic Small Tool cultural groups who inhabited the region beginning in roughly 4500 BCE. In broad regional terms, copper was not a marginal commodity among northern Indigenous people, but circulated widely through the northern reaches of the continent through trade networks and via raids, especially among and between Inuit and sub-Arctic Dene communities farther to the south. Among the Dene, the Yellowknives linguistic group have been called the "Copper Indians," since they gathered the metal in the northern parts of their territory. Their use of knives with a yellow copper hue inspired later explorers to apply the "Yellowknives" appellation; in their own language they refer to themselves as the T'satsąot'inę, the metal or copper people.

To Dene and Inuit, copper circulated not just as a

material commodity but also as an important aspect of their cultural imaginations. Geographer Emilie Cameron's wide-ranging book, *Far Off Metal River*, highlights the significance of the multiple copper stories that have circulated through the Kugluktuk region. Older narratives such as the Kugluktukmiut story of a group of stranded travellers who sacrifice a valuable copper knife to the water in order to reach safety, or the Dene story of a woman who escapes captivity with Inuit, discovers a massive copper deposit, and then foils a group of men who attempt to rape her (after she has revealed her secret) as she disappears into a mountain along with the copper, all attest to the deep cultural importance of copper for these communities.

Cameron's work also reminds us that the search for copper sits at the core of one of the most infamous historical episodes of Indigenous and European contact in the Arctic: the Bloody Falls massacre. In July 1771, as British Hudson's Bay Company explorer Samuel Hearne's expedition from Fort Prince of Wales (on the shores of Hudson Bay) worked its way along the Coppermine River Valley, his party of Chipewyan and "Copper Indians," led by the Chief Mattonabbee, organized a surprise raid on a Copper Inuit camp at Bloody Falls. Catching the Inuit unaware in their sleep, the Dene massacred more than twenty men, women, and children while Hearne watched on in a state of shock. Hearne's published account of the killings spared none of the macabre details, emphasizing the apparent senselessness of the massacre with lurid stories of a naked young woman wrapping herself around the explorer's legs and begging for mercy before she was speared to death, and the killing of an old woman who could barely see or hear what was happening around her. Hearne wrote in his famous published memoir, "even at this hour I cannot reflect on the transactions of that horrid day without shedding tears." Some scholars have suggested that Hearne exaggerated the brutality of the killings as a way to emphasize that both of his own feet were firmly planted in the "civilized" world. Cameron argues it was the larger purpose of Hearne's journey (and not the accuracy of Hearne's account) that is the key

An image taken by photographer R.S. Finnie in the 1930s near Bloody Falls on the Coppermine River, about 15 km southwest of Kugluktuk, the location of the massacre of Copper Inuit in 1771 during the Hearne Expedition.

Late nineteenth/early twentieth-century drawing of Samuel Hearne, who traveled from Hudson Bay searching for the "far off metal river" on behalf of the Hudson's Bay Company.

Bloody Falls National Historic Site of Canada commemorates this traditional fishing site and preserves archaeological evidence of Pre-Dorset, Thule, First Nation and Inuit cultures over the past three millennia.

determining the lines of culpability for the killings. She cites the common view among Kugluktukmiut today that Hearne was personally responsible for the killings because he knowingly brought a party of hostile Dene into Copper Inuit territory. Cameron also reminds us that the Dene under Mattonnabee's command immediately began searching Inuit tents for copper after the killings, suggesting the raid was as much about resource acquisition as it was an act of irrational violence. Add to this the fact that the whole purpose of Hearne's journey was to assess the commercial potential of the rumoured copper deposits at the mouth of the "Far Off Metal River" (the prospects for which he found disappointing), and it becomes apparent that Hearne and his party shared the similar goal (if not the exact method) of dispossessing Kugluktukmiut of their copper resources. A century and a half later, Kugluktukmiut and T'satsąot'inę had ceased mining copper as European metals flooded their homelands in the twentieth century. Each group soon had to wrestle with the potential impacts of copper-mining proposals at

Kugluktuk and the dramatic health and environmental effects of early gold mining developments at Yellowknife (see Chapters 3 and 4).

Mining and Colonial Dreams in the Arctic

Hearne was far from the first European to search for minerals in what is now Canada. That distinction likely belongs to Jacques Cartier, who mistook pyrite and quartz for gold and diamonds on his second St. Lawrence voyage in 1541. Cartier's musings about the mineral potential of the New World did not extend much beyond casual observation. Just over three decades later, however, explorer Martin Frobisher became the first European mining entrepreneur in Canada. His notorious expeditions to the Arctic Islands from 1576 to 1578 resulted in the first European contact with North American Inuit,[1] an initial attempt to establish an English colony in North America, the first English house to be constructed in the Americas, and the inaugural English mine in the New World. For all these endeavours, Frobisher's three voyages to the Arctic

Islands failed on almost every level, resulting in violence toward Inuit, abandonment of the idea of a colony, and (as if that were not enough) the first major mining stock scandal in North America. As the founding European mining developer in what would become Canada, Frobisher provided the industry with a less than honourable origin story, one that in some ways presaged the speculative nature of northern mining and the industry's almost total disregard for Indigenous people prior to the late 1970s.

Frobisher did not originally intend to become the first European mining magnate in the North American Arctic. He had been a sailor since he was a teenager, a veteran of some of the first English expeditions to West Africa, in the 1550s. On the second voyage, in 1554, Frobisher volunteered himself as a hostage during hostilities with local Indigenous people. His captors eventually turned Frobisher over to the Portuguese and he worked his way back to England, possibly after hearing the claims of a fellow imprisoned mariner to have sailed from the Pacific to the Atlantic through the channels that weave among the Arctic Islands. During the 1560s Frobisher became a privateer — veering into piracy at times — though he apparently never lost his curiosity about finding the Northwest Passage.

In 1574 Frobisher and promoter Michael Lok worked tirelessly to obtain licensing from the Muscovy Company and financial backing for a journey to the Arctic Islands. Among merchants and members of the royal court, interest in the Northwest Passage reached a peak in 1576 with the long-delayed publication of Humphry Gilbert's *A Discourse of a Discoverie for a New Passage to Cataia*. Frobisher and Lok soon raised enough money to secure three small ships (the *Gabriel*, the *Michael*, and an unnamed smaller vessel) for a voyage that set sail for the Arctic Islands in June 1576. In August, the expedition reached Baffin Island and sailed up a narrow bay near the south end (now called Frobisher Bay), convinced that this dead end was the fabled passage to the Pacific. As they became blocked by a maze of islands that sit near the end of the bay, Frobisher and his crew spotted seven Inuit

Sir Martin Frobisher, the privateer and explorer who established the first English mine in North America near Baffin Island in the 1570s.

kayaks coming toward them. After some initial distrust (the English sailors had no experience interacting with Inuit), a group of nineteen Inuit came on board eager to trade (as previous generations would have done with other *qallunaat*, the Greenlandic Norse, over the previous three centuries). Relations quickly soured, however, when the ship's crew took an Inuk ashore to retrieve his kayak and act as a guide for the English. Although the shore party was instructed to stay within sight of the ships, they rounded a point and were never seen again. Whether

Museum illustrator Francis Back created these images for the Canadian Museum of History of the Frobisher expedition's ill-fated encounters with Inuit. Above: First contact. Below: The first hostage.

they were kidnapped, killed, deserted, or abandoned amid a misunderstanding remains a mystery, but Frobisher retaliated by kidnapping an Inuk and taking him back to England, where he soon died of illness. The English expedition also brought back samples of black rock from Little Hall Island that Lok distributed to three assayers who pronounced it worthless. Lok chose to believe a fourth assayer, Giovanni Batista Agnello, who claimed to have produced gold dust from the rock.

At this point the motivation for a new expedition to the Arctic Islands took on the bizarre logic that often accompanies speculative gambles. Lok approached Secretary of State Francis Walsingham in a bid for royal support, who then sent ore samples for further assaying that turned out to show only tiny amounts of silver. Nonetheless, Lok and Agnello continued to promote the idea of an Arctic gold-mining venture among a royal court that was well aware of the immense riches of gold and silver that the Spanish had mined in Mexico since the 1530s. By March 1577 the two promoters had raised £3,900 (Queen Elizabeth put £1,000 toward the venture, much of it in-kind support in the form of a large vessel, the *Aid*, and a crew). Lok formed a joint stock entity, the Company of Cathay, as a means to channel the interest of investors, but the Queen refused to grant a charter due to fears that she would lose control over her investment. By May, Frobisher's fleet departed from England, their mission to explore further the route of the fabled Northwest Passage, but only after they had filled the hull of their flagship with gold ore.

They arrived at the Baffin Island region in July, disappointed at their failure to find a worthwhile deposit of the supposedly gold-bearing black rock on Little Hall Island but elated to find large deposits on nearby smaller islands. On July 19, Frobisher's party raised a cross on the northeastern shore of the entrance to Baffin Island and claimed the surrounding lands for England. The ceremony attracted the attention of Inuit, who warily approached to trade with Frobisher. After one initial peaceful exchange, Frobisher decided to kidnap an interpreter, succeeding only after a back-and-forth skirmish in which he was wounded in his backside. Frobisher then proceeded to explore the southern shore of the bay and found signs of European clothing in an abandoned Inuit camp. Racist assumptions convinced the English that these were signs the five missing crew members from the last summer had been victims of cannibalism. Frobisher rashly organized an attack on a nearby Inuit camp and killed five people (one of the expedition crew was badly wounded), taking a woman and her infant son captive. Frobisher then turned back toward his main business, returning to the north shore and setting up a mining operation on a small plot of land dubbed Countess of Warwick Island (now Kodlunarn Island). There his crew used simple tools — wedges, hammers, and picks — to crack rock from a cliff face and load it into the hull of the ship. As the work proceeded, another group of Inuit appeared on the nearby shore to trade. Frobisher thought they knew the whereabouts of the five missing crew and convinced them to take a letter promising their deliverance either by ransom or force. By August 23, however, the expedition had set sail for England with two hundred tons of ore and three captive Inuit, all of whom would be dead from illness within a month. The first European mining operation on Canadian soil proved to be less a voyage of discovery and more a violent raid on local Inuit, not dissimilar to the behaviour Samuel Hearne attributed to Indigenous savagery two centuries later.

Upon Frobisher's return to England, the Baffin Island ore was subject to the immediate scrutiny of the assayers. The first three assayers to test the rock, including Agnello, revealed the catastrophic result: no gold. Jonas Schutz, chief assayer on the voyage, had reported 2.6 ounces per ton of gold in the Baffin rock, though his results may have been skewed by Frobisher apparently threatening him with a knife to speed up his assessment of the ore. A fifth assayer, Bernard Kranich, finally produced the eye-popping result the investors had hoped for: 13.5 ounces of gold and 50 ounces of silver per ton of ore. Kranich's assistant, Robert Denham, claimed, however, that the substance used to

English painter John White created this watercolour depicting a skirmish between the Inuit and Frobisher's men, violence which claimed victims on both sides. The painting was produced between 1585 and 1593 as part of a book of 113 drawings.

Image from a model of Frobisher's mining operation on Countess of Warwick Island (Kodlunarn Island) just off Nunavut's southern Baffin Island as it may have appeared during late August 1578. Frobisher's expedition yielded only worthless ore, lawsuits, and conflicts with Inuit.

separate the metals from the ore contained silver, that the assay had been completed on a very small ore sample of one pound, and that Kranich had added gold and silver to the ore sample to account for its small size. Denham's assertions seemed to matter little as this final assay became the basis on which, against all logic, the Company of Cathay mobilized investors to back Frobisher's final voyage to the Arctic Islands.

In June 1578 a fleet of fifteen ships set out for the territory the Queen had named *Meta Incognita* with a party of four hundred crew, soldiers, and miners. Frobisher's commission for the voyage promised a challenging summer, tasking him not only with returning to mine the supposed gold and silver ore of Countess of Warwick Island, but also with exploring for even more valuable mineral deposits in the area, pushing farther westward to chart the Northwest Passage, and establishing a tentative colony of a hundred men in the area to assess the viability of overwintering on the Arctic Islands. After two months of particularly challenging sailing, the crew began a new mine on Countess of Warwick Island and developed satellite mines throughout the area. They built an assay furnace near their original mine to evaluate ore from the outlying mines. Frobisher conducted occasional forays to capture hostages, perhaps still hopeful of finding out information on the five missing sailors, but the Inuit had learned to be wary of the English interlopers.

As the end of August approached, the miners had excavated twelve hundred tons of ore deemed suitable for shipment to England. With the first signs of winter approaching, Frobisher and his crew prepared for the return voyage to England, deciding not to leave the hundred colonists to overwinter, since their prefabricated houses and supply of beer had sunk along with the supply ship *Dennis*. The workers on Countess of Warwick Island did gamely build the first English house in the New World, one that was never inhabited and was eventually dismantled by Inuit for useful materials. Frobisher and his fellow ship captains also decided that probing for the Northwest Passage was no longer feasible with the onset

of winter conditions. Having failed in many of its key endeavours, Frobisher's mission — not to mention the loss of forty of his men along the journey — would now be weighed solely against the value of the rocks stored in the holds of the transport ships.

All but one of Frobisher's ships found safe harbour in the Thames River (the *Emmanuel* was left derelict in Ireland). Throughout the summer, Lok and other investors had built a smelter in the small town of Dartford downstream from London. Through the fall and early winter of 1578, horse-drawn carts slowly moved the ore up to the smelting furnace — where nothing but disappointment awaited. By the end of December, repeated smelting trials had failed to produce any gold or silver. Some investors blamed the smelting process, or the acumen of metallurgist Jonas Schutz, but as the winter deepened it became increasingly clear that the ore was worthless. One thing the ore did produce was ill will among the investors, as Lok and Frobisher engaged in a very public spat over the handling of the venture. Smelting trials continued until 1583, but whatever faint hope remained was likely dashed when much of the ore was used to construct a wall around the Queen's manor house in Dartford.

While Frobisher went on to a reasonably successful career as a naval officer, Lok spent time in debtor's prison as a result of lawsuits related to the Baffin Island venture. Some might point to subsequent explorations in Baffin Bay by John Davis and Henry Hudson as vindication for Frobisher's misadventures, but from the perspective of Indigenous people his voyages were a harbinger of the often-violent hunger for land and resources that accompanied English colonization in North America.

Early-colonial industry

As the Hearne and Frobisher episodes indicate, early European colonists and explorers in North America were keenly interested in the mineral resources of these territories. However, amid the recurring clashes of European powers during the eighteenth century — wars that also shaped and

The famous Joggins fossil cliffs, on the Bay of Fundy in the province of Nova Scotia, provide a remarkable record of the "Coal Age" period some 300 million years ago; their exposed coal seams also attracted early colonial coal miners.

reshaped the North American colonies and their inhabitants — few efforts to exploit these resources came to fruition. Royal reserves (ie. exclusive privileges) on precious minerals, the lack of markets, and a preoccupation with the fur trade and agricultural settlement limited early-colonial mining activities for all but local uses. However, two notable colonial enterprises emerged in the eighteenth century, one in Acadia and the other in New France, focused on two key commodities of the early industrial era: coal and iron.

Rising dramatically on the eastern shore of Chignecto Bay (part of the Bay of Fundy), the cliffs at Joggins are remarkable both for the profusion of Carboniferous Period fossils on their exposed strata (studied by such famous geologists as Charles Lyell, Charles Darwin, and William Dawson), and as the site of some of the earliest coal extraction in North America. Explorers and colonists had noticed exposed coal seams at several locations around Nova Scotia and Cape Breton in the seventeenth century, and there are references to the sporadic extraction of coal from Cape Breton, the Bay of Fundy, and the Grand Lake region of modern New Brunswick for export to the Massachusetts Bay colony. Early French maps note the Joggins coal seams in Chignecto Bay, and an active, illicit trade with New England arose around 1700,

supplied by Acadian settlers on the Fundy shore. The first coal mined using "regular mining methods," however, is attributed to Port Morien (Cow Bay), Cape Breton, where the French mined coal starting in 1720 to supply the nearby fortress of Louisbourg (as well as to trade with New England). Both the French and the English operated the mine during their alternating tenures at Louisbourg, which culminated with the final French defeat in 1758. Guarded by a blockhouse, the mine followed the exposed coal seam underground using room-and-pillar methods. In the late 1750s, as much as three thousand tons of coal were reportedly mined there annually. However, mining at Port Morien declined with the withdrawal of the British garrison in 1768, and illicit mining anywhere in Cape Breton was prosecuted by the governor.

The first attempt at legal coal extraction at Joggins came under the British, who had captured nearby Port Royal (renamed Annapolis Royal) from the French in 1710, and who exploited local coal deposits for their garrisons. In 1730, the Nova Scotia governor granted a license (and later, land title) to a Boston–Nova Scotia partnership to mine coal from the Chignecto Bay cliffs. The operation employed six British soldiers to protect the diggings, and perhaps a dozen Acadian miners to dig the coal from surface pits and transport it seven miles or so north to a sheltered anchorage at "Gran'choggin" Creek — a likely source for the name Joggins — for loading on to Boston-bound ships. Despite a promising start, the venture came to an abrupt end in 1732 after local Mi'kmaq and Acadians ransacked the incipient mining outpost (the latter incensed by the imposition of fees to dig coal). For the rest of the century, coal digging at Joggins (as in Cape Breton) remained episodic, mainly to supply British forts during periods of disruption, such as the Seven Years War and the American Revolution.[2]

A more substantial and durable colonial enterprise emerged in New France, where deposits of bog iron formed the basis for colonial Canada's first heavy industry: an iron foundry and forge that operated off and on for a century and a half. French colonists had noted surface and near-surface iron deposits in the St. Lawrence lowlands around Bay St. Paul and Trois-Rivières in the late seventeenth century, and samples from the Trois-Rivières area were sent to France for test-forging by the first intendant of the colony of New France, Jean Talon, in 1670. Iron mining drew periodic interest from colonial officials over the next fifty years, but not until the 1720s was the French Crown receptive to proposals for a colonial ironworks. In 1729, Montreal merchant and seigneur of St. Maurice, François Poulin de Francheville, petitioned the King of France (with the support of the colonial governor) to invest in iron mining and establish a forge to supply the growing colony with iron goods. Francheville was granted an exclusive twenty-year privilege for iron production, as well as license to harness waterpower from St. Maurice Creek and harvest resources not only from his own St. Maurice seigneury, but also from the neighbouring St. Étienne seigneury. Francheville's financial partnership collapsed after his death and which, along with the poor design of the initial blast furnace, resulted in low-quality iron and a halt to production. A new partnership was established in 1735, employing French ironmaster Pierre-François-Olivier de Vézin, to construct an even larger blast furnace, two forges, and smithy at the site. Although this partnership, too, ended in bankruptcy in 1741, the colonial

government took over Vézin's forges, which it operated until the Conquest of New France in 1760. Vézin himself ended up in Louisiana where, after an abortive attempt to develop mining prospects, he served in a number of important administrative posts during both the French and Spanish regimes.

Historian Roch Samson, who chronicled the history of the St. Maurice Forges for Parks Canada, argues the forges were essentially "a microcosm of the Old World iron industry" that operated into the modern era with relatively few technical changes (even with the addition of a new blast furnace, axe factory, and rail wheel foundry in the mid-1800s). Ironmaking at St. Maurice was organized along traditional European craft lines, with the secretive ironmaster at its head, but the colonial context meant that the forges also operated as a "vertically integrated" system of smelting and iron-working, processes that were typically separate enterprises in Europe. The result was the establishment of a major industrial complex on the banks of the St. Maurice River, drawing on a large hinterland of resources and labour in the St. Maurice and neighbouring seigneuries. It included the furnace, two forges, casting houses, and other industrial buildings, supported by an industrial village occupied by year-round workers (especially skilled labour) and their families, and swelled by a large seasonal/itinerant workforce.

The raw materials gathered from lands around the forges included iron, wood for charcoal, and clay and limestone as "flux" for the smelting process. Bog iron (*fer des marais*) consists of near-surface veins and nodules of iron oxide, often found in swampy areas and meadows. To locate and harvest the ore, local *habitants* (settlers) and prospectors used metre-long iron rods to probe the surface and delineate deposits. Mining consisted of trenching and removing the iron, often mixed with soil, which was then carted (or in winter, sleighed) to the forges. Smelting the iron oxide required cleaning and combining it with the charcoal and flux, in a precise ratio, in the carefully designed blast furnace to remove oxygen and impurities from the ore and reduce it to a workable metallic

The St. Maurice Forges, located close to Trois-Rivières, Quebec, were the site of early Canada's first heavy industry, an iron-making complex established in the 1730s.

compound (once cooled). Thus all the raw materials for a "campaign" or extended iron production period needed to be on hand at the site, and their constant supply was critical. Charcoal production exploited the extensive upland forests of the seigneuries, which colliers reduced to charcoal in clearings using a pit charcoaling process. Limestone, clay, and sand for iron moulding were also available within a reasonable distance of the forges.

Once the blast furnace was "blown in," or ignited, it operated continuously for six to eight months (typically, it was blown out in late autumn for repairs and to restock raw materials). The furnace was manually charged with raw materials, and the resulting molten iron and slag (waste) were drawn off and the former poured into "pigs" or iron bars, as well as into sand moulds on the floor to produce cast iron goods such as stove plates, cookware, farm implements, and (in times of war, especially)

munitions. Pig iron in turn supplied the forges, where the iron bars were reheated in a hearth (*renardière*) and worked into wrought iron using massive 200–300 kilogram hammers turned by waterwheels. Indeed, much of the operation relied on water power, supplied by millponds on the St. Maurice Creek, which powered bellows for the furnace and forges, the hammers, and other equipment for the settlement.

The St. Maurice Forges required specialized skills unavailable in New France, meaning the earliest workers were recruited directly from the mother country. These included ironmasters (like Vézin) and their assistants, furnacemen, forgemen, and even colliers to produce charcoal. Many of these craft workers had a reputation as being independent and troublesome — and possibly drunkards. After the conquest, when the British Crown took over the operation, perhaps half the skilled

The restored Grande Maison at the St. Maurice Forges National Historic Site of Canada, the site of a major archaeological and restoration effort in the 1970s.

French workers left, but others remained, training subsequent generations of ironworkers in their crafts. These permanent workers formed the core of the small settlement that grew up beside the forges. From the end of the eighteenth century to about 1850, between 200 and 425 people lived in the village surrounding the forges in what was essentially a company town. Housing conditions reflected the hierarchy of labour, with management and skilled workers occupying houses (often shared with fellow tradesmen) and seasonal or unskilled workers living in rustic log huts. The ironmaster, of course, lived in the grande maison, a large residence that also doubled as the business headquarters of the forges and dominated the village landscape. A company store and chapel also served the small community.

The forges entered a period of decline in the mid-nineteenth century, as the enterprise struggled with indebtedness and increasingly difficult access to raw materials. Colonial governments relinquished control in 1846, after which the forges were operated by a series of private investors. But the favourable (essentially free) access to land and resources the forges enjoyed under the colonial regime ended, and the forges increasingly had to transport raw materials over long distances from the foundry. Although early owners updated equipment and attempted to expand production, by the 1860s the forges were struggling under crushing debt loads and legal wrangling, and much of the skilled workforce left. By 1863, a chronicler of the history and decline of the forges for the *British-Canadian Review* declared, "To one who has seen the Forges of St. Maurice in their hey-day of prosperity, their present condition of abandonment and decay is truly a heart-rending spectacle." The forges, in fact, were not quite dead: new owners, the McDougalls, tried to revive the operation through capital investment and expansion, but they, too, succumbed to indebtedness and the forges were blown out for good in 1883. The forges and village were abandoned, but became the focus of a major archaeological and heritage reconstruction initiative led by Parks Canada in the 1970s. The St. Maurice Forges are now a National Historic Site known as one of Canada's most significant industrial heritage sites.

Early and Modern Mining

While stories of daring mining ventures and pioneering operations in New World environments remain alluring, this chapter ultimately serves as a reminder that Canada's early mining history is not merely a story of European colonial plunder or the growing requirements for materials in an emerging industrial economy. Indeed, the colonial and more recent histories of large-scale mining are a mere blip in time when compared to the thousands of years of Indigenous mining that preceded them.

The average Canadian is far more likely to be acquainted with the Klondike Gold Rush (widely commemorated in books, films, and a National Historic Site), or even Frobisher's failed attempt at gold mining, than anything concerning the immensely long and complex history of Indigenous mining. Obviously the lack of a document trail surrounding Indigenous mining makes it difficult for historians to construct a coherent story from an artifactual record that does not reveal key events in the development of the Indigenous copper economy. Until recently, however, the mainstream thread of commentary from settler North America has been to diminish the accomplishments of Indigenous miners while exalting more recent mining initiatives as the forerunner of civilization in hinterland areas. Indigenous mining remains a somewhat hidden history, at least in the popular realm, in part because we do not think of hunter-gatherers as miners. Even when we do acknowledge Indigenous mining, too often we think of it as primitive, archaic, a mere prelude to the more important mining developments that marked the dawn of industrialism in North America.

The obvious differences of scale aside, Indigenous and modern mining share some features. Both modern and pre-contact miners sought minerals as material to build useful tools and to augment their military might through the production of weapons; both used metals to make decorative objects that reinforced prestige and social class; both shaped and reshaped their environments in order to dig minerals; both developed extensive processing chains and trading networks to move raw ore to market as a finished product; and both developed rich, if vastly different, cultural narratives surrounding the value and use of metals. Though the miners inhabited vastly different worlds, many of the same motivations — power, affluence, an affinity for precious metals — unite them.

Of course, it is too simple to conclude that all mining is the same, irrespective of the historical and cultural context in which it occurs. Indeed, the geographer Emilie Cameron has noted how today's mining companies sometimes invoke a crude and problematic continuity with Indigenous mining traditions to promote projects in contemporary Indigenous communities, ignoring the vastly different scale and impacts associated with modern industrial mining. Indigenous mining economies ultimately remained small-scale, and thus lasted so much longer than their modern counterparts, especially in the now largely mined-out Keweenaw. Although a thoroughly modern industrial approach to mining would take time to develop, the arrival of Frobisher signalled a new approach to mining in North America: one characterized by rapid exploitation, the appropriation of Indigenous lands, environmental damage, abandoned mining landscapes, and the accumulation of material wealth beyond what previous generations of miners could imagine.

A group of prospectors work a claim at Bonanza Creek, ca. 1899, during the Klondike gold rush. Using flumes, sluice boxes, and rockers, they attempted to separate alluvial gold from the stream beds and hillsides.

CHAPTER 2
Mining from Colony to Nation

If ancient and early modern societies found many uses for precious metals, minerals, and other products of mining, it was not until the industrial revolution that the demand for minerals of all types skyrocketed. Technological change and industrial expansion from the late eighteenth to the late nineteenth century drove growing demand, especially for coal for energy, iron for industrial and military applications, and copper for ship sheathing and (later) electrification. While European nations found many of these materials in their own countries, the search for coal, minerals, and precious metals (among other resources) also spurred European colonial expansion. It also fuelled the economic ambitions of the new colonies and nations themselves, including those emerging in North America.

The colonies that would become Canada began taking shape in this period. With the conclusion of the

Seven Years' War in 1963, Great Britain had acquired most former French possessions in northern North America. After the American Revolution ended in 1783, the British colonies in North America were reduced to the thin strips of Upper and Lower Canada along the St. Lawrence River and Great Lakes, the historic Acadian colonies in the present-day Maritimes, insular Newfoundland, and the coastal strip of Labrador. To the north, the vast territories of Rupert's Land remained a fur supply zone under the nominal economic control of the Hudson's Bay Company (HBC). These British colonies and fur trade outposts were isolated and thinly populated, dependent mainly on semi-subsistence agriculture and trade in staple commodities, not only furs from the

Illustration of the Caledonia Colliery in Glace Bay, Nova Scotia, appearing in *Picturesque Canada: The Country As it Was and Is* in 1882. Coal was a key colonial-era industry in British North America.

Mining in the Klondike, Yukon. The Klondike Gold Rush helped consolidate Canada's national expansion to the west and north.

interior but also fish on the coasts. British North America in the late eighteenth century hardly seemed a candidate for the development of a new transcontinental nation, but within a century dramatic social, economic, and political changes culminated in Confederation of the Dominion of Canada in 1867, Canada's purchase of Rupert's Land in 1869, and the extension of this new nation across the continent to the Pacific coast when British Columbia joined Canada in 1871.

The pursuit of mining riches played its part in fostering dreams of a transcontinental nation. Looking back, in his 1863 book *Eighty Years' Progress of British North America*, pro-Confederation geologist Henry Youle Hind touted the spirit of improvement the colonies had shown since the 1780s and enumerated the great natural endowments that secured their "magnificent future" — including the "inexhaustible mineral resources" of the northwestern territories. For many European colonists, agricultural settlement represented the civilizational ideal, and in Hind's volume agriculture enjoys pride of place in the account of the colonies' achievements and potential.

But as Great Britain and, increasingly, the United States, rapidly industrialized, mineral resources were recognized as increasingly important to colonial — and potentially national — economies and settlement. So it's not surprising to find in this volume an extensive review of "the nature, extent and value of the metals and other useful minerals found" in the colonies, along with "an account of the progress of mining industry in these provinces." While highlighting the challenges of a lack of capital investment and access to markets, Hind's book nevertheless conjures the image of a territory poised for industrial glory based on vast mineral riches.

Indeed, as historian Suzanne Zeller argues, geological and mineral exploration in British North America was central to the process of colonization and in promoting the idea of Canada. In the nineteenth century, geologists played a dual role as scientific explorers of new territories and discoverers of potential economic mineral deposits. British colonists and administrators brought with them a strong background in natural history and an interest

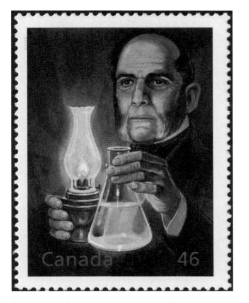

Postage stamp commemorating Abraham Gesner, New Brunswick's first geological surveyor.

Perhaps the most iconic image of the Klondike gold rush: packers and prospectors ascend the treacherous Chilkoot Pass in the winter of 1897-98. Crossing from Alaska, prospectors were required to bring with them a year's worth of supplies and pay duties to Canadian officials at the summit.

in scientific questions of the day, such as the origins of fossils and the age of the earth. They also professed Hind's faith in technology and progress, and a recognition that Britain's rise to industrial dominance was based firmly on mineral resources — particularly coal and iron. For contemporary observers, the discovery and development of these resources, as well as precious metals, were key to British North America's economic future. To this end, colonial governments promoted geological exploration, including the appointment of geological surveyors in New Brunswick (Abraham Gesner) in 1838 and Newfoundland (J.B. Jukes) in 1839, culminating in the establishment of a Geological Survey of the united Province of Canada in 1842 under Montreal-born William E. Logan.

In spite of these industrial visions, colonial mining grew fitfully in the first half of the nineteenth century. Much of British North America remained rugged and remote, little explored by Europeans other than fur

traders and, in any case, distant from any sort of market. Imperial mercantile policies ensured that prices for coal favoured British producers in Cornwall and Wales, and precious-metal finds of real significance eluded colonists. As historian Morris Zaslow has noted, in this period — and for much of the century — "ignorant optimism on the score of mining success was the rule rather than the exception." Many mining plays turned out to be as much promotional schemes as solid prospects, and many early developments were marked by failure. Nevertheless, mining developments in today's Maritime provinces and Central Canada provided early impetus to the further expansion of the industry after Confederation, by promoting frontier industrial development and settlement, attracting British and American capital investment, and spurring the economic integration of the new provinces of Canada. Discoveries of coal and gold in western Canada, culminating in the global phenomenon of the

Mechanics employed by the General Mining Association, Sydney Mines, Cape Breton, 1894. Cape Breton and Nova Scotia hosted colonial Canada's earliest coal mining complexes, dating to the mid-eighteenth century.

Klondike Gold Rush, further cemented the emergence of a nation stretching from coast to coast in the second half of the century. In so doing, mineral development also spurred treaty-making with Indigenous peoples on whose territories valuable minerals were found. As in earlier periods, however, mineral development frequently became a source of conflict with Indigenous people and, ultimately, contributed to the colonization of their lands.

Cape Breton and Nova Scotia Coal

In spite of coal's importance as a domestic and industrial energy source, coal mining developed only slowly in Nova Scotia. For most of the eighteenth century, only sporadic coal mining took place along exposed coal seams and outcrops around Chignecto Bay at Joggins and on the northern coast of Cape Breton Island (see Chapter

1). In 1784, Cape Breton became a separate colony; the following year, Loyalists fleeing the American Revolution settled at Sydney. A small outcrop mine on the north side of Sydney Harbour reopened to supply the British naval yards at Halifax and St. John's, Newfoundland, as well as the tiny local demand. For the next forty years, production remained halting. The British Crown retained control of mineral resources, colonial leases were short and royalties high, and the mines failed to attract significant capital investment. The poor quality and high price of the coal meant that it struggled to compete against British imports, even in regional markets.

Mining techniques remained primitive, even at organized diggings. Adits were driven into the exposed seams from the foreshore, but these shallow workings left much valuable material behind. These were pre-industrial

Underground miners at the No. 5 Mine, Cumberland County, Nova Scotia. By the 1870s, the Cumberland collieries became Nova Scotia's most productive - and deadliest.

mines reliant on the muscle power of men, boys, and horses to cut away the coal with picks and shovels and haul it to a shipping wharf by cart. They were also seasonal operations: ice-locked ports meant that the mines virtually ceased operations in winter, and many miners combined summer work at the diggings with farming or fishing in the spring and fall. This small workforce — only about fifty to a hundred miners worked the Sydney Mines colliery — included Irishmen drawn from the Newfoundland fishery and recently arrived Loyalist settlers carving out new lives in Cape Breton. During operations, miners were housed in cookhouses that doubled as rough bunkhouses; mostly unskilled, the men were poorly paid and dependent on the company for supplies of food and rum, purchased on credit from the company commissary at inflated prices. When the mining season ended, few left with cash in pocket.

Mining on the Nova Scotia mainland was, if anything, further behind. The "coal cliffs" at Joggins saw mining activities virtually cease in the decades after the Seven Years' War. Colonial policy restricted coal production to protect British exports, and Loyalist settlements around Chignecto Bay after 1760 seem to have ignored the presence of coal at their doorsteps, though it is likely a small bootleg coal trade continued well into the late eighteenth century. The historian Ian McKay argues weak local markets, export restrictions, and the presence of an alternate

staple for trade — extensive grindstone quarrying took place around Chignecto Bay — thwarted the early development of Cumberland County coal resources. Similarly, while coal deposits around Stellarton in neighbouring Pictou County were known as early as 1798, they were exploited on only a modest basis between 1807 and 1825. Though visible for all to see, and favourably located near tidewater for shipping, the colony's coal deposits remained undercapitalized, poorly administrated, and without a significant market, even as the Coal Age dawned.

The modernization and development of Nova Scotia's coal industry emerged from somewhat bizarre colonial circumstances. In 1788, King George III had granted his favoured son, the Duke of York, the mineral rights for the Nova Scotia colonies — which the King and Duke both promptly forgot or neglected until after the former's death in 1820. Facing a loss of personal income from his father and mounting debts (attributed to his penchant for jewellery and gambling), the Duke rediscovered this bequest and promptly transferred the rights to a mining syndicate that included his London jewellers. The General Mining Association (GMA) dispatched a Cornish mining

Working the coalface underground at the I.R. and C. mine, Inverness, Nova Scotia, 1906. Underground coal mining in the nineteenth and early twentieth century was specialized work initially undertaken by skilled colliers from England and Wales.

engineer to the colony, but instead of finding the copper deposits they hoped for, they had to settle for Nova Scotia's extensive coal resources — not all of which the GMA controlled. Using its colonial influence, the GMA quickly moved to secure control over the neighbouring Cape Breton fields (not part of the Duke's original grant) and snapped up existing mainland leases as they came up for renewal, giving the company a virtual monopoly over mineral development in Nova Scotia by 1828.

In addition to British merchant capital, the GMA

brought modern British mining technology and methods to Nova Scotia. Under the stern direction of young mining engineer Richard Brown, the Sydney mines transformed from primitive, dangerous, and largely unprofitable diggings to modern, industrial mines which, while still dangerous and unpleasant workplaces, incorporated updated technology and production methods. Underground mining employed the "bord and pillar" system, which entailed opening a series of interconnected underground rooms in the coal seam, supported by pillars of coal and flanked by shafts that provided access for workers, ventilation, and hoisting of coal to the surface. The introduction of steam power for pumping and hoisting, along with improved ventilation, enabled the mines to sink deeper underground shafts and undertake more efficient working of the "deeps." Production increased steadily, from 12,000 tons in 1827 to 68,000 in 1837. Though the company courted American customers for its bituminous coal, markets remained largely regional until the conclusion of the Reciprocity Treaty with the United States in 1854, which drove production from the Sydney coalfields higher still, to 126,000 tons in 1857.

Accompanying these modern technologies was the imported skilled labour required to exploit the resource effectively. Few Nova Scotians, nor many in the waves of displaced Highland Scots arriving in this period, possessed knowledge of underground mining techniques, so the GMA recruited colliers from northern England and South Wales, skilled workers who perched atop the highly stratified division of labour in the mines. These men worked the coalface singly or in pairs, hewing out and sorting coal from rock using augers, picks, and shovels, their work illuminated only by whale-oil lamps or, later, Davy safety lamps, whose enclosed wicks eliminated the danger of combustion from underground gases. While their work was difficult and dangerous, and their payment tied to their productivity, colliers nevertheless exercised considerable freedom in their underground workplace. Unskilled labourers included loaders, who transferred

Company store at Sydney Mines, Nova Scotia (1909). Early Cape Breton coal mining settlements were typically company towns.

the coal to tubs to be hauled out along underground roads by horses (which often spent their entire working lives underground). Horse-drivers and doorkeepers underground were often boys as young as ten, for whom labouring served as an apprenticeship to becoming miners themselves. A series of other specialized, if low-skill, labourers performed myriad duties at or near the surface, from timbering and ventilation below ground level, to "banking" or unloading coal above it. This backbreaking work was poorly paid, and remained highly seasonal before the advent of shipping coal by rail.

In this way, the GMA implanted in Nova Scotia, as one contemporary observer noted, "a colony of miners." Coal mining quickly became the single largest employer in Cape Breton, and settlements around the Sydney coalfields grew accordingly. The villages of Sydney Mines, Bridgeport, and Lingan were more orderly and comfortable than the former seasonal mine camps; they were effectively company towns, with housing provided by the GMA (which could be withdrawn in the event of the company's displeasure). At the largest, Sydney Mines, the settlement included schools; Roman Catholic,

Presbyterian, and Methodist churches; and mine buildings clustered around the pithead. Historical geographer Stephen Hornsby notes the demographic changes from earlier camps: some of the skilled miners brought families, and the community included a range of cultures and languages from around the British Isles, as well as increasing numbers of Cape Breton– and Newfoundland-born workers. Miners' wages were generally higher than those across the Atlantic, but problems of indebtedness to the company store persisted and mining in Cape Breton, especially for low-skilled labourers, was frequently a transient occupation: many left for better opportunities "down the road."

The GMA rapidly extended its dominance of the provincial coal industry to the mainland coalfields of Pictou and Cumberland counties. In fact, the GMA's general manager, Richard Smith, set up the company's headquarters at Stellarton in the Pictou field, where he oversaw a similar transformation of that county's coal mines through steam power and industrial organization. At Albion Mines, the company installed the first steam engine in Nova Scotia and, by 1829, it completed the first

The coal-fired locomotive Samson, preserved at the Nova Scotia Museum of Industry. The first colonial railways were built to serve coal mines in the region.

to a lack of inland transport connections and the GMA's general discouragement of development of the nearby seaside deposits at Joggins.

For this and other reasons, the monopolistic GMA, while helping modernize Nova Scotia's coalfields, excited considerable opposition in the colony. Reformers seeking to wrest back control over the colony's resources finally succeeded in abrogating the company's exclusive mineral rights in 1857, enabling local entrepreneurs and other developers to take up undeveloped coal leases. Still, full development of all three major Nova Scotia coalfields awaited that key technology of the industrial revolution: the railway. The completion of the Intercolonial Railway in the mid–1870s opened new coalfields in Cumberland County, provided a new domestic coal consumer, and integrated the province's nascent industrial centres as never before, while redirecting coal exports (thanks to Confederation and the high tariff walls of the National Policy protecting domestic coal) to the St. Lawrence market in Canada.

Freed from the GMA monopoly and given new impetus by Confederation and industrialization, the Nova Scotia coal fields expanded rapidly in the 1870s. Independent companies opened a series of mines in the Glace Bay area of Cape Breton, and the Cumberland coalfield, previously virtually dormant, sprang to life. Most notable was the dramatic rise of the Springhill mines, where a new branch line to the Intercolonial opened in 1873. Backed initially by Saint John investors, the Spring Hill Mining Company consolidated claims in the area, opened the Springhill No. 1 Mine, and later acquired four square miles of former GMA mining concessions atop the rich seams of this district. The company later merged with railway interests, backed by Montreal capital, to become the Cumberland Coal and Railway Co., and Springhill became the nation's largest coal producer in the 1880s. Looking back to this period from the turn of the century, one writer for the Mining Record noted, "A little over a quarter of a century ago the town of Springhill was not in existence; now it has a population of about 6,000 people, who have

steam railway in British North America, a short line to move coal between the mines and the wharf at tidewater. By contrast, before the 1860s the rich coal deposits of neighbouring Cumberland County remained stranded, due

Bankhead and surface works IR & C. Co. coal mine, Inverness, Nova Scotia, 1906. Coal mines were voracious consumers of wood for underground supports and surface buildings.

been drawn to the locality by the great success attending the Cumberland Coal and Railway Co.'s operations."

Coal mine outputs expanded in spite of the economic downturn in the 1870s, with the railway providing a degree of built-in demand, but also (by the next decade) because of the rise of manufacturing across Nova Scotia at towns like New Glasgow, Truro, and Amherst. Even the struggling Joggins coalfield, with its thin seams and poor-quality coal, enjoyed a revival of sorts after the arrival of a rail line in 1888.

Springhill also gave birth to the earliest labour organizations in the Nova Scotia coalfields, indeed the province. By the 1860s, the dominance and paternalism of GMA had given way to fragmentation among mine operators, which bred confrontation between owners and workers, including irregular strikes and walkouts. Mining remained dangerous work, while skilled miners

themselves found their autonomy undermined and pay packets threatened. In response to the imposition of a wage cut at the Springhill Mine in 1879, Scotland-born Robert Drummond founded the Provincial Miners Association (later the Provincial Workmen's Association), Canada's first province-wide union. Formal labour organization spread rapidly, in spite of the resistance of mine managers. Although the union struck scores of times in its first decades, it was hardly a radical force, according to historian Ian McKay. Drummond himself wrote, "Our object is not to wage a war of labour against capital, nor to drive trade, by oppressive measures, from the locality; on the contrary, by mutual concessions between master and man, we seek to have it carried on with advantage to both." The PWA succeeded in improving mine safety conditions, but had rather less success in achieving collective bargaining or improving overall standards

"The Drummond Mine Horror," an illustration from Harper's Weekly of the Drummond Mine explosion in 1873, which claimed 60 lives. Gases known as "firedamp" released by mining underground could suddenly ignite, causing massive explosions.

of living for miners. Though increasingly drawn from the ranks of native-born Nova Scotians, many miners continued to be transient, indebted, and apt to leave the province altogether.

Working-class organization and labour actions built upon a mining identity that was rooted in hazardous and demanding work and that, to some extent, transcended the hierarchy of job status. Entire families and towns depended on the mines, and this dependency bred a fierce solidarity. Coal mining work was beset with daily risks and frequent tragedies: in the late nineteenth century, an average of four workers per thousand lost their lives every year in Nova Scotia coal mines, from causes ranging from roof collapses to collisions with mine cars and locomotives to explosions large and small. The gas-filled Pictou County mines produced the most gruesome death tolls, including sixty dead in the 1873 explosion at the Drummond Mine and the horrific Springhill mine explosion on February 21, 1891, which claimed 125 lives, including twenty-one boys under eighteen years old. "The majority of the bodies bear no marks of violence, death having apparently been caused by firedamp [poisonous gas]," noted one news report on the Springhill disaster, while "others are horribly mutilated and almost unrecognizable." As McKay observes, "Death, this palpable presence underground, intensified the solidarity of workers menaced by a common enemy." Mine workers responded with both labour militancy and community-based mutual aid for injured or fallen comrades and their families.

Beginning in the 1880s, another round of changes swept the Nova Scotia coal industry. Deeper and more

At the morgue, a worker awaits identification after the Springhill mine disaster, 1891. Of the 125 dead in the explosion, twenty-one were boys under eighteen.

technology-intensive mines required greater investments to start and to operate, and this period saw a wave of British and American capital into the Nova Scotia coalfields, investing in smaller mines and more speculative exploration plays. A series of large collieries in Pictou County amalgamated in 1886, but the most significant development came in 1893, when wealthy American street railway magnate Henry Whitney and his "Boston Syndicate" consolidated nearly all of Cape Breton's coal mines under the control of the Dominion Coal Company. Through political connections with Premier William Fielding, Whitney engineered a ninety-nine-year lease over its Cape Breton properties, with a fixed

royalty of 12.5 cents per ton. Over the following decades, fragmentation gave way to corporate consolidation in the Nova Scotia coal industry and integration with the province's nascent steel industry, a story taken up in Chapter 3.

Mining in the Atlantic region was not confined to coal. The nineteenth century saw gold (in Nova Scotia), graphite (in New Brunswick), and iron (in both) mines operate, often sporadically, in the mid to later parts of the century. Of these, Nova Scotia gold was the most notable: during the peak years (1885–1903), Nova Scotia mines produced more than twenty thousand ounces annually. Further east, though the colony of Newfoundland

An illustration of the first mine in Ontario at Marmora, Hastings County by Susanna Moodie. Iron was the key colonial resource in both Upper and Lower Canada.

rejected Confederation with Canada in 1869, it remained a British colony and Newfoundland mines became an important source of copper ore for Empire smelters in the latter part of the century. Newfoundland copper production centred around Notre Dame Bay on the island's north coast, where deposits were discovered in 1857. With copper prices high during the American Civil War, Nova Scotian Smith McKay and St. John's merchant (and later, anti-Confederate premier) Charles Fox Bennett opened a mine at Tilt Cove in 1864, direct-shipping ores to the massive smelters at Swansea, Wales. Within a decade, the decline of high-grade ores shifted the locus of copper mining to nearby Betts Cove, where, through remarkable circumstances, German-born Baron Francis von Ellershausen established a copper mining and smelting operation in 1875. Backed by English capital and employing imported German and Cornish miners (as well as a good number of Newfoundlanders), the Betts Cove Mining Company installed six coal-fired cupola blast furnaces to smelt the lower-grade ore to a regulus (concentrate) of 20 to 30 per cent copper for shipping to Swansea. Primitive smelting at Tilt Cove, Betts Cove, and later Little Bay mines bathed their associated communities in sulphurous smoke and left behind a noxious molten slag, dumped around the towns or into the bay (where, at times, it exploded). Along with several smaller operations, the Notre Dame Bay mines experienced fitful booms and busts over the final decades of the century, each closing in the wake of declining copper prices after the high-grading of deposits.

Mining Upper Canada
Marmora and Hastings County

The earliest colonial efforts to exploit the rich array of minerals of the Precambrian Shield (the exposed portion of continental crust stretching across central and northern Canada) occurred on its southern flanks, in the eastern counties of Upper Canada (modern-day Ontario) between Georgian Bay and Lake Ontario. If coal was the key energy source driving the industrial revolution, iron was its critical material, and as at Trois-Rivières in Lower Canada (Chapter 1), iron provided the impetus for the first industrial mine in Upper Canada. Before the 1820s, there had been a few abortive attempts to establish ironworks in the thinly settled upper St. Lawrence and Lake Erie regions, but a combination of distance from markets and Imperial restrictions against large-scale industrial production meant these efforts failed quickly. After the War of 1812, however, non-Indigenous settlement grew in the territory and the Lieutenant Governor of Upper Canada, Sir

Peregrine Maitland, moved to relax restrictions on colonial industry and to induce local production by offering military contracts for iron goods.

At Marmora, in Hastings County, just north of Lake Ontario's Bay of Quinte, Maitland's efforts succeeded — to some extent. Maitland's offer of land grants and contracts was taken up by an enterprising Dubliner, Charles Hayes, a linen merchant with no experience in ironmaking who became, for a short time, Upper Canada's first industrialist. Arriving in the colony in 1820, within two years Hayes had raised a furnace, casting house, and small village at Marmora: the province's first mining town. Blown by a pair of twenty-eight-foot German bellows, the furnace burned charcoal made from the region's hardwood forests to melt and purify ore into pig iron before casting it into moulds for ballast as well as for finished cast-iron consumer goods. Poor-quality ore from Marmora was first used, but quickly replaced by high-quality magnetite from the "big ore bed" three miles away (later known as Blairton), and the ironworks boasted smelting technology and finished products equal to those elsewhere in North America. The settlement of Marmora grew to four hundred or so by 1824, and exhibited classic mining town characteristics: a mainly immigrant, male population (many, like Hayes, Irish-born), entirely dependent on mine-related work and on the company store for goods and services.

However, far from launching an industrial revolution in Upper Canada, the Marmora Ironworks struggled from the outset to become economically viable. Hayes quickly squandered his modest fortune in the construction of the ironworks, as well as road-building and surveying in this newly settled district. In spite of some political connections, Hayes failed to attract colonial government support, and by 1825 he returned to Ireland deeply indebted, leaving the Marmora enterprise in the hands of Peter McGill, his somewhat reluctant partner and financier. McGill, a Scottish Montrealer and a director of the Bank of Canada at Montreal, recognized transportation as Marmora's key limitation, but he, too, failed to attract support for a canal or railroad to the site. By the 1830s

Peter McGill, financier of the Marmora ironworks, pictured in 1866. McGill was a significant Montreal capitalist and politician, but lost a considerable sum in his Marmora venture.

the ironworks sat idle and McGill's efforts to sell the works and town remained frustrated until 1847, when the Marmora works were purchased by Joseph Van Norman, an American who had previously operated a small but profitable bog iron furnace at nearby Madoc. Less than a decade later, Van Norman also left Marmora, defeated by the failure to overcome the lack of efficient transport connections (and, perhaps, his inexperience in smelting the sulphurous magnetic ore). Thereafter, the Marmora ironworks operated sporadically, but never profitably, closing for the last time in 1875.

After the decline of Marmora, an attempt to establish an iron-mining operation at Blairton proved equally ephemeral. After decades of failed attempts to raise capital for a rail connection to the region, in 1866 the Cobourg, Peterborough and Marmora Railway syndicate (which included the Marmora Iron Co.) pushed a road fourteen kilometres to the mine pithead from the Trent River, enabling the newly established Blairton Mine to direct-ship ore to American smelters. The mine expanded rapidly, as did the new settlement of Blairton, becoming for a short time the new Dominion of Canada's largest iron producer. The mine attracted residents from nearby Marmora and recruits from as far away as the Cornwall, England, mining district. But by 1874, competition from Michigan's iron range pushed Blairton to the brink of insolvency, and after a few final years of halting production, the mine closed permanently in 1883 after winter damage to the rail line. Blairton was rapidly abandoned thereafter, earning it the distinction of being Ontario's first mining ghost town. The end of Blairton and Marmora did not signal the end of early Ontario iron-mining, however; through the early 1880s no fewer than thirty-three small iron mines were in operation around the southern and eastern districts of the province, most taking advantage of new rail links to direct-ship ore to American smelters.

Beyond iron, precious metals also generated a mini-rush to Hastings County, though somewhat later. Before 1864, the colonial governments of Upper and Lower Canada followed the long-standing imperial practice in granting land titles of reserving both base and precious metals to the Crown. In the wake of the short-lived (and ultimately disappointing) gold rush to the Chaudière River south of Quebec City in 1835, pressure mounted on colonial administrators to ease these restrictions. In the 1850s, Crown reserves were relaxed on base metals and with the 1864 Gold Mining Act, miners and landowners were permitted to work and claim ownership of gold on property to which they held title. The late-colonial policy of granting mineral rights outright with land ownership (and with little or no royalties due to the government) carried over to the early mining legislation of the new provinces of Ontario and Quebec.

Ontario's first gold rush was launched by a search for copper in the Madoc district of Hastings County by local prospectors in 1866. In a cave located on the farm of one John Richardson, a man named Marcus Powell discovered what he first thought were "leaves and nuggets" of copper. These were confirmed by Geological Survey of Canada geologist H.G. Vennor (who was exploring the area himself) as gold and, in spite of his cautions to keep the discovery quiet, word quickly spread. By 1867, the region flooded with prospectors and other chancers seeking to profit from gold, or from those seeking it. The farmer Richardson, himself, was tricked out of at least a few barrels of ore by American would-be financiers; later, he sold his property to other American investors, who opened the Richardson Mine to work the deposit. A boomtown called (optimistically) Eldorado sprang up on the former farm, within a year boasting eighty buildings, and prospectors from as far away as the Cariboo in British Columbia fanned out across the county.

Unlike western placer gold deposits (discussed below), however, the lode gold of southeastern Ontario occurred in difficult sulphide quartz formations. Would-be miners struggled to extract the gold from the ore, much of which contained significant quantities of arsenic. In spite of some considerable technological experimentation in ore processing, small, undercapitalized operations (including the Richardson Mine) struggled to install the stamp mills, grinders, and roasters needed to release the gold. By the end of the rush in 1871, only about seven mines produced significant quantities of ore, mostly from shallow workings. The Richardson Gold Mining Co. went bankrupt, and the boomtown of Eldorado faded into obscurity.

Gold production enjoyed a brief resurgence in Hastings County in the 1880s, when New York capitalists formed the Canada Consolidated Gold Mining Co. and acquired the Deloro mine from the former Gatling Gold and Silver Mining Co. Ironically, it turned out to be not gold but arsenic, the byproduct of ore processing, that sustained industry at Deloro. Arsenic production from arsenopyrite ore and recovered from tailings totalled 440 tons in 1885 and 120 tons in 1886, and until 1901 Deloro was the only commercial arsenic producer in North America. By the 1890s, the mine itself was left to flood, while a new mill for processing arsenical ores was erected. Thereafter, a company called Canadian Gold Fields operated the

Silver Queen mica mine near present-day Perth, Ontario, 1912. This short-lived mine produced industrial minerals mica and apatite (phosphate).

Deloro mill as a custom mill for arsenical ores shipped from elsewhere, including from the new mines at Cobalt, Ontario, and, by 1907, the reopened Deloro mine itself. In that year, the Deloro Mining and Reduction Company was incorporated, launching a new era as a major producer of cobalt and arsenic products. Though the Deloro operation lasted for decades afterwards, it also created a "grossly contaminated" site with arsenic and arsenical compounds, refining slag, mine tailings, heavy metals, mercury, and low-level radioactive wastes.

Upper Great Lakes

By contrast with southeastern Ontario, where mining tended to follow agricultural settlement, mining was a significant driver of non-Indigenous settlement along the Great Lakes shores of modern-day Northwestern Ontario. Before the 1840s, this vast region of lakes, forests, and rugged Precambrian rock was the territory of diverse First Nations peoples including Anishinaabe-Ojibway and Cree. These groups engaged in fur trade and small commercial fishing activities, but by the 1830s a reorientation of the fur trade to the north (through Hudson Bay) marked the beginning of the end of this industry's dominance of the region. Before 1850 (and indeed for some time thereafter),

colonial society regarded the Shield as largely unsuitable for non-Indigenous (i.e., agricultural) settlement.

Copper deposits on the Lake Superior shore were known to both Indigenous people (as noted in Chapter 1) and traders, but distance from markets and almost non-existent transportation links rendered mining an uncertain venture until well into the latter half of the century. Nevertheless, surging demand for copper, not only for its traditional industrial uses but for the growing electrical industry, eventually attracted miners to this remote region.

Geological reports from the Upper Peninsula of Michigan in 1842 first sparked a wave of interest in the Superior region's copper deposits, which were somewhat speculatively assumed to extend to the Canadian side of Great Lakes. A flurry of mineral exploration and speculation followed between 1845 and 1850, as colonial capitalists formed companies large and small to purchase huge mineral exploration tracts in the vicinity of Sault Ste. Marie. Few of these ventures actually explored their holdings, much less exploited any deposits, with the notable exceptions of the Quebec-Superior Mining Association at Mica Bay north of the Sault rapids, and the Montreal Mining Company's (MMC) Bruce Mines on Lake Huron some fifty river miles below them. While neither mine proved an enduring

One side of a stereoscopic photograph showing a group of miners at Silver Islet, near Thunder Bay, Ontario, circa 1877. Miners employed there were a diverse group, including Americans, Cornishmen, and Norwegians.

venture, the short but dramatic life of the Mica Bay mine in particular provoked dramatic changes in the relationship between Indigenous people and settlers in the region.

Encouraged by the American copper boom and supportive statements by Geological Survey of Canada head William Logan, prominent Montreal capitalists (including Peter McGill of Marmora fame and Sir

George Simpson, Governor of the HBC) formed the Montreal Mining Company to promote exploration and development of the Canadian side of the Great Lakes. Initially, the company concentrated its efforts on the quartz-copper deposit at Bruce Mines, which it purchased in 1847, and by the following year had constructed the first engine house — which promptly collapsed that winter. This proved to be the first of many difficulties in the first few years, the mine enduring remoteness, weather conditions, challenges in retaining skilled labour, and even a cholera outbreak. Although a small townsite was established and a stamp mill constructed, high production costs, low-grade ore, and low prices in the 1850s meant Canada's first copper mine faltered and, by the early 1860s, the MMC sold the mine to the operator of the nearby Wellington Mine. The Bruce Mines site closed in 1876, reopening only sporadically thereafter.

Even less successful, but arguably more significant for the region's history, was the Mica Bay mine. Title to the lands around Mica Bay north of Sault Ste. Marie was held by the Quebec-Superior Mining Association, which financed construction of mine buildings and accommodations in 1847, with a view to producing ore the following year. But by this time, the combined developments at Bruce Mines and Mica Bay had stimulated an influx of labourers, prospectors, and other enterprises to the Sault region, drawing the ire of local First Nations. Chiefs in the region had agitated since the early 1840s for protection from land developers and would-be settlers, and in response to mining developments, chiefs Shingwaukonse and Nebanaigooching protested further incursions into their territory without treaties. The chiefs received support from unexpected quarters, including a former backer of the Quebec-Superior Mining Association, lawyer Allan Macdonell. Joining forces with Macdonell, the chiefs pressed their case with colonial officials in Montreal and Toronto, and made petitions to the governor general, including claims to the existing mineral leases on Lake Superior and demands for benefits from mining activities.

When the chiefs' demands were ignored, they resorted to direct action. In November 1849, a small armed party including the chiefs, along with Macdonell and his brother, sailed from Sault Ste. Marie to the Mica Bay mine, which they promptly seized. Mine workers and their families were evacuated, and the occupiers shuttered the operation before abandoning the site in advance of the arrival of government troops in December. While the authorities apprehended (and later released) leaders of the "insurrection," including the chiefs, the protest did successfully prompt the colonial government to undertake treaty negotiations in the Lake Superior country. The resulting treaties with upper Great Lakes First Nations, known as the Robinson Treaties, were concluded in 1850. Although the treaties excluded existing mineral leases and claims, they included reserve lands, cash payments, and annuities for First Nations, and secured colonial (and mining) access to tens of thousands of square miles along the Superior and Huron shores. It would not be the last time that mineral development directly spurred treaty-making between settler governments and First Nations.

As for the mine itself, the Mica Bay operation was closed again by 1853, undone by low copper prices; it was described by one traveller as "the grave of 40,000 pounds [sterling], a monument to crass and ill-directed enterprise . . . [now] fast going to decay." Indeed, the rampant copper development on the American side of Superior virtually flooded copper markets, and even the completion of a canal through the St. Mary's rapids at the Sault could not improve the fortunes of Canadian mines. Desultory exploration and prospecting continued through the 1850s, but low prices, poor transportation, shifting colonial mineral regulations, and large tracts controlled by mining syndicates stymied development, with only a few modest exceptions. A small silver rush attracted prospectors to the lakehead area between Fort William (Thunder Bay) and Lake Nipigon in the early 1860s, but this was a mere prelude to one of early Canada's most storied developments: the Silver Islet Mine.

The setting for Canada's first major lode silver operation

Chief Shingwaukonse (Anishinaabe), along with Chief Nebanaigooching, led resistance to miners' incursions into the territories around Sault Ste. Marie in the 1840s. The resulting "Mica Bay Affair" led to their arrest, and eventually the first treaties in the region with Crown, known as the Robinson Treaties, in 1850.

could hardly be more daunting or improbable: a tiny islet offshore of Lake Superior's Thunder Cape, rising only eight feet above the waterline and smaller than the infield of a baseball diamond. However, the rich geology of this outcropping included several "bonanzas" of rich silver veins and orebodies, a number of which were visible and easily worked at the surface; others extended hundreds of feet below the lake. Exposed to the brutal storms of Lake Superior, establishing a mine on tiny Silver Islet entailed huge investments and remarkable ad hoc engineering,

The abandoned Silver Islet Mine shortly after its closure in 1884. Constructed atop a tiny island in storm-tossed Lake Superior, the mine was a remarkable feat of engineering and Ontario's earliest successful precious-metal mine.

while mining and milling activities generated important technological advances.

Spurred by new Ontario legislation in 1868 and 1869, which relinquished the Crown reserve on gold and silver while applying a levy on mineral lands, the Montreal Mining Company dispatched exploration crews to its extensive Superior holdings to determine which, if any, areas held mineral promise. While surveying the eastern side of Thunder Bay in 1868, the company's crew discovered remarkably rich, clear veins of galena extending from the surface of the islet out into the lake. Rapid preliminary workings proved the richness of the silver ore, but, from the beginning, extraction was a struggle. Initial attempts to blast rock below the waterline failed, and the first winter's work consisted of a shallow shaft just deep enough to work surface showings. These modest efforts yielded enough ore — and the promise of more — to allow the Montreal Mining Company to

sell out to a group of American investors led by Detroit financier and Civil War veteran Alexander Sibley.

Sibley's Silver Islet Mining Company brought American capital and mining expertise to bear on this tricky prospect. Arriving from the Houghton, Michigan, copper fields in 1870, engineer William Bell Frue oversaw the construction of a massive cofferdam and system of breakwaters around the islet to protect the mine workings from stormy lake waters. Meanwhile, initial mining raised over 155,000 tons of ore shipped for processing at smelters in New Jersey. That winter, Frue's first breakwaters were destroyed by violent Lake Superior storms, flooding the pit: "It seemed as though the water would surely succeed in regaining the whole of its territory and in driving its invaders from the ground," Frue recalled. The following year, a larger breakwater eighteen feet high and cribwork filled with fifty thousand tons of rock were constructed to protect the mine, permitting the construction of a shafthouse and mine buildings equipped with a steam-powered hoist and mine pumps. This allowed subsequent elaborate underground development of levels (or drifts) off of a main shaft to intersect with the deeper veins of the ore body, making the Silver Islet Mine resemble, below ground at least, the advanced hardrock mineworks of the western US.

Silver Islet proved a mining pioneer in other ways. In 1872, the mine was one of the first to use compressed-air drills as it pursued silver veins to ever-greater depths, heralding the beginnings of mechanization of skilled mining labour. The company also rapidly adopted the new diamond-drilling technology to locate ore bodies in its underground workings. As the mine encountered lower-grade ore at lower depths, it also turned to milling to produce concentrates for shipping. The company installed a stamp mill on the mainland near the mine settlement, where Frue put his engineering background to work on a new process for mechanically separating valuable ore from "slimes," or crushed rock. The "Frue Vanner," developed and patented at Silver Islet, went on to wide application in the North American mining industry and made Frue, who left the company in 1875, a rich man.

Like many mining settlements before and since, Silver Islet Landing, the shoreline townsite housing workers and their families, was an "instant" company town. It also reflected the predominantly male but relatively cosmopolitan qualities of mining settlements — mine workers at Silver Islet were recruited from Michigan, Cornwall, and even Norway. Cornish workers, recruited by mine captains Richard and John Trewtheway (the former succeeded Frue as superintendent), sat atop the mine's skill hierarchy, but they also proved highly independent and prone to strike. Most workers boarded in bunkhouses operated by the company, while a few mine officials lived in houses with their families. The little settlement boasted Methodist and Catholic churches, a small hospital, a jail, a customs house, and the inevitable company store. By 1873, the mine employed some three hundred workers, but, as at most mines, the workforce

waxed and waned over the years with the company's fortunes, and as miners left for better pay or working conditions. Nevertheless, the mine took on an air of permanence, and Silver Islet became the base for other silver prospects in the area.

Silver Islet realized its last bonanza in 1878, intersecting a rich deposit yielding 800,000 ounces of silver. Yet by 1880, production declined rapidly as richer veins "pinched out" and lower-grade ores, requiring concentration, predominated. Teetering on the edge of solvency, the Silver Islet operation folded in 1884 after the winter's supply of coal was lost in a shipwreck on Lake Superior, halting the water pumps and allowing the mine to flood. In all, the mine produced around three million ounces of silver with a market value of $3.5 million, making it Ontario's earliest successful precious-metal mine. Halting attempts to revive the mine in subsequent decades failed, and little remains of the mine today, although remnants of the town are still visible on the landscape at the tip of Sleeping Giant Provincial Park.

Mining Moves West and North

As in the Maritime colonies, in the nineteenth century mining played a role in driving British colonial interest in the Pacific coast territories that would ultimately join Canada. While coal deposits on Vancouver Island fired visions of an "even Greater Britain" on the Pacific Ocean, it was gold that ultimately drove mass migration to British Columbia and later the Yukon, and the incorporation of these remote colonial territories into Confederation with Canada. Though often considered more orderly and peaceful than the American "wild west" mining frontier, the mining booms of the Canadian west were also characterized by social instability, aggressive displacement of Indigenous peoples, and the sometimes violent confrontation of capital and labour.

In the 1830s, as Nova Scotia's General Mining Association was consolidating its monopoly on colonial coal resources and constructing its first steam railway, Vancouver Island remained a distant outpost of the fur trade. European

The Brechin Mine near Nanaimo, BC, operated in the early twentieth century. Coal mining around Nanaimo on Vancouver Island dates to the 1850s.

presence in the colony was limited to the vicinity of Hudson's Bay Company forts; beyond interactions at these trading posts, Indigenous peoples remained substantially independent in their homelands. In 1835, observing a blacksmith's use of coal shipped from Britain, Kwakwaka'wakw traders brought coal from deposits well known to them to Fort McLoughlin. Later, the presence of easily worked surface coal near the shoreline of Beaver Harbour prompted the establishment of a small coaling station at Tsaxis on northern Vancouver Island, worked by Kwagu'ł people. Near the newly established Fort Rupert (1849), Indigenous men cleared shallow trenches and dug coal, while women delivered coal by canoe to waiting HBC ships, principally for local use.

Keen to develop additional resources to promote colonization, the HBC expanded coal mining activities in the 1850s, with an eye to supplying both the Royal Navy's Pacific Fleet steamers and the expanding settlements of the United States Pacific coast. The company imported Scottish colliers and their families to

work the seams at Fort Rupert; in what would become a familiar pattern, the miners almost immediately struck, dismayed at having to undertake manual trenching work rather than hew coal. Their leader, Andrew Muir, was briefly imprisoned; most of the remaining miners left for the California goldfields. Efforts to revive the enterprise faltered due to low-grade coal and remoteness, but despair over Vancouver Island's coal turned to delight with developments further south at Fort Colville (later Nanaimo). As at Fort Rupert, Indigenous people introduced the British to the presence of coal near Nanaimo. Snuneymuxw traders first brought coal to Fort Victoria from nearby surface outcrops, attracting the interest of HBC chief factor James Douglas, who travelled from Fort Victoria in 1852 to inspect the deposit, declaring Vancouver Island "one vast coal field."

Encouraged to try its hand at mining again, the HBC established a small settlement and worked the deposits using a combination of Indigenous and imported labour (including some transferred south from the abandoned

Army Service convoy during the Great Strike of 1912-14. Strikes and violence at Dunsmuir-owned coal mines on Vancouver Island led the BC Premier to call out the militia at Dunsmuir's behest.

Fort Rupert). One of the newcomers was Robert Dunsmuir, a Scottish miner whose rise to become Vancouver Island's coal magnate began in the Nanaimo fields. In the 1850s, Dunsmuir worked both for the HBC and as a "free miner," honing his ability to locate and work the region's complex seams. In 1862, with its commercial monopoly dissolved, the HBC sold its mining interests to London investors, who made Dunsmuir superintendent of the Vancouver Coal Mining and Land Company (VCMLC) Nanaimo operation. Dunsmuir continued to pursue his own ventures, however, and in 1871 discovered the massive Wellington coal seam, on which he built his fortune. By 1878, production at the Wellington Colliery eclipsed that of the more established VCMLC mines. Drawing on investors from the elite of the new province of British Columbia, Dunsmuir acquired or discovered other mines across Vancouver Island, most notably at Cumberland in the Comox Valley.

Dunsmuir's empire — which continued under his son's direction after 1889 — was built on political influence and fierce opposition to organized labour. As historian John Belshaw describes, "forceful personalities, an aggressive attitude toward expanding output in their mines, and an antipathy to trade unionism combined to make the Dunsmuirs stereotypical robber barons and, inevitably, targets for industrial unrest and controversy." Beginning with his Wellington colliery, Dunsmuir established small, closed mining settlements that enabled him to break strikes by tying access to housing and stores to employment. Unlike the VCMLC at Nanaimo, which endured strikes in the 1870s but tried to reach an accommodation with labour unions, Dunsmuir (and, later, his

son) vigorously resisted the growing unionism imported by British and American workers to the Island coal fields. In 1877, 1883, and 1890–91, the Wellington colliery suffered bitter strikes, which the Dunsmuirs fought with evictions, blacklists, replacement workers, and even Royal Navy troops. Elected to the BC legislature in 1882, Dunsmuir consolidated his status as coal magnate and one of the richest men in British North America in 1884, when he secured a massive land grant and subsidy from the provincial and federal governments for the construction of the Esquimalt and Nanaimo Railway.

Coal workers on Vancouver Island were a diverse body, divided along lines of age, skill, and race. An "aristocracy" of skilled hewers, mainly imported from Britain and Scotland, sunk the shafts and worked the coal face and pits, while Indigenous and later Chinese haulers pushed the coal to the surface, where a mixed force of unskilled white, Indigenous, Chinese, and later Japanese workers sorted, transported, and loaded the coal onto ships. The growing presence of Asian workers, particularly those working underground, sparked controversy in the coalfields. Subscribing to the broader anti-Asian prejudice in BC society, white workers also resented the lower wages accepted by many Chinese workers and believed (erroneously) that they were dangerously irresponsible underground. Dunsmuir eagerly employed Chinese workers in his mines to offset a scarcity of labour and to drive down wages, reinforcing these negative attitudes. Anti-Asian sentiment was a feature of many job actions in the nineteenth century, and while there was little racial violence, white workers achieved a ban on Asian underground workers following underground explosions at Nanaimo in 1887 and Wellington in 1888 that some colliers blamed on Chinese workers.

Nevertheless, the brutal and dangerous conditions of the

Craigdarroch Castle, in Victoria, BC, was built by coal magnate Robert Dunsmuir as a home for his wife, though he never lived to see its completion. Coal made Dunsmuir one of early Canada's richest men. Today the mansion is a National Historic Site.

Vancouver Island coal mines did not discriminate in taking miners' lives. John Belshaw refers to the death rate in Island coal mines as "terrifying," even compared with mines in Wales, Britain, or Nova Scotia. In addition to the major disasters at Nanaimo and Wellington (which killed 147 and 60 men, respectively), a steady toll of death and disfigurement was registered by falling roofs, collapsing timbers, and the presence of noxious methane, or "firedamp." While some improvements in mine safety

Flumes and sluices of the Cariboo Gold Mining Co. near Barkerville, BC, 1897. In placer gold mining, flumes carried creek water often great distances to "wash" streambeds and benches to separate gold from alluvial deposits.

were achieved through ventilation and mechanization of pumping and hauling, BC coal mines remained twice as deadly as those in Nova Scotia and the United States well into the twentieth century.

A year after Robert Dunsmuir's death in 1889, his wife moved into the ostentatious Craigdarroch Castle he constructed in Victoria, a fitting symbol of the coal magnate's power and the wealth extracted from his Island coalfields and workers. Yet twenty years later, Dunsmuir's empire was liquidated: son James sold the Esquimalt and Nanaimo Railway to Canadian Pacific in 1905 and by 1910 had sold the family's coal interests as well. The massive Wellington seam had begun to play out by century's end, and though coal mining (and its fractious labour relations) would continue on Vancouver Island (see Chapter 3), it would never again generate the spectacular profits of the Dunsmuir era.

Gold fever on the Fraser

While coal mining began the transition away from the fur trade on the Pacific Coast, gold mining completely upended colonial economy and society. Though never as rich as the California or later Klondike gold rushes, the BC gold rushes were part of the global flow of fortune-seekers in the nineteenth century that ranged from Australia to California to the Transvaal and the Yukon, transforming settlement patterns, economies, and local environments along the way. As economic historian Harold Innis noted, "Placer gold acted as the most powerful conceivable force in mobilizing labour and capital for an attack on the difficult Pacific Coast region." The Fraser River and Cariboo gold rushes of 1858 to 1863 brought tens of thousands of migrants to the Vancouver Island and New Caledonia (mainland) territories, leading to the extension of formal British authority to the mainland, the unification of the Pacific Coast colonies and, ultimately, to the entry of British Columbia into Confederation in 1871.

HBC officials became aware of prospective gold diggings on the coast and in the interior in the early 1850s. Haida traders alerted the HBC to the presence of

A First Nations family placer mining with sluice boxes and gold pans at the confluence of the Thompson and Fraser rivers near Lytton, BC, ca. 1890. Gold mining and trade by Indigenous peoples preceded the Fraser River gold rush of 1858.

gold in their territory, Haida Gwaii (Queen Charlotte Islands), and in 1851 the company sent the brig *Una* to explore the outcroppings. The Una ran aground on its return to Fort Victoria, but word of the sixty ounces of gold recovered spurred a miniature rush to the island — mainly by American miners from the Oregon Territory. Conflict with the Haida ensued and neither the Americans nor the HBC recovered much gold, but the incident alerted senior HBC officials to the potential threat of American incursions. As a result, the Colonial Office extended Governor Douglas's authority to Haida Gwaii, and declared all minerals found within British Pacific territories property of the Crown, their exploitation subject to licensing.

This authority was put to the test during the Fraser River gold rush in 1858. Gold from the Fraser and Thompson valleys had been traded by Interior Salish peoples since the early 1850s, and the HBC quietly promoted Indigenous mining by supplying tools and supplies. A steady drip of American miners into the New Caledonia interior soon became a flood, however, after the SS *Otter* docked at San Francisco in February 1858 carrying 800 ounces of Fraser River gold. As rumours of a "new El Dorado" spread, legions of California miners, facing diminishing returns in the Sierra Nevada, streamed northward, flooding the streets of tiny Fort Victoria (the main port of entry to the colonies). The sleepy colonial capital was transformed into a boomtown, as a mass of gold-seekers arrived and outfitted for the journey into the interior. Indigenous and British residents now jostled with black and white Americans, Australians, Chinese, and Europeans seeking to reach the goldfields.

Some thirty thousand migrants swelled in the colony in 1858, most by steamer, docking at Fort Victoria and Esquimalt before crossing the Strait of Georgia to the Fraser River, others via arduous overland trails through the mountainous Oregon Territory and New Caledonia interior. Miners swarmed the river banks in search of alluvial (placer) gold, most ignoring the British licensing system. Operating largely beyond the reach of colonial authority, the miners organized themselves along the lines of the California goldfields, establishing claims to sections of river bank and adjudicating disputes among themselves, sometimes violently. The rising tide of American "Argonauts" — rootless, armed, and disdainful of British authority — spurred the British Parliament to proclaim the mainland HBC territories as a new Crown colony: British Columbia. The Colonial Office installed Douglas (who resigned from the HBC) as its governor and the new colony's capital was established at Fort Langley, an HBC post on the lower Fraser.

The presence of thousands of miners along the riverbanks and moving through inland trails provoked episodic but intense conflicts with Indigenous people. Along the lower Thompson, Nlaka'pmux attempted to defend their diggings (as well as important salmon fishing sites) from invaders even before the rush. "They have openly expressed a determination to resist all attempts at working gold in any of the streams flowing into the Thompson," Governor Douglas reported to the Colonial Office, "both from a desire to monopolize the precious metal for their own benefit, and from a well-founded impression that the shoals of salmon which annually ascend those rivers . . . will be driven off. . ." The summer of 1858 saw a series of revenge raids and killings (and at least one "treaty") between miners and Indigenous people, sometimes referred to as the Fraser River War. The HBC and colonial authorities intervened when they could to impose law and order, but soon the

balance of power and population in the BC Interior had shifted decisively. As historian Tina Loo noted, "From the perspective of the Sto:lo and Nlaka'pamux, who were the first to discover and mine gold on the river, the fortune-seekers of 1858 were not just claim jumpers but foot soldiers in an army of invasion."

Alluvial gold, washed down smaller rivers and creeks and deposited on the sandy bars of the Fraser and Thompson, provided relatively accessible "pay dirt" for miners using simple methods. Prospectors scraped away surface layers of gravel and sand to reveal gold-bearing clays, which they washed in pans or, working in pairs, in a small rocker or sluice box to recover small flakes of gold. When it was available, some used mercury to amalgamate smaller particles, but inevitably recovery rates remained low. Few nuggets or large deposits were discovered; nevertheless, in that first summer many miners compared daily returns with those realized in California. The main challenges for miners along the Fraser were the high price and uncertain availability of supplies, particularly food, and the vagaries of the river itself. American miners bitterly complained about the cost of food and supplies at HBC posts like Fort Langley and Yale; further upriver, there were few supplies to be had at all, and the line between subsistence and starvation was thin indeed. In addition, miners struggled to work the banks of a large river with extreme seasonal flows: in the summer of 1858, summer rains and snowmelt waters swelled the Fraser, closing the diggings for weeks at a stretch. Idle, hungry miners prowled makeshift camps at Yale and Lillooet, while others left the region altogether, declaring the Fraser rush a "humbug."

Nevertheless, the official production tally for 1858 topped a hundred thousand ounces, and both colonial and private pack roads were quickly constructed to transport and supply miners further up the river. Renewed, if more modest, rushes followed in subsequent years. The banks of the Fraser continued to be exploited, increasingly with larger sluice systems consisting of elaborate ditches or flumes carrying upland water to wash the sand and gravels.

Chinese prospector operating a "rocker" to recover gold on the Fraser River. Over a thousand Chinese miners, migrating from California or directly from China, joined the nineteenth-century gold rushes to BC.

Later, in the 1880s, hydraulic mining was undertaken, using tributary streams directed through pipes or hoses to a nozzle called a "monitor" to wash sediments from hillsides and river terraces into sluice boxes. This technique, developed in the California and Comstock mining districts, filled the river with sediments and left behind eroded terraces and boulder fields still visible on the landscape along the middle Fraser today.

Other independent miners, particularly First Nations and Chinese miners, remained long after many rushers moved on. The latter, arriving from the California fields or frequently directly from China, were greeted by the colonial administration as a necessary, if not especially preferred, source of labour in the goldfields. Chinese miners found a niche in working over diggings abandoned by white miners, labouring long hours rewashing river bar deposits. In common with most gold rushers, Chinese migrants were "sojourners," lured by the prospect of the riches found in Gum Shan ("Gold Mountain," their name for British Columbia) but intending to return home to China. By 1860, an estimated twelve hundred Chinese people worked in the Fraser river goldfields, and many pursued the subsequent rush further northward.

Miners moving up the Fraser River into the colony's interior made their next big strike in the "Cariboo" region of central British Columbia, precipitating another, albeit smaller, rush. Prospectors arriving in the Quesnel River region after 1860 faced very different circumstances, however. Harsh interior winters and long distances from settlements and supplies made travel, living, and mining

A flume crossing the Cariboo landscape, carrying water to gold claims. Placer deposits in the Cariboo were typically found below glacial sediments, requiring intensive hydraulic methods to recover the free gold.

conditions extremely difficult; most miners left the district to return south for the winter in the first years, as it was nearly impossible to work the frozen diggings. By 1862, with some six thousand miners prospecting the creeks and gulches of the region, supplies grew very short — and incredibly expensive, with some suggesting flour earned the same on the scales as gold dust. In response, Governor Douglas launched the construction of the Cariboo Wagon Road northwards from Lillooet, skirting the wild and unnavigable Fraser Canyon.

Once completed, the road eased freight rates and opened access to the Cariboo, but by the time it reached the gold rush boomtown of Barkerville in 1865, opportunities for individual prospectors — always limited — were on the wane. Unlike the Fraser's alluvial gold, which could be easily sifted using a gold pan or rocker, the placer deposits in the steep gulches of the Cariboo were largely found at depth, under layers of post-glacial

sediment and old stream beds. To get at this gold required dredging stream beds, sinking small shafts, or blasting away hillside overburden with hydraulic hoses, all techniques requiring time, organization, and capital — resources in short supply among prospectors. Experienced miners from the Fraser River and California fields adapted accordingly. For instance, in August 1862 Englishman Billy Barker famously struck paydirt on Williams Creek, but only after prospecting for more than a year in the Cariboo and after trenching his claim to a depth of fifty-two feet. Though some men working in small teams profited from such early discoveries, Cariboo historian Richard Wright notes "most of the companies committed huge financial investments" in labour, shaft-sinking, and flume construction. Gold production peaked in 1864, marking the end of the boom phase, but mining around Barkerville continued in its more capital-intensive form until the 1880s. South of Barkerville, a large hydraulic operation on the Quesnel River called the Bullion Pit was established in 1894, yielding well over a million dollars in gold during its heyday before 1905.

Still, a boom it was in the early years, attracting would-be miners and merchants not only from the Fraser and California goldfields, but also from the US, Britain, Europe, and Eastern Canada. The latter included the storied "Overlanders," a group of 250 small-town Canadians that banded together in 1862 to cross the Prairies to the Cariboo gold fields. Their harrowing five-month trek from Fort Garry (Winnipeg) to Quesnel ended just as most miners were departing for the south — many Overlanders joined them to overwinter on the coast and return the following spring. They arrived to find a mining camp organized into three main towns: Richfield, home of the Gold Commissioner; Cameronton, a miners' residential community; and Barkerville, the commercial centre of the Cariboo goldfields. The latter, with its saloons, shops, and supplies, eventually supplanted the other towns as the heart of the goldfields — but only after it burned to the ground and was rebuilt in 1868. By that time, the boom had subsided and the population

Images of Barkerville, BC, hub of the Cariboo gold rush. Barkerville was burned and rebuilt in 1868, even as gold mining declined. Today it is a major heritage attraction featuring historical re-enactments.

of the Cariboo rapidly contracted. Barkerville today remains a prominent mining heritage attraction, its false-fronted buildings and historical re-enactments evoking the romantic era of the individual prospector and the gold rush boomtown (see Chapter 6).

The Cariboo development reinforced the rapid

Gold rush camp at Lake Lindeman, BC, near the Yukon border in 1898. After crossing the mountain passes in winter, stampeders would build boats while awaiting the ice break-up that would allow them to travel downriver to Dawson City.

social and political transformation of the Pacific Coast colony. Epidemic disease had preceded miners into this Indigenous territory, bringing significant depopulation and migration of First Nations within the region. As in the Fraser River region, Indigenous people also resisted the changes gold mining brought to their territory. At the end of April 1864 a group of Tsilhqot'in warriors killed twelve members of a crew working on the extension of the Cariboo road that would cross over their land to connect Barkerville and the surrounding gold fields to the coast. Although now referred to as the Chilcotin War, the two colonial militia parties sent to confront the Tsilhqot'in wandered somewhat aimlessly through the BC interior, getting lost, retreating in the face of ambushes, and inflicting friendly fire casualties on each other. By the end of May, the Tsilhqot'in had killed a total of twenty non-Indigenous people. The conflict came to an end in

August as Gold Commissioner William Cox ordered the arrest of several Tsilhqot'in chiefs who arrived unarmed, not to surrender, but to discuss peace terms. The colonial authorities hanged six of the chiefs in October as murderers, an act for which the British Columbia and Canadian governments have recently apologized, recognizing that the Tsilhqot'in were defending their land militarily from provocative intrusion rather than engaging in criminal acts. For the Tsilhqot'in, the execution of the chiefs served as a rallying point for subsequent struggles to assert title over a traditional land base, and for their more recent legal fight against the New Prosperity gold and copper mining project near their territory (see Chapter 5).

Other Indigenous groups adapted to the new mining economy in the Cariboo region. Historian Mica Jorgenson has shown how the Cariboo rush attracted Dakelh and St'at'imc (Lillooet) people to the Barkerville area for work and trade. In combination with trapping and subsistence activities, First Nations men worked as guides, packers, and mining labourers, though seemingly less frequently as individual miners in comparison with the Fraser and Thompson river rushes. At Barkerville, Indigenous people

Miners were not the only ones who risked the harsh journey northward to profit from Klondike gold in the Yukon. Here a group of actresses fords a river as they head for the gold fields surrounding Dawson City.

joined the polyglot settlement of miners, merchants, and "camp followers" (from Chinese laundrymen to German hurdy-gurdy girls) that grew rapidly in the early 1860s. This migrant flow was also accompanied by the institutions of British colonial control of land and people, embodied in the local gold commissioner and the feared itinerant judge Matthew Baillie Begbie. While the Indigenous population remained larger than that of newcomers for some years yet on the mainland, the massive changes inaugurated by the gold rushes would not be reversed. In the wake of the Fraser and Cariboo rushes, British Columbia, only recently declared a Crown colony, would soon be incorporated into the new Canadian federation, in 1871, mining being a decisive factor in the political, economic, and demographic incorporation of the territory.

The Last Great Gold Rush

Few episodes in Canadian — or any — mining history are swathed in as much romanticism and lore as the Klondike Gold Rush. Though neither the final nor the largest of the Pacific Coast gold rushes of the nineteenth century,

the 1897–98 rush to the Yukon was a truly global cultural and economic phenomenon. In addition to profound local impacts on the Yukon/Alaska borderlands, the Klondike provoked seemingly endless fascination for outsiders, stoked by an emerging mass media and popular culture. Coming as it did amid a deep economic depression and an international fiscal crisis, the discovery of gold in the creeks and rivers tributary to the Yukon River attracted many thousands of fortune-seekers to travel to this hitherto remote region, few of whom would find reward. As gold rushes had in California and British Columbia, the Klondike pulled the Yukon Territory into a new national, political, and social order. As a mining phenomenon, the Klondike was also emblematic of the decisive shift away from individual and small-scale mining and toward highly capitalized, technology-intensive extraction methods.

The stampede of would-be prospectors to the remote Yukon territory was very much the product of the tumultuous end of the nineteenth century. Throughout the century, transportation, trade, and colonial expansion brought greater integration of markets and economies, such that when economic downturns gripped France, Germany, and England in the late 1880s, recessions and financial crises spread to Australia, South America, and the United States. The Panic of 1893 in the US provoked large-scale unemployment for much of the rest

Californian prospector George Carmack who, along with spouse Shaaw Tlaa (Kate Carmack), brother-in-law Keish (Skookum Jim), and Keish's nephew Kaa Goox (Dawson Charlie), filed the first claims on Bonanza Creek, sparking the Klondike gold rush.

of the decade. It also fuelled a national debate in the US around whether to tie that country's currency to gold, versus a "bimetallist" policy that would also use silver to back its currency. While previous global gold rushes had encouraged European adoption of the gold standard (in turn fuelling ever-wider searches for more gold), fears of a tightening or unreliable money supply gripped the US in the wake of the 1893 crisis. The Klondike discovery thus fired the imagination of a world beset by the rolling crisis in industrial capitalism.

Prospecting in the Yukon River watershed preceded the Klondike gold rush by a couple of decades. The 1870s saw forays into the region from St. Michael and Fort Yukon in Alaska, but access to the Yukon interior was restricted in part by Tlingit control of trade routes through the coastal mountains before 1880. A minor rush was triggered in 1886 by the discovery of coarse gold at Fortymile River, drawing several hundred prospectors and miners to the territory of the Han, or People of the (Yukon) River. Two small communities arose on either side of the as-yet unsurveyed Alaska-Yukon border: Circle City, Alaska, and Forty Mile, Yukon. Both were rough-and-tumble mining camps, but the latter assumed permanence enough to receive a detachment of twenty Mounties in 1894, in an early attempt to stamp Canadian authority on this disputed borderland. A series of other small strikes in the region confirmed the emergence of a small but productive placer mining district before the bonanza was struck in 1896.

In August of that year, California-born prospector George Carmack and his Tagish partners, spouse Shaaw Tláa (Kate Carmack), brother-in-law Keish (Skookum Jim), and Keish's nephew Káa Goox (Dawson Charlie), discovered gold on a small creek tributary to the *Tr'ondëk* (Klondike) River, near its confluence with the Yukon. There is some historical debate about who actually discovered the gold, with some giving credit to George, and others promoting Shaaw Tláa or Keish as the true founders of the Klondike gold rush. Regardless, the group hurriedly returned to Forty Mile to register their claims

Steamer *Excelsior* leaving San Francisco for the Klondike, July 28, 1897. *Excelsior* was the first steamer to carry passengers to the Yukon after news of the Klondike gold discovery reached California. She was laden with 350 passengers and 800 tons of supplies.

on the creek they dubbed Bonanza, freely sharing their good news with the camp. The Bonanza strike, along with the more moderate nearby find by Nova Scotian Robert Henderson (who had tipped Carmack to the Klondike River prospect to begin with) prompted an initial rush to stake claims along the Klondike and associated creeks. Under territorial mining law (following BC precedents), claims could be staked for a five-hundred-foot length from "rim-rock to rim-rock" along the creeks; Carmack, as official discoverer, could stake two, and his partners (and subsequent prospectors) one apiece. Bonanza and neighbouring creeks were quickly staked, and by June 1897 some eight hundred claims were recorded, which included many of the richest locations.

Over the winter of 1896–97, as local miners staked and worked the creeks, the region's centre of operations shifted from Forty Mile to a flat, bankside location at the confluence of the Klondike and Yukon rivers. Dubbed

Dawson City, the town was established on the site of a fur trade post (Fort Reliance) and associated village of Tr'ondëk Hwëch'in (Han) people; the latter were forcibly relocated downstream to a site known as "Moosehide Village." Already by spring 1897, residents of Dawson (named after the Geological Survey of Canada's George M. Dawson) numbered about 3,500, as merchants, innkeepers, saloon keepers, and government agents arrived to service (and exploit) the miners. Within two years, this muddy camp would be transformed into a roaring city of nearly 30,000, as it swelled with the hordes of fortune-seekers and camp followers from around the globe.

Though word had begun to seep out over the winter, the Klondike truly came to the world's attention in July 1897, when the first steamers arrived in Seattle and San Francisco from Alaska bearing newly rich miners laden with hundreds of thousands of dollars in gold. From there, recently completed telegraph wires rapidly spread word

of the discovery across the continent and beyond, news that was amplified and exaggerated by the popular press. The Klondike story not only reached a world hungry for economic relief, notes Yukon historian Ken Coates, but it also resonated with the period's fascination with exotic frontiers and adventure tales. Historian Kathryn Morse similarly suggests gold rush stampeders of all classes and backgrounds were motivated by "ideas of cutting loose, making a mark, and escaping from dwindling opportunities" in the highly regimented industrial economy. Coates argues the Klondike was perceived a "democratic" gold rush, where anyone armed with a shovel and gold pan could, by dint of initiative and hard work, strike it rich — though few actually did so.

Whatever their motivations, perhaps a hundred thousand people began the long journey to the Yukon

Typical mining claim setup in the Klondike goldfields. Finding gold often took weeks or months of backbreaking work all winter to dig out gravel for "washing" in the spring.

Advertising poster for the Belfast theatrical production of "The Klondyke Nugget," ca. 1898-1904. Thanks to telegraph communications and mass media, the Klondike gold rush was a cultural phenomenon that captured people's imaginations worldwide.

between 1897 and 1899; fewer than half that many actually made it. Whether travelling from Sweden, Eastern Canada, South Africa, New Zealand, or simply California, the stampeders' tales of hardship, toil, and death along the route to the Yukon are legion and form as much of the mystique of the Klondike as the actual mining. Of the four main routes to the Yukon, by far the most-travelled involved steaming to Alaska before either travelling up the Yukon River (in summer, if wealthy enough to afford the passage) or docking at the Alaska panhandle towns of Dyea or Skagway (at the head of the Lynn Canal) before travelling over mountain passes into the Yukon watershed. (Two arduous "all-Canadian" routes wound overland through British Columbia or via Edmonton and the Northwest Territories; relatively few reached Dawson via these difficult trails). As staging points for the most-travelled routes, Dyea and Skagway were themselves wild Klondike boomtowns, with shifting populations in the thousands, many of whom profited from the greenhorns outfitting their overland journey to the Yukon. The towns were patrolled by gangs of thugs

Gold prospectors and packers climb the summit of Chilkoot Pass, likely 1898-99. Thousands of prospectors and others braved the steep and treacherous pass en route to Dawson and the Yukon goldfields.

and gamblers led by one "Soapy" Smith — at least until 1898 when Smith was killed in a shootout with vigilante Frank Reid.

Would-be Klondikers were required by the Canadian government to enter the Yukon with a year's worth of supplies — about a thousand pounds' worth of goods. Having assembled their provisions, travellers could take one of two mountain pass routes: from Skagway up the White Pass Trail, or from Dyea over the famed Chilkoot Trail. Both were gruelling and deadly. The White Pass was less steep, but longer, and rapidly turned to an impassibly muddy trail in summer, along which pack horses died by the score. By contrast, the Chilkoot Trail rapidly became too steep and narrow for horses — at a way station called Sheep Camp, stampeders abandoned their beasts of burden and either began ferrying their

Gold rush prospectors waiting to register their claims in Dawson City, Yukon, 1898. Thousands of would-be miners rushed to the Yukon in search of gold, but relatively few struck it rich.

own loads (of a hundred pounds per load), or employing packers — mainly Indigenous men and women. The final climb up the Chilkoot Pass, along a boulder-strewn trail in summer or up steps cut into the ice in winter, brought weary stampeders to the summit — and the border with Canada, where they had to check in with the North-West Mounted Police, pay duty on their supplies, and cache them before scrambling down to collect another load. Although winter made the transit over the pass somewhat easier, it also presented dangers: travellers endured storms and frostbite, and in April 1898 an avalanche near Sheep Camp killed more than sixty people. In 1898 enterprising businesspeople installed a tramway to ferry goods to the top of the pass, though few travellers could afford the additional expense.

Once over the passes, stampeders still needed to get to Dawson, some nine hundred kilometres down the Yukon River watershed. At Lakes Lindeman and Bennett, gold rushers turned to boatbuilders, often working in small teams to construct rafts or boats to float the lakes and rapids to the main river, once the ice went out. Here, too, were obstacles and peril: the small armada heading for Dawson encountered canyons and rapids that wrecked more than a hundred boats (and drowned several men), to the point where the NWMP required inspections of boats entering Miles Canyon, and insisted women and children walk around the rapids. Little wonder, facing these obstacles, that relatively few of the thousands who set out for the Yukon in the summer 1897 actually made it to Dawson before freeze-up that winter.

Even as the rush slowed in 1899, the trek to the Klondike goldfields was significantly improved. Steam navigation was introduced on the upper Yukon connecting Dawson with the nascent settlement of Whitehorse (the limit of navigation on the river). The summer of 1899 saw the first train run between Skagway (on the coast) and Carcross in the Yukon, along the White Pass and Yukon Railway line. Financed by British capital and built with remarkable speed in a little over a year, this narrow-gauge line was extended to Whitehorse the following year. These connections not only made travel to the Klondike easier and safer, they slashed the cost of goods and supplies, and permitted the importation of mining machinery, contributing to the transformation in mining technique described below.

As the ranks of would-be miners swelled in spring 1898, it soon became apparent that most of the richest locations in the Klondike had already been staked. New arrivals were forced to follow creeks and gulches far upstream to find claim locations, often resorting to prospecting small "pups" or tributary creeks. Others, realizing that the location of creek channels (and therefore gold deposits) had changed over the years, began staking hillside claims — many of the benches above Eldorado, Bonanza, Dominion, and Hunker creeks proved to be productive. In some cases, late-arriving miners could purchase claims, or work a "lay" on behalf of a claim-owner for a specified percentage of the proceeds. In others, prospectors staked "fractions," or small spaces between improperly measured claims, which sometimes proved to be surprisingly high-yielding. Nevertheless, results were highly variable: many experienced miners were left frustrated while greenhorns (or "cheechakos" as they were known) hit paydirt, reinforcing the myth of instant Klondike riches.

Having acquired a location, a miner was required to work it regularly, and Klondikers quickly adapted classic placer gold mining methods to the particular challenges of the Yukon environment. As in the Cariboo, alluvial gold deposits were found in highly variable "pay streaks" below gravelly creek beds (as well as under surface dirt and

Panning for gold during the Klondike gold rush in the Yukon. Although a romantic image of placer gold mining, these techniques were rapidly replaced by hydraulic mining and steam dredges.

vegetation on the benches). But unlike the Cariboo, much of this ground was permafrost and required thawing in order to remove overburden and get at gravel for washing and gold recovery. This entailed much preparatory work over the winter months. As Dominion Surveyor and Commissioner of the Yukon William Ogilvie described, "The miner, instead of putting in the winter months in the towns and saloons, remains on his claim all winter, cutting wood in the earlier months with which he builds fires and thaws the frozen ground, piling it up to be washed as soon as the flow of water will permit." Miners struggled to keep underground fires burning amid cold temperatures, infiltrating water, and collapsing shafts and drifts. If they located paydirt (determined by washing excavated gravels in a pan), miners drove open-cut drifts along the former streambeds as best they could. They also prepared for spring by building rockers, sluice boxes, and coffer dams to hold back creek waters for washing the gravel.

In spring, miners hoped this strenuous (and unpaid) labour would see profit when water flow resumed and the accumulated gravels could be washed. Water availability proved a major challenge, prompting miners to build dams and flumes to direct creek waters through their sluices and rockers, into which they shovelled their paydirt. Sudden freeze-ups could idle the "washup" process. Hillside claims proved a greater challenge still due to water scarcity, forcing miners to haul water for their rockers or build communal flumes, often hundreds of feet long, to transport water. Rocking and sluicing washed gravels over riffles or sometimes small holes, which captured the heavier gold along with black sand, which was washed out in a pan. In these ways, miners produced an estimated $2.5 million in gold in 1897, and $10 million the following year in the Klondike district. In so doing, Kathryn Morse notes, they also nearly completely disassembled the local landscape by deforesting hillsides, removing soils, rerouting and sedimenting creeks, and leaving huge piles of mud and "spoils."

By 1899, mining moved into an early phase of mechanization, with the introduction of steam thawing, using steam boilers to direct hot air underground to hasten shaft work in the frozen ground. Steam engines also permitted mechanization of hoisting from shafts and shovelling of paydirt into sluices; eventually, small steam shovels were employed to remove overburden. Some hydraulic mining was undertaken, though limited on the creeks by water availability and space to store the vast amounts of tailings and overburden (which, after all, couldn't just be washed onto a neighbour's claim). These more intensive operations employed miners as wage workers rather than independent producers, the labour force drawn from the hundreds of disappointed prospectors remaining in the Klondike.

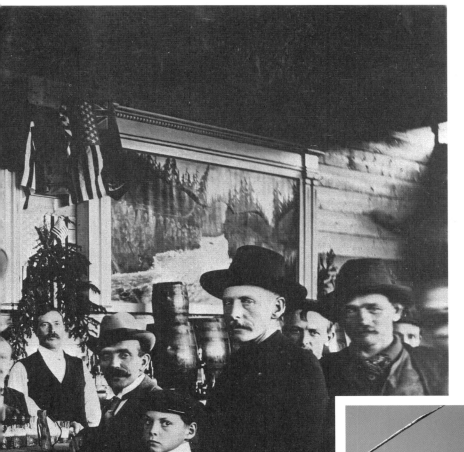

LEFT: Bar at the grand opening of the Opera House, Dawson City, Yukon Territory, July 4, 1899. American Independence Day was as big a holiday as Canada Day in Dawson, where Americans initially dominated.

BOTTOM LEFT: Huge steam-powered dredges like this one scoured riverbeds for gold deposits, making mining a capital-intensive enterprise. They also left behind massive tailings deposits visible on the landscape around Dawson City today.

BELOW: The reconstructed Palace Grand Theatre, one of many entertainment halls in the gold rush boomtown.

Church in Dawson City. Although its population rapidly declined after the gold rush era, Dawson City remains a vital Northern community.

While active miners often lived in cabins on their claims for much of the year, the epicentre of gold rush society remained Dawson City. Rapidly constructed — and reconstructed, after annual fires from 1897 to 1900 — the city briefly became the largest Canadian city west of Winnipeg, though its population in the early years was highly transient. Historian Charlene Porsild paints a portrait of Klondike-era Dawson as a bustling, cosmopolitan society, rejecting the popular image of the boomtown as simply "a gang of unruly American miners tamed by Mounties in red serge." While Americans initially dominated Dawson, over half the city's population included forty other nationalities, from English and French Canadians to northern and southern Europeans, Chinese, Japanese, and Russians. In addition to housing the gold commissioner and the North-West Mounted Police detachment (headed by the legendary Superintendent Sam Steele), the city provided all the services and delights demanded by fortune-seekers and newly enriched alike. In the short summertime season, Dawson's riverside docks hummed with activity as goods and people were unloaded. Merchants, laundries, restaurants, and saloons sprang up to serve the male-dominated populace, though goods and food were often scarce and prices were high — gold dust served as virtually the only currency in the community.

Much of Dawson's historical colour and character is rooted

in the city's dancehalls, theatres, and saloons — as well as its "demi-monde." Theatres such as the Opera House, Monte Carlo, and Palace Grand (the latter supposedly holding up to 2,200 patrons) served the miners and townsfolk imported entertainments and liquor. The city's famous dancehall girls put on shows six nights a week, and doubled as hostesses to sell the miners drink and dances — and sometimes more. Although illegal in the rest of Canada, gambling and prostitution were tolerated in Dawson's early years, the Mounted Police reasoning they were too popular and well-established to shut down. The romantic image of the city's red-light districts, particularly Lousetown or "Paradise Alley," obscures an often harsh reality of illness, addiction, and exploitation experienced by the immigrant and Indigenous women who worked in the sex trade.

For all the mania, mythology, and real-life drama, the Klondike rush dissipated in a short few years. By summer of 1899, more people were leaving Dawson than arriving: many disappointed fortune-seekers, unable to find gold or stake claims, headed back south or joined the smaller rushes to Nome (1899) and Fairbanks (1903), Alaska. Individual miners using relatively inefficient methods increasingly found diminishing returns, and more technology- and capital-intensive approaches to mining came to dominate. Small dredges, capable of processing seven hundred cubic yards of gravel per day, appeared as early as 1900, but large-scale dredging and hydraulicking was limited by the fragmented landscape of individual mining claims. In 1905 and 1906, backed by American capital, Joe Boyle's Canadian Klondyke Mining (CKM) Company and A.N.C. Treadgold's Yukon Gold Company obtained large concessions and constructed dredges for washing the streambed gravels of the Klondike. Floating dredges dug gravel from as deep as seventeen metres below the surface for washing through a long, rotating sieve (a "trommel") along the dredge's centre line. CKM dredges could process eight thousand to ten thousand cubic yards

Dawson City is an enormously popular tourism destination that has come to symbolize the last great gold rush.

per day, leaving behind a distinctive landscape of snaking, conical spoils piles still visible in the Klondike valley today. While these methods boosted gold production to new heights in the first decade of the twentieth century, historian David Neufeld notes they also signalled the decisive shift toward corporate-driven mineral extraction in the Canadian North and elsewhere in the country.

Conclusion

From Cape Breton coal at the end of the eighteenth century to Klondike gold at the end of the nineteenth century, mineral development was a regionally significant, if at times halting and unsteady contributor to Canada's journey from colony to nation. Mineral resources — particularly coal, iron, and precious metals — fuelled geological exploration, territorial expansion, and dreams of a transcontinental British imperial dominion. In territories marginal for agricultural settlement, the expansion of the industry brought contact and conflict with Indigenous communities, who in varying ways resisted, accommodated, or participated in mineral developments, but who ultimately saw their territorial sovereignty undermined. Mining itself underwent revolutions in technology and

industrial organization, such as the shift from labour-intensive, craft-based mining techniques of early coal miners to the increasing mechanization of deep, underground workings and the development of rail transportation. Hardrock mining saw similar developments in drilling, stoping, and ore-processing technologies. In the western goldfields, the romantic image of the individual sourdough prospectors flourished, but ultimately gave way to capital-intensive, large-scale alluvial mining of hydraulicking and dredging. Through these changes, mining produced diverse "workscapes" of labour and community associated with different mines, from the closed, paternalistic company coal towns of Cape Breton and Vancouver Island, to the remote boomtowns associated with precious metal mining. The underlying trends of nineteenth-century industry — enhanced technology, corporate organization, and labour militancy — would only increase as mining moved into "Canada's century."

Shift change at the Hollinger Consolidated Gold Mine in Timmins, Ontario, 1920. Mining grew into a cornerstone of Canada's industrial boom around the turn of the twentieth century.

CHAPTER 3

Mining and the Industrial Boom

If a group of travellers visited Canada in 1880, left, and then returned in 1913, they would be astonished by the radical transformation. While they may have travelled by rail in Eastern and Central Canada during their first journey (along the intercolonial and Grand Trunk Lines), the transcontinental Canadian Pacific Railway (CPR) now linked the western part of the country to the cities of Central Canada. From the passenger cars they might remark on the dramatic changes to the western prairie: a sparsely populated grassland where, by end of the 1870s, hunters had destroyed once-vast herds of bison and the Canadian government had begun the process of confining Indigenous people to reserves. The prairie had now become the ecological engine behind a major wheat boom in Canada, with production rising from 56 to 225 million bushels of the grain between 1901 and 1913. New western cities had grown rapidly amid the seemingly endless fields of grain and farther west along the Pacific Coast. From 1891 to 1914, Winnipeg's population expanded from 25,000 to 136,000, while Vancouver experienced a remarkable tenfold growth from 15,000 to 155,000. Even the older, established cities of Central Canada doubled in size during the same period, Toronto from 181,000 to 382,000 and Montreal from 219,000 to 490,000. Many came to the cities to fill the demand for labour in the rapidly expanding manufacturing sector, toiling in the garment factories, steel

The Falconbridge nickel mine at Sudbury, Ontario in 1930. Falconbridge grew to become one of Canada's biggest mineral producers with mines in Canada and eighteen other countries.

Mining exploration party at the Hollinger property in the rich Porcupine gold region of Northern Ontario, ca. 1909. Noah Timmons, second from right, became a famous mine financier as president of Hollinger Mines Ltd.

mills, and machine shops that formed the base of Canada's industrial takeoff. Indeed, from 1896 to 1913, Canada's manufacturing heartland shifted from the Maritimes to the Great Lakes and St. Lawrence basin and drove (along with the wheat boom) an explosive quadrupling of the country's gross national product between 1896 and 1913. The twentieth century belonged to Canada, or so it may have seemed to our imagined group of travellers in the midst of the most rapid period of economic expansion the country had ever seen.

Mining contributed enormously to fulfilling the voracious energy and material demands of industrialization in Canada and in key export markets such as Great Britain and the United States. Certainly, production boomed across all sectors in the mining industry. In an age when oil was a bit player, coal production increased nearly fivefold from 1896 to 1913 (from just over 3.7 million tons to 15 million tons) to meet the ever-increasing energy demands of the expanding railway network, factory sector, and cities.[3] The venerable precious metals also continued to flourish, as annual Canadian silver production increased tenfold from 3.2 million to nearly 32 million troy ounces (a measurement unit specific

to precious metals) from 1896 to 1913. Annual gold production rose and fell more erratically during the same period — from 133,000 to 1.35 million troy ounces between 1896 to 1900 and then back down to 406,000 troy ounces in 1907 — due to the rapid boom and bust of Klondike production. Nonetheless, new gold mines at Rossland, BC, in the 1890s and in northern Ontario in the 1910s pushed production back up to 803,000 troy ounces by 1913.

More than any other mineral sector, however, base metals exploded as the mining industry took advantage of new demands associated with the Great Transformation. Annual copper production increased approximately sevenfold (from almost 9.4 million to 77 million pounds) between 1896 and 1913 to feed the insatiable demand for electrical wiring. Mining companies targeted other metallic minerals because of their value to a burgeoning steel industry and the production of other industrial alloys. Iron production doubled and nickel increased by a factor of fifteen during the boom years (reflecting nickel's ever-greater importance as an alloy to make reinforced steel in preparation for the global war that was soon to come). Cobalt production increased remarkably from 32,000 pounds to 1.6 million pounds between 1904 and 1913. By 1896 the metallic minerals began to eclipse coal and other fuels as the top cash earner within the Canadian mining industry, accounting for more than 60 per cent of total revenue in the industry four years later. It is unlikely coal producers resented this shift, however, as the mineral industry expanded broadly and in most sectors without pause during the industrial boom, with revenues growing from $20 million in 1896 to over $140 million in 1913. While the boom period must be kept in perspective (production rates for many minerals multiplied even more impressively in the 1950s and 1960s), it signalled the development of a modern industrial society that became increasingly reliant on a material base of non-renewable minerals.

Such hunger for minerals encouraged the industry to reach into previously remote regions, most notably western Canada and the Canadian Shield country of northern Ontario. Nickel and copper at Sudbury, silver and cobalt at the aptly-named Cobalt, and gold at Timmins and Kirkland Lake all became significant prior to the First World War. In southern Alberta, Lethbridge became the self-proclaimed "coal city in the wheat country" as Alexander Galt financed new mining activity beginning in 1882. In British Columbia, several gold, silver, and copper mines opened in fits and starts in the Boundary-Slocan district in the British Columbia interior in the 1890s, and in 1904 the Britannia copper mine near Vancouver began a seven-decade production run. In 1896, the massive smelter complex at Trail began to process ore from the nearby Rossland mines, and in 1909, feedstock from the massive Sullivan lead-zinc mine in Kimberly. In the late 1880s Vancouver Island coal production expanded from its original epicentre near Nanaimo to Comox, reaching peak production between 1910 and 1930. Mining activity in the far north was minimal during the boom years, but the industry did make a new foray into the territories as the Keno Hill district in the central Yukon became a

Slag pot train dumping smelter waste near Copper Cliff, Ontario. As mining and mineral processing grew, so did their impacts on the local environment.

major silver producer beginning in 1913. Although the mines themselves occupied relatively small spaces, by the early years of the twentieth century the Canadian mining industry had expanded its networks of regional extraction from coast to coast.

In all but the most remote cases, new railroads helped drive mining development to these distant corners. The three new transcontinental lines constructed between 1885 and 1915 — the Canadian Pacific, the Canadian National, and the Northern Transcontinental/Grand Trunk Pacific lines — opened vast stretches of northern Ontario and the West to development. Smaller branch lines were perhaps even more of a spur to mining activity. The Crowsnest Pass line, for example, was constructed with a large public subsidy to provide southern BC, particularly the smelter in Trail, access to the coal-rich regions of southern Alberta. The discovery of silver during the construction of the Temiskaming and Northern Ontario Railway precipitated the Cobalt mining rush in 1903, and then gold rushes near Porcupine (now Timmins) in 1910 and what became Kirkland Lake in 1911 as construction moved northward. The provincial government had built the Temiskaming line as a state-owned enterprise to promote agricultural settlement and timber harvesting in eastern Ontario, but it quickly became known more for sparking a mineral bonanza beyond the government's wildest dreams. Just as

Freight cars hauling ore from the Britannia Mine on Howe Sound in British Columbia. Railway construction often accompanied major mining developments in remote regions.

importantly, the public railroad provided the means for private capital to access northern Ontario's mineral wealth, a "pleasant train ride that united Toronto physically and psychologically with the booming mining frontier," as historian H. Vivian Nelles described it. Throughout Canada's boom period, private mining capital spread along the tentacles of thousands of kilometres of publicly financed railroads, stitching the financial interests of the metropolis to the mineral resources of the distant hinterland.

Such massive expansion in output and geographical reach brought structural changes to the industry. As mentioned in the previous chapter, the Klondike gold rush proved to be the last days of the plucky and adventurous individual miner panning for gold amid fluvial sands. The precious and base metal deposits of the Canadian Shield required driving into hard rock, a geological challenge that demanded heavy investment in labour, machinery, and complex ore-processing facilities, especially as it became feasible to mine the minute percentage of valuable minerals contained in lower-grade ores. Miners worked in underground and surface environments that increasingly resembled highly mechanized urban factories. To finance and facilitate this transition, and as a reflection of broader trends in Canadian industry toward factory production and

heavily capitalization, the mining industry began to adopt a large-scale corporate structure in the late nineteenth century. Although individual prospectors could still stake mineral claims, or perhaps even raise capital on the stock exchange to start a "junior" company, more often than not these smaller claims were swallowed up as the large companies consolidated control over mineral supply and production networks. Prior to the First World War, the American-financed International Nickel Company (Inco) dominated the Sudbury nickel deposits and became the first mining giant in northern Ontario, beginning in 1902. Canadian-controlled companies became key players in northern Ontario: Algoma Steel controlled major iron holdings around Sudbury after incorporation in 1901; Hollinger quickly became the corporate giant of the Timmins goldfields after 1910; and Falconbridge provided some competition to Inco in the Sudbury nickel fields after 1928. In the West, the Consolidated Mining and Smelting Company (CM&S, later Cominco), a subsidiary of the Canadian Pacific Railway, became the most important large corporate player after its creation in 1906 due to its control of several mining properties in the BC interior, including the large Sullivan lead-zinc mine, that fed the crucial central smelting facility in the town of Trail. Mining in Canada had become synonymous with big business by the turn of the century, as investment capital flowed into the country (much of it from Britain and the United States) to build emerging corporate empires.

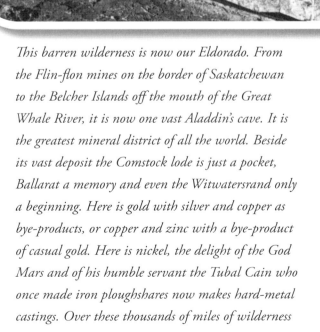

RIGHT: Early electric locomotive underground at the Hollinger Mine. Mining technology changed rapidly in this period, enabling the construction of deeper and more efficient mining.

Governments of all political persuasions supported the expansion of mining in tangible ways. In addition to the aforementioned railroads, provincial and federal politicians provided generous royalty regimes, royalty holidays for the early years of a mine's life, and tax incentives. Although some provincial governments attempted to enforce a "manufacturing condition" in certain cases (mandated refining of raw material in Canada prior to export), in general the state was reluctant to force companies to process raw material prior to export. Federal and provincial governments generally became a client of industry during the boom years, as Nelles has argued so famously in the case of Ontario, deferring to private interests as opposed to making a substantial claim to the "people's share" of resource revenues from private lands. In rhetorical terms, provincial and federal politicians touted new mining development as being at the vanguard of expanding civilization, bringing new towns, settlers, and industries to areas that were thought of as a barren wilderness. The equation of mining with progress was a widely held sentiment in public circles as well. In 1937 humourist and economist Stephen Leacock wrote with unbridled optimism about mineral developments on the Canadian Shield:

This barren wilderness is now our Eldorado. From the Flin-flon mines on the border of Saskatchewan to the Belcher Islands off the mouth of the Great Whale River, it is now one vast Aladdin's cave. It is the greatest mineral district of all the world. Beside its vast deposit the Comstock lode is just a pocket, Ballarat a memory and even the Witwatersrand only a beginning. Here is gold with silver and copper as bye-products, or copper and zinc with a bye-product of casual gold. Here is nickel, the delight of the God Mars and of his humble servant the Tubal Cain who once made iron ploughshares now makes hard-metal castings. Over these thousands of miles of wilderness

Miners on strike at South Porcupine in the winter of 1912, with the Western Federation of Miners union hall in the background. The early-century mining industry was the scene of intense, often violent confrontations between capital and labour.

aeroplanes float in the sky and flurry on the frozen lakes, carrying a new race of men, as Hyperborean as the cold itself.

Even the social scientist Harold Innis, most famous for his pessimism about economic dependence on raw materials in hinterland regions, wrote in extremely positive terms about the potential for mineral-led development to bring infrastructure and economic development to Canada's northlands.

Of course, the picture was never so rosy as the mining boosters proclaimed. One of the major claims of this chapter (and subsequent ones) is that the expansion of mining activities during the boom years often carried dire social and environmental consequences, the brunt of which was sometimes borne by First Nations communities in remote areas newly opened to development. Mining activity created

new resource towns where none had existed, and provided work and/or trade opportunities for some Indigenous people, but in other cases displaced hunting and trapping. Indigenous communities also had to contend with a settler population that imported with them new food, alien cultural norms, and new methods of economic exchange. Among the settler community, miners had to ride the roller coaster of the commodity cycle, running flat out during booms and weathering the slowdowns of the busts as best they could. Mine closure and abandonment was traumatic for mining towns, leading to a hollowing-out and possible total collapse of the community. As the industry consolidated into larger companies, mine managers constantly sought to wring more concessions and efficiencies from workers to satisfy the push for profitability among owners and/or shareholders. Bitter strikes ensued across the industry, especially during the broader labour unrest after the First World War.

Environmental problems were also endemic to the industry. Hardrock mining broke and crushed the rock of the Canadian Shield to get at tiny percentages of ore; the result was a virtual Pandora's box of waste rock and fine dust known as tailings that could contain dangerous heavy metals (arsenic, cadmium, lead, copper, etc.) or in some cases radioactive material. Sulphide-bearing waste rock tended to oxidize in the open air, a chemical reaction that produced acidic water, or acid rock drainage, that could in turn lead to the mobilization of more heavy metals into nearby lakes and streams. Such material worked its way into soil, streams, and lakes, and sometimes into the bodies of the workers in the mines or of the people who lived nearby. Mineral smelting produced additional airborne toxic compounds such as arsenic trioxide and sulphur dioxide that spread far beyond the processing site, often destroying vegetation and impacting human health for miles around. Governments imposed few environmental regulations on the mining industry during this period of rapid expansion, a long-term subsidy that often left the public bearing the cost of cleanup many years after closure and abandonment (see Chapter 6). If mining represented industrial progress, it also threw into bold relief all of the explicit and hidden costs associated with hinterland resource development; a barometer, if you will, of the ecological and social consequences of modernity at the margins of Canada's settled geography.

ABOVE: Example of square-set timbering used to construct underground drifts, or tunnels.

BELOW: Drilling underground at Garson Mine, Sudbury, Ontario. Well into the industrial era, underground mining remained one of the most dangerous industrial occupations.

The Nickel Empire of Northern Ontario

In 1854 land surveyor Albert P. Salter noticed his compass needle moving anomalously when running a survey line near what is now known as the Sudbury basin. Provincial geologist Alexander Murray took samples at the site and confirmed the magnetic anomaly indicated a geological formation containing potentially large deposits of nickel, copper, and iron. At this time, however, the site was so remote there was no interest among government or private investors. In 1883 Thomas Flanagan, a blacksmith working in the Sudbury area on the construction of the CPR, noticed rusty signs of oxidization on a recently blasted area. With a major railroad set to run though the area, the rediscovery of Salter's ore body prompted a staking rush as prospectors quickly marked claims and began to dig ore at several small mines.

In 1886 American investor Samuel Ritchie formed

Evans Mine, Canadian Copper Co., Copper Cliff, Ontario, 1898. In spite of the name, it was nickel that propelled the Copper Cliff/Sudbury region to global prominence as a mining region in this period, as demand for industrial minerals grew.

the Canadian Copper Company and quickly moved to consolidate mining activity in the region, buying up the McAllister, Stobie, Creighton, and Copper Cliff mines. These purchases set the tone for mining in the Sudbury region, where big American capital sought to retain monopoly control over production to serve American industrial and military appetites. Ritchie found a US partner to refine his ore in the Orford Copper Company of New Jersey, quickly discovering through processing that his copper ore was extremely rich in nickel, a versatile metal growing in importance as an alloy in steel-making and other industrial applications. Seizing the opportunity to promote nickel's virtues, Ritchie effectively lobbied politicians on both sides of the border. Prime Minister John A. Macdonald visited the region and was convinced in 1889 to lift duties

on mining and smelting machinery and smelting coke. At Ritchie's behest the US secretary of the navy, B.F. Tracy, became enamoured of nickel's military potential, providing the biggest customer for Canadian production. Indeed, the US government dropped tariffs on semi-refined nickel matte (while maintaining a duty on refined nickel) to reinforce the mineral conduit from Sudbury to the American industrial heartland. Although other minerals were mined in the Sudbury Basin, including copper and gold, it was the growing demand for nickel that drove extractive activity in the region for decades.

In 1901 the famous American captain of industry J. Pierpont Morgan moved to consolidate his various holdings into the giant US Steel Company, securing an all-important nickel supply though the acquisition and merger of Canadian Copper and Orford into the International Nickel Company (shortened to Inco in 1919). The result was a virtual monopoly over the Sudbury deposits, as ineffectual competitors such as the British company Mond, which Inco absorbed in 1928, failed to dent the dominance of American capital. Even the arrival of Falconbridge to

The main shaft of the Falconbridge Mine in Sudbury, Ontario in 1929.

the area in 1928 provided little threat initially — at least until the US military wanted to diversify sources of nickel supplies after the Second World War. Inco remained the dominant corporate player in the Canadian nickel industry for decades, exercising control over what was quickly becoming the world's largest source of the mineral.

Any attempts to level a nationalist critique at International Nickel's practice of channelling Canadian nickel to American processing facilities met with only limited success. From the earliest days of Sudbury mining until the First World War, nickel processing at Sudbury was limited to the production of matte through smelting, a partially refined product that was then shipped to the United States for final refining. Somewhat ironically, it was the American Samuel Ritchie who worked with Canadian businessmen throughout the 1890s to lobby for export tax on partially refined nickel to encourage Canadian refining after he was ousted from the board of Canadian Copper earlier in the decade. *The Canadian*

Mining Review summed up industry opposition to the export tax in 1899, claiming that Canadian Copper already made major contribution to the economy through the operation of four smelters in Canada and associated mines that employed a thousand men. The editorial argued that, "neither the copper mines nor the nickel mines can stand the proposed exaction. Let the mining industry have a free chance to develop and strengthen itself; to gather a population of consumers around it; to give natural birth to associated industries." Not until 1916, when the media widely reported that Canadian nickel had been shipped through the United States to Germany on two occasions aboard the submarine *Deutschland*, did the resulting public outcry and threat of government expropriation force Inco's hand. Although it would continue to produce feedstock for US mills, the company completed a nickel

Workers sorting nickel matte (an intermediate refined nickel product) at a smelter near Sudbury, 1925. Nickel production and export was frequently the subject of controversy between Canada and the United States in the first quarter of the twentieth century.

refinery at Port Colborne in 1918 to produce 99 per cent pure electrolytic nickel from nickel oxides that had been partially processed at smelting facilities in the town of Copper Cliff (a small mining town that would be absorbed as a neighbourhood of Sudbury regional municipality). If the war had forced Inco to fully refine nickel along a Canadian production chain, breaking its monopoly over global nickel supplies was more difficult. Just prior to its takeover of Mond in 1928, Inco managed to avoid the then-powerful US anti-trust laws through a simple share conversion to make the company nominally Canadian.

Inco's lock over nickel supplies was mirrored in its resolute control over the people that worked in the mines. In satellite company towns such as Copper Cliff, the company used the threat of eviction from leased land or housing as a means to maintain control over workers. The men who worked the mines faced difficult conditions: dust, noise, long working hours, the potential for rockfall

and other accidents all undermined their health and safety. The cyclical boom-and-bust nature of the industry meant frequent layoffs, undermining worker solidarity as the unemployed often moved on to find work elsewhere. In addition, Inco actively and successfully thwarted all attempts at unionization until 1942, using tactics ranging from outright intimidation to the exploitation of ethnic divisions among the diverse groups of Scandinavians, Poles, Ukrainians, Italians, and French Canadians. As with other mining companies in northern Ontario, Inco refused even to recognize labour unions until after the Second World War, when changes to Ontario's labour legislation in 1943 compelled companies to negotiate with independent workers' associations. The company banned labour publications, dismissed workers who joined or even discussed a union, and employed the American security firm Pinkerton to keep union organizers away from workers. When the first local of the International

Mine, Mill, and Smelter Workers (known simply as "Mine Mill") was chartered in 1936, a gang of company thugs wrecked the office and attacked organizer George Anderson, precipitating the collapse of the organization. When a new local began to organize in 1942, another gang of thugs raided the office, breaking furniture and windows, and beating two organizers, Forrest Emerson and Jack Whelahan, who were working that day. During the same year, Inco also organized a company union, the United Copper Nickel Workers, though a certification vote in 1943 overwhelmingly swung in favour of Mine Mill Local 598. After four decades, Inco workers finally had a legal union, forcing management to relinquish at least part of their complete control over their working conditions.

The road ahead was not easy for organized labour in Sudbury. Communist sympathies among some Mine Mill leaders did not play well during the Cold War among the political elite and the mainstream labour movement in Canada and the US The Canadian Congress of Labour expelled Mine Mill in 1948, isolating the union from the mainstream labour movement. A failed strike in 1958 helped set the stage for the United Steelworkers of America to attempt a takeover at Inco's Sudbury operation. In 1962 the Steelworkers won a certification vote by fifteen votes, but Mine Mill did retain control over the Falconbridge workforce. Buoyant nickel markets in the 1960s (partly to feed Vietnam War production) and a successful wildcat strike in 1966 meant higher wages and increased revenues at the Inco Sudbury plant. But the development of alternative laterite (soil-based) nickel sources in other countries (with Inco expanding into Indonesia and Guatemala), meant that the Sudbury operation lost its control over the global nickel market. A global glut in nickel production resulted in mass layoffs at Sudbury: fifteen hundred workers in 1974 and three thousand in 1977, though a 261-day strike in 1978 managed to save a thousand positions. By 2010 a Sudbury workforce that had numbered seventeen thousand at Inco in 1969 had been reduced to only three thousand under a new owner, Brazilian mining giant Vale. During a strike in 2009, employees did make wage gains but lost the fight to keep a defined benefit pension plan despite spending a year on the picket line. Seventy years after unionization, and management still largely held the upper hand in Sudbury's nickel basin.

Sudbury's nickel mining operations also exemplified, perhaps more than at any other place in Canada, the widespread environmental damage associated with mining. Beginning in 1888, the Canadian Copper Company and then Inco roasted ore in large, open beds, called sintering yards, essentially placing mounds of mined rock up to thirteen feet high on piles of burning logs, often leaving them to smoulder for months. Logging for such large amounts of firewood cleared large areas of forest, but even worse was the resulting sulphur dioxide (SO_2) gas, a noxious fume that destroys vegetation and causes respiratory diseases in humans and other organisms. Between 1890 and 1930 Canadian Copper and then Inco burned 900,000 tons of cordwood to roast 28,040,068 tons of ore on eleven open beds, producing 8.4 million tons of SO_2 (in addition to toxic arsenic, lead, and selenium) with absolutely no pollution controls. Because there was no smokestack to disperse emissions over a broader area, the SO_2 stayed low to the ground, completely denuding areas surrounding the roasting yards of vegetation, which in turn caused soil erosion. As the roasted ore was sent through an additional smelting stage at Copper Cliff to produce nickel concentrate, Canadian Copper and Inco produced additional SO_2 emissions and huge piles of molten slag — 119 tons spread over 240 acres at Copper Cliff. Local farmers protested against the damage to their property due to SO_2, prompting the Ontario government in 1916 to declare a dozen townships unsuitable for settlement and cultivation. The farmers pressed the case for compensation all the way to the Supreme Court of Ontario in 1917, where Justice Middleton awarded only minor damages for the loss of crops. A spate of additional legal action inspired the provincial government to pass the Damages by Fumes Arbitration Act in 1921, which granted an arbitrator primary authority to grant compensatory damages to farmers due to SO_2 (though the provincial minister of mines

Inco smelter at Copper Cliff, circa 1925. Nickel smelting in the Sudbury region denuded local vegetation and resulted in lawsuits over smoke damage to local farms from sulphur dioxide.

could overrule these awards). The government also created a system of smoke easements under the Industrial Mining and Land Compensation Act that permitted companies to pay landowners for damage SO_2 pollution caused to their property. While Inco did make small payments under the arbitration system, the underlying purpose of these legislative initiatives was to curtail the rights of landowners to pursue more extensive damage payments in court. When it came to pollution, the Ontario government made only small concessions to the "polluter pays" principle that was just beginning to emerge in the 1920s, ultimately protecting the interests of the mining industry rather than the citizen farmers of the Sudbury Basin.

The practice of open roasting ceased in 1929, not because

of the farmer protests but due to its inherent inefficiencies and the tightening of the local wood supply. The damage from SO_2 emissions and other sources of pollution only worsened over time, however, as Inco commenced operations at the Coniston smelter and constructed more expansive smelting operations at Copper Cliff in 1929. A reporter visiting from London in 1933, quoted in the *Sudbury Star*, described the environmental damage: "There were the same forlorn buildings [as in British smelter towns] against a background of dun hills, the same baked earth and slag heaps; all the vegetation killed by sulphur fumes from the smelter." Falconbridge began to operate its own smelter a year later, ensuring that still more SO_2 would be dispersed over a larger area surrounding Sudbury in the coming decades. Due to major increases in production, SO_2 emissions peaked in the 1950s and '60s, with Inco roughly quadrupling pollution releases to between roughly 1.5 to just over 2 million tons annually (Falconbridge added another 200,000 to 300,000 tons of SO_2 during the same period). The result was

LEFT: Inco constructed its "superstack" at Copper Cliff in 1972 to mitigate pollution by dispersing pollutants into the atmosphere, leading to acid rain generation.

BELOW: In the wake of local pollution reductions, Sudbury underwent a "regreening" thanks to local environmental restoration efforts detailed further in Chapter 6.

Sudbury's infamous moonscape: twenty thousand hectares of boreal forest reduced to bare rock and another eighty thousand hectares degraded to a semi-barren state.

In 1972, Inco attempted to mitigate the problem through the construction of a 380-metre superstack at Copper Cliff (the largest smokestack in the world and the second-tallest freestanding structure in Canada, next to the CN Tower) to disperse SO_2 from the immediate Sudbury area. Although the superstack helped create the conditions for Sudbury's remarkable regreening program that began in 1974 (see Chapter 6), the wider SO_2 plume also made it the biggest point source of acid rain deposition in North America, with direct impacts on southern Ontario and the northeastern United States. Inco achieved dramatic SO_2 reductions beginning in the 1980s and 1990s due to a combination of equipment improvements, a decline

in production, and steady pressure from governments eager to meet obligations to reduce acid rain pollution under the Canada–US Air Quality Agreement. By 2013 Inco and then Vale had reduced total SO_2 emissions to approximately 130,000 tons annually with plans for further cuts to 20,000 tons as part of a $1 billion pollution-control program. As the scourge of the SO_2 became less of a threat over time, Sudbury has slowly transformed its reputation from one of Canada's worst polluted places to a centre of environmental innovation.

Precious Metals and Empire Ontario

Minerals were hardly foremost in the mind of the Ontario government when it began construction of the publicly owned Temiskaming and Northern Ontario Railway in 1902. Running initially from North Bay to

Locomotive of the "Muskeg Special," a branch line of the Temiskaming and Northern Ontario Railroad that carried prospectors, miners, financiers, and camp followers to Golden City (Porcupine). The mines and camps were destroyed by devastating fires in 1911.

New Liskeard (and all the way to Moosonee by 1932), the T. & N.O. was conceived as a colonization railroad that would bring waves of agricultural settlers to the supposedly fertile clay belt north and northwest of Lake Temiskaming. If visions of a new "Empire Ontario" based on agriculture proved too extravagant, the railroad sparked a mineral rush in the region that had enormous consequences for industrial growth in northeastern Ontario and the spread of mining know-how and investment capital to other parts of the country.

In August 1903 two forest workers, James McKinley and Ernest Darragh, discovered metallic rock — later confirmed to be silver — while walking the railroad line in search of timber to cut ties. A few weeks later T. & N.O. blacksmith Fred LaRose made a separate silver discovery, with local legend suggesting he discovered silver after narrowly missing a fox with a hammer and turning over a telltale rock. Willett Miller, a provincial geologist, visited LaRose and found rich silver veins near the surface at Long Lake. He then confirmed a third find

by French Canadian railroad worker Tom Hébert. Miller returned to Long Lake the next summer and conducted a full survey with prospectors Alex Longwell and William Trethewey. Very quickly Trethewey discovered two massive silver deposits that would become the Coniagas and Trethewey mines. By 1905 a full-scale silver rush was on: Long Lake became the largest silver producing region in the world as production reached a peak of 31,507,791 ounces in 1911 and the population of the town exploded to over ten thousand. Even if silver output began to decline after a massive fire in 1922 and slowed to almost nothing during the Depression, the Cobalt mines produced a remarkable 460 million ounces of silver during the bonanza years.

At Cobalt, geology and legislation worked against the kind of mineral monopoly that had developed at Sudbury. The Ontario Mines Act of 1903 prevented the registration of claims until the presence of a commercial deposit was confirmed, precluding the pre-emptive buying up of claims prior to exploration by large and well-financed mining interests. Moreover, most of the narrow silver veins at Cobalt were either at or near the surface, meaning little capital

Mine owners often used pictures of exposed precious metal veins (in this case silver) to entice investors to support new mining projects.

ABOVE: Inside a miner's hut, Cobalt, Ontario, 1902. Workers in Cobalt's boomtown silver mines faced harsh living and working conditions.

RIGHT: Fred LaRose, a blacksmith, was credited with finding one of the Cobalt silver mines during railway construction.

investment was required for what were often pick-and-shovel operations. In addition to Trethewey's mines, three independent operations, the LaRose, the McKinley-Darragh, and the Nipissing mines, also began shipping silver along the completed railroad in 1904. A year later twelve new mines were established at Cobalt; over one hundred mines operated at one time or another during the boom. In many cases it was individual prospectors who, following the example of McKinley, Darragh, LaRose, and Trethewey, developed their own claims, gaining valuable technical experience as

Cobalt station on the Temiskaming and Northern Ontario Railroad. Cobalt's boomtown phase lasted until the First World War and the town began to decline in the interwar period.

surface operations began to move underground. Indeed, several mining historians point to Cobalt as the epicentre of Canadian mining expansion in the ensuing decades, a source of domestic capital and Canadian experience with hardrock mining that accelerated expansion into new areas ranging from Quebec to the Northwest Territories.

For all the buoyant confidence ascribed to Cobalt, life in the town was at best tenuous in the early years. If some of the newly rich silver magnates built spectacular homes, many miners in the early days lived in shacks meant only to last for what was thought (due to the shallow ore base) to be a flash-in-the-pan boom. And despite the massive wealth that was exported from Cobalt, the disorganized nature of the town militated against a viable municipal tax base and

thus the provision of basic water and sewage services during the early years. So hastily was the town established, municipal infrastructure often conflicted with new mineral claims as trenching cut into streets and blasting occurred within earshot of town residents. The trenches became dumping grounds for sewage and other waste, with little thought to the impact on the town's water supply. In 1905 a Provincial Board of Health report predicted major public health problems for Cobalt:

> *Garbage, wash water, urine and faeces all mixed together in frozen heaps out in the open, on top of the rock practically bare in its greater area. The cold has been steady so far and all is frozen, but when the thaws come the accumulations will all be washed into the valleys*

and the lake, polluting all water sources. If nothing is done . . . then in all human probability there will be a severe outbreak of disease in and about the settlement.

A massive fire the summer of 1909 left two thousand people homeless and reliant on contaminated water. Sure enough, a typhoid outbreak hit the town later that summer, the worst in Ontario's history: 1,119 were sickened and 111 died. Although Cobalt today is, like Dawson City, heavily invested in its heritage as mining town and national historic site, the quality of life for the earliest town residents was far from perfect.

Working conditions in the mines were hardly better. Labourers faced ten-hour shifts and dangerous conditions as the mines began to move underground. Accidents ranged from collapsing stopes to the untimely ignition of explosives, with the Cobalt mines accounting for 114 deaths from 1904 to 1913 (41 per cent of the total mining accidents in Ontario). Miners did receive relatively competitive wages of $1.50 to $2.25 per day in the early years, though attempts by the local Mine Managers Association to impose a single wage structure for all Cobalt mines did provoke Ontario's first general mining strike by the Cobalt Miner's Union, which management had resisted recognizing because of its ties to the radical Western Federation of Miners (which later became Mine Mill). Cobalt was large enough (with more than ten thousand people at its zenith in 1911) that miners could console themselves in part through recreational sports, especially hockey, or at one of the many illegal drinking establishments, the infamous "blind pigs" common to many northern Ontario mining towns. But ethnic divisions among miners, particularly as the First World War heightened divisions between British Canadians and "foreigners," undermined social cohesion and labour solidarity in Cobalt. Workers in the silver mines did organize a major strike in 1919, a reflection of the broader worker's revolt in Canada that included such key events as the Cape Breton coal miners' strikes in 1923 and 1925 and the Winnipeg General Strike in 1919. The Cobalt mine managers successfully defeated the strike, however, pitting Canadians of British origin against foreign workers, especially

Cobbing (hand-sorting) and stacking sliver ore underground and the LaRose Mine near Cobalt, 1904. Like most of the area mines, LaRose closed by 1930.

those who were deemed Bolsheviks or "enemy aliens" from the recently concluded war. Organized labour never regained its footing in Cobalt, especially as the mines began to close and miners quit the town beginning in the 1920s.

Despite its relatively short period of intensive production, silver mining at Cobalt produced major long-term environmental consequences. Exploration and trenching for silver scraped the land clear; at times exploration crews used high-pressure hoses to clean away the overburden of soil and vegetation so as to expose the bare rock below. The mining companies also rapidly cut the surrounding forests in the early years to produce steam power. If lakes stood in the way of silver production, they could be removed; Cobalt, Peterson, and Kerr lakes were all drained and their beds washed with hydraulic machinery to reveal the silver-bearing rock. A report on Cobalt Lake in 1913 described "disagreeable odours emanating from the lake," the residual waters "tainted or a yellow green," with "a portion of the south end of the lake now being rapidly filled up by the slimes or tailings from the mills." Indeed, the mining companies routinely dumped ton after ton of waste rock and tailings

The underground environment at the McIntyre mine in Timmins, Ontario. Company officials at the McIntyre Mine developed the technique of dousing miners with aluminum dust as a supposed prophylactic against silicosis, a debilitating lung disease caused by silica dust. This medical treatment then spread to mines and other dusty workplaces in several countries, likely the cause of increased neurological diseases among exposed workers.

Prospector's shack, Porcupine district, no date. The Porcupine/Timmins region north of Cobalt spawned three of Canada's richest gold mines: Dome, McIntyre and Hollinger.

on land and into nearby water sources, contaminating them with arsenic, cobalt, nickel, and cyanide (the latter used in processing ore to recover silver). Over a century has passed since the first mine wastes were dumped in the area, but waste rock piles and tailings deposits remain a major concern because runoff from these sites still contaminates local streams, rivers, and lakes. The Cobalt mines remain among the worst sites in Canada for arsenic runoff into surface water, with many sites showing contamination levels above drinking-water standards and exceeding guidelines for sustaining aquatic life. Agnico-Eagle, the mining company that currently holds rights to many of the properties in the Cobalt area, has undertaken remediation activities since the 1990s. The widespread and pervasive nature of the pollution problems, combined with the fact that addressing basic safety issues (uncovered stopes, exposed trenches,

subsidence under buildings) often takes priority, has ensured that a legacy of environmental damage from the mines will persist into the foreseeable future.

Even as Cobalt reached its heyday in the 1910s, the epicentre of the Ontario mining boom was shifting further north. With prospectors fanning out from Cobalt almost from the beginning, it was only a matter of time before somebody made the next big find in the highly mineralized rock of the Precambrian Shield. Geological reports from the nineteenth century pointed to the area around Porcupine Lake as promising, but a prospecting expedition in 1906 led by former Klondiker Reuben D'Aigle proved disappointing. One small gold mining operation — the Scottish-Ontario Mine — established in the Porcupine region in 1907 was a poor producer and was eventually destroyed in a fire. The resulting pessimism quickly turned to euphoria, however, as three impressive finds in 1909 provoked a gold rush and laid the basis for the big three mines that established the Porcupine region as one of the world's most important gold mining complexes. Jack Wilson led a large party of four other prospectors and three Indigenous guides (four canoes total) into the Porcupine Lake area in June 1909, where they staked spectacular gold showings in a dome of quartz. Next to arrive on the scene was Haileybury barber Benny Hollinger and associate Alec Gillies. Wilson directed them to an unclaimed area west of the Dome claims, where Hollinger eventually stripped away a patch of moss to discover a large quartz vein flecked with visible gold. Almost immediately after they staked the area, two additional parties of prospectors arrived on the shore to hear of the finds. One of these parties, Sandy McIntyre and George Buttner, found visible gold to the north. In rapid succession prospectors had found the big three mines in the Porcupine/Timmins area: the Dome, Hollinger, and McIntyre gold mines.

News of the spectacular finds triggered a staking rush the following summer as prospecting canoes flooded into the region. Small communities such as Golden City, Pottsville, South Porcupine, and Timmins sprang up, and the Ontario government dutifully addressed transportation challenges in 1911 by completing a branch line of the T. & N.O. across the nearly fifty kilometres to the new camps. Prospectors quickly staked new finds, with several sites becoming producing mines over the next few years. But the Porcupine rush was not as open to individual opportunism as the shallow Cobalt deposits; much of the gold was found at depth and considerable financial investment was required to blast and dig through the hard rock of the Porcupine area. Indeed, it was not the breadth of participation that solidified the significance of the Porcupine Rush, but the massive production rates and longevity of the big three mines. The Dome mine, originally worked as an open pit, then an underground mine, and later as a super pit near Timmins, produced over 14.5 million troy ounces of gold and has only recently begun to wind down. Although the namesake of the McIntyre mine tragically sold his claims for a pittance to finance his love of the bottle, the mine produced 10.7 million troy ounces of

Steam donkey in operation at Dome Mine, near Timmins. The region's gold was found at depth, requiring investment in mechanical drilling and underground development.

gold before shutting down in 1988. The biggest of the three, Hollinger, was quickly bought up by the owner of Cobalt's LaRose Mine, Noah Timmins, and became the largest gold producer in Canadian history before shutting down in 1968 after miners had dug six hundred miles of tunnel and produced over nineteen million troy ounces of gold. Although some finance capital for these mines came from Britain and the United States, majority ownership remained in Canadian hands.

The exhilaration that accompanied discovery and growth in Porcupine was tempered by disasters and safety issues during the early decades. In the hot, dry summer of 1911 a catastrophic forest fire ripped through Porcupine region, destroying the fledgling mining camps and killing as many as two hundred people, some indirectly through drowning or asphyxiation as they tried desperately to escape the flames in Porcupine Lake or in the apparent safety of a mine shaft. In February 1928 fire again hit the Porcupine region, this time in the underground workings of the Hollinger mine as flammable waste

Diamond drilling underground at Kirkland Lake, Ontario. Compressed air drills enabled more efficient underground mining, but also produced dangerous silica dust that resulted in the scourge of miner's lungs, silicosis.

(crates, discarded fuse, wrapping, etc.) dumped in a forgotten chamber ignited for unknown reasons. Although twelve miners managed to escape, thirty-nine died in the fire; the nearest mine rescue team was rushed in by rail from Pittsburgh. A coroner's jury ascribed the deaths to negligence on the part of the company for storing combustible material underground. Justice T.E. Godson conducted an inquiry and recommended several improvements to mine safety that became standard within the industry: the provision of proper mine rescue and safety and equipment, rescue training for mine workers, and a system of mine rescue stations to be established within mining regions.

The fire also spurred a broader discussion among workers about the dangers of the underground environment in Porcupine. Miners especially feared the debilitating and often fatal effects of silicosis, a lung disease brought on by the inhalation of silica dust that caused extreme shortness of breath to fibrosis in the lung, and increased susceptibility to tuberculosis. Moreover, the rock body in the Porcupine Mines contained the highest density of silica of any mines in Ontario. In response, the provincial government mandated annual chest x-rays after 1928 (with afflicted workers removed immediately to work on the surface) and underground crews sprayed water to dampen dust while drilling. Silicosis rates in the Porcupine continued to worsen in the 1930s, however. With the cost of workmen's compensation claims rising, James Denny, the chief metallurgist at the mine, set up a research program in partnership with the Banting Research Institute at the University of Toronto. After animal tests

Workers standing next to gold ore in the interior of a processing facility in Timmins, Ontario, circa 1910s.

Nine coffins are laid to rest in a common grave after a disastrous fire underground at the Hollinger Mine in 1928 that claimed the lives of thirty-nine workers. After an investigation, the company was charged with gross negligence; the disaster also resulted in new mine rescue training and procedures.

involving twenty-six rabbits and clinical trials involving thirty-four workers showed promise, Denny concluded in a 1937 issue of the *Canadian Medical Association Journal* that aluminum dust prevented silica from being absorbed in the lungs. The McIntyre Mine quickly patented the treatment, using sale proceeds to fund ongoing research through a non-profit spin-off called McIntyre Research Limited (renamed the McIntyre Research Foundation in 1946). The foundation promoted the treatment throughout

Weighing a refined gold brick at the Hollinger Mine, 1936. Hollinger was the richest gold mine in Canadian history, producing 19 million troy ounces before closing in 1968.

Women's march in support of striking miners at Kirkland Lake, 1941. Four thousand miners struck for several months as labour militancy grew in the mining sector.

Canada, the US, and Australia, where miners typically were sprayed with "McIntyre Powder" in their change rooms as they left their shift. Mine managers claimed a spectacular knockdown effect for the new treatment, but it is more likely that dust mitigation and improved ventilation efforts lowered the silicosis rate. Subsequent research has failed to replicate the McIntyre research team's results; such short-term clinical trials provide a poor indication of therapeutic effect on a disease that can take decades to develop. The mining industry abandoned aluminum therapy in the 1980s due to mounting concerns over the linkages between long-term exposure and neurological conditions such as Alzheimer's and Parkinson's disease. In October 2017 the Ontario government announced $1 million in funding to study the effects of the treatment on surviving miners, recognition that the mining industry and the medical profession had treated the underground workers at the McIntyre and other mines as guinea pigs, exposing them to a metallic dust with insufficient clinical research into the potential long-term health consequences.

The paternalism exemplified in the aluminum dust experiment was symptomatic of broader management attitudes to labour in northeastern Ontario. Prior to the Second World War, mining companies refused even to recognize labour unions, often organizing company unions to foil Mine Mill and its affiliation with the radical wing of the labour movement. Mine owners throughout northern Ontario worked tirelessly to disrupt organizing drives, weakening unions and successfully thwarting strike activity from 1919 to 1941. In broader legislative terms, no provincial labour laws in Canada granted unions the right to bargain collectively with employers (as had the Wagner Act in the United States). The issue came to a head in 1941 at Kirkland Lake, a gold mining complex discovered in 1911 and similar to Timmins in terms of longevity, notoriety, and total production rates. The war had taken a severe toll on the gold mining sector as production shifted once again to the industrial base metals, but recognition was the key issue for Mine Mill Local 240. In November 1941, four thousand miners went on strike after managers of the twelve mining companies refused to negotiate, and snubbed even the recommendation of a provincial conciliation board to recognize the union. The striking miners abandoned the picket lines on February 12, 1942, with none of their demands met and facing layoffs as gold production declined. But growing militancy within the Canadian labour movement — buoyed by the slogan "Remember Kirkland Lake" — finally forced the government to act, and Ontario guaranteed the right to collective bargaining in April 1943 (the federal government followed suit with a cabinet order in February 1944). If the metal mines of northern Ontario exported mining capital and know-how throughout Canada, they also bequeathed a modern framework for labour relations in this country.

Quebec's Valley of Gold

In 1923 a Canadian government publication surveying the natural resources of Quebec lamented the fact that little had been done to develop the "vast potentialities" of mineral resources beneath the huge swath of Canadian Shield that cut through the province. While Quebec was already a global leader in asbestos mining by this point, and some small gold deposits had been found in the Shield region, the province was laggard when it came to production of metals most important to the new industrial economy. Just six years later, however, the same annual resource survey trumpeted the development of mineral resources in the Abitibi-Témiscamingue region in the near northwest of the

province, particularly the copper-gold mine and smelter at Noranda, as heralding a new dawn in the development of metallic mining in Quebec.

Perhaps it was inevitable that the northern Ontario mining boom would spill across the border to Quebec. After all, geological borders often do not match their political counterparts; the mineral-rich formation that sustained the Ontario mining boom, the Abitibi greenstone belt, stretches east for more than two hundred kilometres from the dividing line between the two provinces. When gold prospector Ed Horne began to explore the area around Lake Osisko, Quebec, from his base in New Liskeard, Ontario, in 1911 he reasoned that, "it didn't seem sensible that all the good geology would quit at the Ontario border, just because somebody had drawn an imaginary line there." It took three more visits and ten more years of scrambling for

Colourized image of Sullivan gold mine, Val d'Or, Quebec. Development in the Abitibi-Témiscamingue region followed quickly on the heels of the northern Ontario mining boom.

O'Brien gold mine
near Rouyn-Noranda,
Quebec. By the 1930s,
the "valley of gold"
stretched along the
Abitibi greenstone belt
from Rouyn eastwards to
Malartic and Val d'Or.

grubstake money before Horne was able to confirm valuable deposits of gold and copper at Lake Osisko. By 1922, news of Horne's discovery had leaked out and he was anxious to find financial backing before somebody might attempt to jump his claim. The first buyer was a US interest, the Thomson-Chadbourne Syndicate, which paid $320,000 for the Horne property. The syndicate found a Canadian partner, James Murdoch, to manage the mine, and formed a new company, Noranda Mines, to work the claim in May 1922. The American backers has always envisioned the Horne Mine as a source of feedstock for American mills, so when the Quebec government passed legislation enforcing a "manufacturing condition" for raw mineral and timber extracted in the province they quickly divested their shares in the company. Two years later, Noah Timmins saw an opportunity and invested $3 million from his Hollinger empire to construct a copper smelter at Noranda, convinced that no other mining company in the area was well-financed enough to produce a competitor. The transition from American control was confirmed by 1926 when six of nine Noranda directors were Canadian. The acquisition of large stakes in the Aldermac and Waite-Amulet mines near

Noranda in 1927, Pamour Mine in the Porcupine in 1935, and the Compania Minera La India gold mine Nicaragua in 1938, set the stage for Noranda's continued domestic and international growth up to and through the 1970s. The Horne mine also laid the groundwork for the expansion of a network of mines eastward along the Abitibi greenstone belt to the gold mining complexes of Val d'Or and Malartic in the mid-1930s, and to the multi-metallic mines of the Chibougamau region in the early 1950s. From Horne's small prospecting foray by canoe across the Quebec border a new mining region and one of Canada's most significant mining behemoths had been born.

The Canadianization of Noranda did not preclude interprovincial rivalries from emerging. In the 1920s Quebec was eager to promote colonization of the near-north through lumbering, mining, and (often ill-conceived) agricultural resettlement schemes. As the richness of the Horne Mine ore body became clear, the Quebec government was determined to build a rail link to the area, offering $250,000 to the Canadian National Railway to build a branch line that would ultimately link Montreal to Rouyn, the second town (besides Noranda) adjacent to the mine. At the same time, Noranda was

ABOVE: Lake Osisko and the company town of Noranda, Quebec. Noranda and its sister town Rouyn emerged as the regional mineral processing hub after two railways connected the town and mines to southern markets in 1926 and 1927.

RIGHT: Legendary prospector Ed Horne, who discovered the Lake Osisko gold and copper deposits and for whom Noranda's Horne Mine and Smelter were named.

negotiating with the Ontario government for a rail line that would draw the new Quebec mine into the Temiskaming and Northern Ontario rail network through an extension of the existing Nipissing Central Railway. The race was on to build the first rail line to the Abitibi region, a contest the Quebec government won, delaying the Nipissing Central through court action questioning the authority of an Ontario government–owned railroad to cross provincial boundaries (a legal

The company town of Noranda reflected era's trend toward modern, planned industrial towns rather than boomtown mining camps. The predominantly French-Canadian town of Rouyn emerged beyond Noranda's limits (and beyond company control).

battle Quebec ultimately lost because the Nippissing Central Railway had been established under a federal charter and then acquired by the T. & N.O). On October 25, 1926, the CNR completed its branch line to Rouyn; the first train from Kirkland Lake along the Ontario Line did not reach Rouyn until December 1927. Nevertheless, most supplies for the mining and commercial operations in Rouyn-Noranda arrived from Toronto via the shorter Ontario route. Noranda created Canadian Copper Refiners Ltd. in 1929 to take advantage of the Montreal link, establishing a processing facility near the docks at the east end of town. One year later, Noranda acquired a large share of the Canada Wire and Cable Company with factories in Hamilton and Toronto's Leaside neighbourhood. With ample government assistance, Noranda had built an integrated production and supply network that remained resolutely Canadian, pulling raw material from northwestern Quebec and propelling it through Canada's industrial heartland toward domestic and US markets, all the while reinforcing the dependence of this relatively isolated mining outpost on outside food supplies and manufactured goods.

Noranda the company exerted almost absolute control over Noranda the town. The company decided on the layout of the community, hoping to make it a modern and ordered settlement for mine workers and executives rather than a dishevelled nineteenth-century camp. The company controlled town politics as well: Noranda company chair James Murdoch was the first mayor (1926–29) and Noranda executives held this office until 1949. Rouyn, on the other hand, was a retail commercial centre and more chaotic mix of prospectors, fortune-hunters, and the economically marginalized (a squatters' camp on the south end of town expanded rapidly during the Depression). Noranda's population tended to be English-speaking (from the upper tier of the company hierarchy) or eastern European members of the working class, while Rouyn contained more French Canadians.[4] Although important to Noranda as a retail supply centre, the company did not play an active role in Rouyn's politics, preferring to focus its political energies on the town where the vast majority of its workers lived.

Indeed, the company exerted iron-fisted control over its labour force, fighting union organization and recognition at every turn. Mine Mill began active organization drives in the early 1930s, signing up enough workers by June 1934 to present a set of demands that included an eight-hour day, union recognition, and a 10 per cent wage hike. The company broke the strike in just a few days, bringing

The twin smokestacks of Noranda's Horne Smelter pictured above the towns of Rouyn and Noranda. For decades, the smelter was a major source of air pollution.

Rue principale, Rouyn, mid-1930s. Though prosperous, the towns also experienced their share of labour unrest over the years.

in replacement workers from the legions of Depression-era unemployed. Mine Mill was officially accredited as the representative of Noranda workers in 1944; a subsequent strike around the issue of the "check-off" (the automatic deduction of union dues from workers' pay) extended from November 1946 to February 1947 with no resolution of the issue from the union's perspective. The failure of the strike, combined with Mine Mill's expulsion from the Canadian Congress of Labour, brought on a successful raid by the United Steelworkers in 1950. But even with a more mainstream union representing workers at Noranda, management dug in its heels during another lengthy (147-day) strike over the "check-off" issue in 1953–54. It was not until 1964 that Quebec workers won the right to the "check-off" system through amendments to the Labour Code pushed through in part because of pressure from a sympathetic minister of natural resources, René Lévesque.

The Horne mine closed in 1989 after producing 1.13 million tons of copper and 260 tons of gold, considered a world-class production rate within the mining industry. But, as with so many mines, the Horne also left a legacy of

pollution. For decades Noranda's smelter emitted a veritable stew of contaminants up its stack: arsenic, lead, cadmium, selenium, zinc, copper, and sulphur dioxide. In 1983 a study concluded that high rates of mortality between 1965 and 1974 due to lung cancer and respiratory illness could not be attributed to smoking alone but also involved airborne pollution. Certainly the fact that, as in the Ontario mines, workers had very little protection from silica dust in the early years also must have contributed to the high incidence of lung disease. Other studies cited critical concerns about

The Horne smelter at sunset. Today, the smelter is known for its role in reprocessing metals from electronic waste and other feedstock.

lead exposure among children because of contact with contaminated soils and airborne pollutants, problems that were addressed only in the 1980s with emissions reductions and soil remediation programs. The Horne and other mines in the area also produced contaminated tailings and acid mine drainage, issues that have been partially addressed through remediation programs but which also continue to pose threats to aquatic ecosystems as heavy metals leach into lakes and rivers. Today the Horne smelter has acquired a green hue as a recycling facility for metals from electronic and other wastes, and continues to process "custom" ores from Quebec and elsewhere. As with the Sudbury smelter, however, the Horne operation reminds us of the tremendous environmental costs that accompanied mining and mineral processing along the fringes of the Canadian Shield.

Mining the Cordillera

With the completion of the Canadian Pacific Railroad in 1885, the nascent explosion of industrial base-metal mining in Ontario began to spread west, spawning countless new mines and mining companies. As historian Jeremy Mouat has remarked, "in addition to mining's economic importance — the number of people employed in or dependent upon the industry, its relationship to the key task of 'opening up' the country, the profits that it generated, and so on — mining was also *the* metaphor for the settlement of the West." Mining may have played second fiddle to agricultural settlement as a driving colonial force in western Canada, but the promise of mineral riches brought new people, new forms of transportation, and new communities to many regions.

The epicentre of western Canada's share of the industrial mining boom lay close to the southern edge of British Columbia's stunning Kootenay Mountains. The Rossland gold rush (with some copper ore) began in 1889, when prospector

Joe Bourgeois located the gold deposit on Red Mountain that would become the Lily May Mine, and then a year later staked claims (with another prospector, Joe Morris) to the future War Eagle, Centre Star, Idaho, Virginia, and Le Roi mines. By 1895 the Le Roi had paid a first dividend to shareholders. Despite setbacks from a bitter strike in 1901 and a major fire in 1902, the rich Rossland mining complex had by then reached peak productivity and was known throughout the world.

As it had during the Fraser River and Cariboo gold rushes, the expansion of settlement into the West Kootenay region carried dire impacts, this time for the Sinixt First Nation, or Arrow Lakes People. These people had inhabited the Upper Columbia basin on both sides of the Canada–US border for generations. They had already faced severe crises due to the devastating death rates associated with smallpox outbreaks in the 1780s. The arrival of the first prospectors in the 1850s resulted in violent conflict, an adversarial relationship that intensified with the larger mineral rush of the 1890s. Although many of the conflicts between the Sinixt and settlers remain undocumented, in 1894 miner Sam Hill killed

Miners riding ore cars into the Sullivan lead-zinc mine in 1938 near Kimberly in the southeast corner of British Columbia. The Sullivan Mine was the main source of feedstock for the Trail Smelter.

a Sinixt man named Cultus Jim over a land dispute. More broadly, settlement for mining and agriculture throughout the West Kootenays, hydroelectric development, and deforestation to feed smelters and sawmills in the area around Arrow Lakes degraded hunting and fishing opportunities and left the Sinixt largely landless. Unable to secure a reserve in Canada, many migrated south to the Colville Lakes Confederated Tribes reserve, an amalgam of many nations including Sinixt from the US side of the border. In 1956, the Canadian government declared the Sinixt people "extinct" in Canada, though some remained or have returned and currently are pressing for recognition and land claims in the West Kootenays.

Heedless of First Nations concerns, the industrial development of the West Kootenay region continued at a rapid pace. American capital and labour poured into this district and others in southeastern BC, making the region a virtual outpost of the Western US "Inland Empire." In Rossland and Trail, the stage was set for an international battle over control of Canadian mineral wealth and the creation of one of Canada's dominant corporate mining conglomerates, Consolidated Mining and Smelting (CM&S, later Cominco).

The Rossland mines are less important for the ore they produced than for the smelter they spawned at Trail, a major processing facility that helped keep BC's mineral wealth from being exported as a raw resource to the United States. Ironically, it was an American copper baron, Frederick Augustus Heinze, who is most responsible for diverting Rossland's riches from US business interests. In 1895 Heinze secured an agreement with the Le Roi Mine managers to smelt their ore at a new gold and copper smelting facility he was building, along with a tramway to shuttle the ore to smelter site just west of Rossland at Trail Creek. One year later, American railway entrepreneur Daniel Chase Corbin hatched a very different plan: to freight Le Roi ore along his new Red Mountain Railway from Rossland to Spokane, one of several spur lines he was building to connect the southern Kootenays with the Northern Pacific Railway and US processing facilities. Corbin enticed the Le Roi Mine owners

to build a smelter in Northland, Washington in 1906, where their ore could be processed more cheaply than at Trail. The Canadian ore from the Kootenays, Corbin believed, was destined to flow into the more modern transportation and industrial processing networks in the United States.

As far back as the 1880s, Prime Minister John A. Macdonald's government took a dim view of Corbin's railway activities, seeing his north–south network as a menace to the long-standing dream of a national trade network oriented east to west along the Canadian Pacific Railroad. The CPR shared the prime minister's anxiety, and actively attempted to develop a rival network in the Kootenays beginning in the late 1880s (building a line between the Arrow and Kootenay lakes in 1889), starting a figurative tug-of-war for the resources of southern British Columbia. In 1898 the CPR bought Heinze's Trail smelter and railway charter and dubbed the new subsidiary the Canadian Smelting Works. That same year the Crowsnest Pass agreement provided the CPR with a massive public subsidy of $3.5 million (in exchange for low shipping rates on agricultural goods) to punch a railway through the Rocky Mountains from Lethbridge to Nelson, simultaneously connecting the minerals of the Kootenay region to the CPR mainline and providing access to a new fuel source of coal and coke from the Crowsnest Pass mines.

To manage the Trail smelter, the CPR installed the talented mining engineer Walter Hull Aldridge, with a mandate and funding to modernize the operation. Aldridge replaced the steam boilers with a connection to the emerging electrical grid, and in 1902 stunned the metallurgical world when, after purchasing the Canadian rights to A.G. Bett's electrolytic method of lead extraction, he created the world's first large-scale electrolytic lead refining facility at Trail. Aldridge then aggressively swooped in on the Rossland mines, convincing the CPR in 1906 to buy up the War Eagle and Centre Star mines. In 1911 the Le Roi Mine finally succumbed to CM&S's ownership and Canadian interests had won the long battle for control of Rossland's ore.

Hand-cobbing ore at the Sullivan Mine, Kimberly, BC ca. 1914-16. The massive Sullivan lead-zinc deposit formed the basis for the emergence of the mining giant Consolidated Mining and Smelting, Ltd.

From all these acquisitions came western Canada's first major corporate conglomerate, under the banner of the Consolidated Mining and Smelting Company, an integrated network of mines, railroads (in which the CPR retained majority ownership for decades), the Rossland Power Company, and the Trail smelter. Gradually, the Trail smelter became one of the largest metal processing facilities in the world, capable of smelting gold, silver, copper, lead, and zinc. According to one newspaper report in 1916, the Trail smelter was "one of the metallurgical meccas of America," and certainly the most important mineral processing facility in western Canada. As part of the original consolidation in 1906, for instance, CM&S acquired the St. Eugene Mine at Moyie, BC, as a source of lead ore. When the smelter at Nelson closed in 1907, Trail became the processing centre for the tail end of the rich silver-lead boom in the Slocan Valley, which ran from 1892 to the early 1910s. The massive lead and zinc deposits at the Sullivan Mine near Kimberly, BC, were discovered in 1892, but nobody had developed a practical method of separating the zinc from the lead in this complex ore body. In 1909 CM&S acquired the rights to the Sullivan ore. The wartime demand for zinc spurred CM&S to develop a research program (largely unheard-of in the Canadian mineral industry during this period)

Ore dump near the Consolidated Mining and Smelting Company of Canada lead refinery at Trail, BC The smelter processed lead, zinc, and other minerals from a large network of Kootenay region mines.

from 1917 to 1920 under the direction of metallurgist Randolph W. Diamond. The result was the breakthrough technique of differential flotation, where lead was actively brought to the surface and zinc depressed at the bottom of a chemical treatment circuit, allowing the metals to be recovered separately. With a viable technique for ore processing in place, the Sullivan became the mainstay of CM&S's lead and zinc supply and the richest mine in BC history in dollar value, producing 17 million tons of zinc,

8 million tons of lead, and 286 million ounces of silver before it closed in 2001.

As the Trail smelter grew, so did the magnitude of the environmental problems associated with it. As with the Inco smelter at Sudbury, the major problem with Trail was sulphur dioxide emissions and attendant damage to vegetation, animals, and human health. CM&S paid out damages to local farmers near Trail from 1916 and aggressively purchased much of the Columbia Valley bottomlands toward the US border as a means of sidestepping conflicts with agriculturalists. As Sullivan ore began to pour into the smelter in the 1920s, SO_2 emissions increased from 4,700 to 9,000 tons of SO_2 per month between 1924 and 1926, prompting further complaints

A lead slag furnace inside the Consolidated Mining and Smelting Company smelter at Trail in southern British Columbia. The Trail Smelter was a major source of sulphur dioxide pollution beginning in the 1920s, resulting in a dispute and settlement with the United States to compensate farmers in the state of Washington.

from local farmers for whom smelter smoke had turned from a sign of progress to a threat. In 1926 CM&S decided to raise the height of the smelter smokestack to 409 feet to disperse the SO_2 over a wider area, but this had the unintended consequence of sending smelter fumes wafting down the Columbia Valley toward the farmlands of Washington State. As damage to crops and livestock became obvious, the U.S farmers formed the Citizens' Protective Association to enlist help from local, state, and federal politicians to press their case against the foreign company damaging their lands. In 1931 the International Joint Commission — a Canada–US body

created to manage transboundary water and pollution issues — awarded $350,000 in damages to the farmers (much less than anticipated) but included no provisions for controlling pollution. The US State Department rejected the IJC ruling; a subsequent three-member Arbitral Tribunal awarded the farmers a further $78,000 and mandated pollution reductions. CM&S did implement a program of further dispersion and monitoring while cutting emissions by two-thirds by diverting sulphur toward the production of fertilizer and sulphuric acid. While the case established important precedent in terms of the "polluter pays" principle and the rights and

Cominco's Trail smelter complex long dominated the town's landscape. The town's famous junior and senior hockey teams were known as the "Smoke Eaters."

obligations of states in transboundary pollution issues, historian John Wirth has argued that the settlement was "impressively limited" because it still allowed CM&S to pollute and failed to engage in scientific assessment of the long-term impacts of residual, widely dispersed smelter smoke. Indeed, recent studies from the US Environmental Protection Agency suggest high levels of lead and arsenic contamination remain in soils on the Washington side of the border due to air pollution from the Trail smelter (now operated by Teck Resources).

Water also carried pollution south. The Confederated Tribes of the Colville Reservation won a lawsuit in 2012 alleging that the company knowingly polluted the Columbia River with millions of tons of harmful smelter slag, waste rock, and other waste containing arsenic, cadmium, copper, mercury, lead, and zinc from the smelter for over a century, dating from 1896. Although Teck ceased dumping slag in 1996 and some remediation projects have proceeded, the residue from decades of air and water pollution remains woven into the soils and sediments of northern Washington's portion of the Columbia River Valley, and accumulated in the Lake Roosevelt reservoir behind a Columbia River dam. Despite prior knowledge of pollution impacts and international legal action, the Canadian government granted the Trail smelter a licence to pollute so long as the impacts were not short-term and immediately apparent to the surrounding population.

At least some significant mining areas in British Columbia operated outside the orbit of the Trail smelter. The Boundary Country between the Kootenays and the Okanagan briefly became one of the most important copper mining regions in the world in the first decade of the twentieth century. Based on promising assessments of the Boundary mineral formations, the CPR pushed a railway line to the area in 1898 (and the Great Northern arrived six years later); the

town of Phoenix subsequently emerged in 1900 as a base for several mining operations, and the most important of the many mines and three smelters that dotted the regions. The Boundary copper ore was very low grade, too costly to ship in a raw form to Trail. For this reason the Miner-Graves Syndicate built a smelter in 1900 at the North Fork of the Kettle River and, as had CM&S, consolidated several mine holdings into the Granby Consolidated Mining and Smelting Company. At the height of production, in 1918, the Phoenix mines were the largest copper mining complex in the British Empire, sending 4,500 tons of raw ore to the Granby smelter every single day. To extract such large volumes of rock at a profitable rate the miners of the Boundary region created one of the earliest examples of open pit mining operations in Canada. Historian Tim LeCain has described this extraction method as a highly mechanized and energy-intensive process of mass destruction, where steam shovels, ore removal trams, explosives, and high-volume smelting are used to move and process massive amounts of rock and earth. Such mining techniques scarred the Boundary landscape, leaving huge pits contoured with access roads, waste rock piles, and tailings ponds. A severe downturn in copper prices in 1918 led to

the decline and abandonment of most copper mines in the Boundary region (though the Phoenix Mine reopened in sporadic spurts of production from 1959 to 1976). As prices recovered in the 1920s, the core of the BC copper industry shifted to underground mines on the Pacific coast, where the Britannia Mine (1904–74) in Howe Sound north of Vancouver and Granby's Bonanza and Hidden Creek mines (1912) at the planned smelting community of Anyox (near Prince Rupert) emerged as the key producers in the province.

Prairie and Coastal Coal

The precious and industrial metals of British Columbia were undoubtedly the poster children for mining's westward expansion during the industrial boom years. But, as mentioned previously, coal production also increased dramatically during this period, providing the spark for new mining activity in Alberta and Saskatchewan as well as significant production increases and expansion on Vancouver Island. Indeed, coal remained Canada's principal energy source in the late nineteenth century and would not yield this mantle to oil until after the Second World War. It was critical for rail and steamship transportation, the

production of coke for smelters, and home heating. From its beginning days in Coalbanks (later renamed Lethbridge) in 1883, coal mining expanded throughout the badlands, foothills, and mountain country of southern Alberta along the transcontinental railway and its spur lines. Coal mining in Edmonton, for instance, had occurred for local use since the 1850s, but developed on a large scale with the completion of the Calgary and Edmonton Railway in 1891 and especially with the arrival of the transcontinental Canadian Northern Railway in 1905. The aforementioned railway extension though the Crowsnest Pass spurred a large complex of coal mines high in the Rocky Mountains at the turn of the century. The first coal mine began operations near the town of Frank in 1901 (only to be wiped out by a massive rock slide in 1903), and expanded to places such as Bellevue, Fernie, and Coleman on either side of the provincial border. Further to the east, coal production in the badlands near Drumheller commenced in 1911 at Newcastle, and one year later at the present-day tourist draw,

the Atlas Coal Mine National Historic Site. Production in the Drumheller Valley expanded to 139 coal mines that produced fifty-four million tons of coal by the time the last of the mines, Atlas #4, shut down in 1979. Commercial coal production began in southeastern Saskatchewan in the early 1890s with mines such as the Roche Percée and the Souris Valley (the region surrounding the coal mining towns of Bienfait and Estevan) in 1896. Even the well-established coal mining region of Nanaimo experienced something of a renaissance as James Dunsmuir managed to effectively replace his declining Wellington mines with the large Extension Mine and the instant mining town of Ladysmith at Oyster Harbour beginning in 1898. The list could go on: some four hundred coal mines dotted the landscape of western Canada by 1930, producing roughly eight to twelve million tons of the fuel annually between 1915 and 1950.

As with earlier periods of mining in Canada, in the early twentieth century collieries remained the most dangerous of all mines for the workers who toiled underground. The

The ore dump and rail tracks at Britannia Mine, BC Perched in the Coast Mountains along Howe Sound, Britannia was for a time one of the British Empire's largest copper producers.

Destruction in the aftermath of the Hillcrest Mine explosion in 1914, one of the worst coal mining disasters in Canadian history.

danger from rockfall or the collapse of a room was always a threat, particularly when mining teams "robbed the pillars," taking on high risk (sometimes with premium pay) to take up the one-half to two-thirds of the coal that might be left behind as supports in a mined-out room. Coal mines also contain the omnipresent danger of explosions; ambient coal dust and the methane (known as firedamp) gas that is often released from the ore body could be ignited by the tiniest spark or flame. Often a methane explosion kicked up enough dust, heat, and flame to initiate a second shockwave. Miners died not only from the blast but also from the rockfall and carbon monoxide gas that was a byproduct of many explosions. Although proper ventilation and dampening dust with water helped mitigate the risks of explosions, they remained an inherent if dramatically reduced risk of working underground coal seams. Casualty rates were extremely high in some cases: 125 miners killed at Springhill, Nova Scotia, in 1891; 63 at the Union Mine near Courtenay, BC, in 1901; 128 at Coal Creek near Fernie, BC, in 1902; and, in Canada's worst-ever mining disaster, 189 at the Hillcrest Mine on the Alberta side of the Crowsnest Pass in 1914. These examples only scrape the surface of the many large and small coal mining accidents in Canada, producing death tolls that are shocking when aggregated over time and region. In Cape

Miners standing outside the entrance to a tunnel at the Brule Coal Mine, 1917. An Alberta coal mining boomtown supplying the railway, Brule was abandoned by 1932.

Breton alone, 1,321 miners died in the coal mines between 1866 and 1987. On Vancouver Island, at least 416 coal miners perished in explosions between 1879 and 1923. As if these catastrophes were not enough, many other miners suffered debilitating injuries or illness, primarily black lung disease (more formally termed coal miners' pneumoconiosis), a severe respiratory condition similar to silicosis that is caused by repeated exposure to coal dust. The coal-based energy regime that dominated Canada and the rest of the industrial world during the nineteenth and early twentieth centuries were built on a foundation of human misery; hundreds, if not thousands, of sick and broken bodies could not keep the coal barons from pushing forward with business as usual.

As in other mining sectors, the mine owners and managers also harboured a fervent antipathy toward unions. Nowhere in Canada was the struggle between labour and mine owners as violent as the low-level shooting war that erupted in Colorado's coalfields and culminated in the infamous Ludlow massacre in 1914. Coal miners' strikes in Canada were also often intense and violent as the industry expanded westward. In 1906 over five hundred members of the United Mineworkers of America walked off their jobs in the coal mines of the Alberta Railway and Irrigation Company (AR&I) at Lethbridge. Their demands both mirrored those in other mining sectors and reflected the unique conditions of the coal industry: an eight-hour day, protection from dismissal for union membership, union recognition, the "check-off" system for collecting union dues, a minimum wage ($3 per day) regardless of the weight of coal mined, independent weight checkers supervising the coal scales, and better ventilation in the mines to improve health and safety conditions.

Miners killed in the Hillcrest disaster are laid to rest. Nearly half the mine's workers were killed in the blast.

Crowds gather in the wake of the devastating explosion at the Hillcrest Mine, in the Crowsnest coal region of Alberta in 1914. The blast and tunnel collapse killed 189 workers in Canada's worst-ever mine disaster.

Shortly after the strike began in March, AR&I convinced the local Royal North-West Mounted Police detachment at Lethbridge to support the company, along with several non-striking miners appointed as special constables. From the strikers' perspective, the police used intimidation tactics ranging from breaking up demonstrations (in one case with pistols drawn), raiding the homes of strikers, and arresting a striker in April for using profane language. The strikers also used violence, beating one strike-breaker and possibly dynamiting the homes of three others (nobody was killed and the union claimed management was responsible so as to discredit the strike). As a coal shortage loomed in the fall of 1906, the federal government sent Deputy Labour Minister Mackenzie King to mediate. The future prime minister produced an agreement shortly after his arrival, granting the miners the minimum wage, independent weight checkers, a per-ton pay increase, and the eight-hour day, but failing to grant the all-important "check-off" clause (which, combined with a non-discrimination clause, allowed non-union workers to benefit from union contracts). King's experience at Lethbridge prompted him to push through Parliament the Industrial Disputes Investigation Act, legislation that required both sides of labour disputes in key industries (rail, coal, etc.) to submit to an arbitration board before going on strike, depriving unions of the power to determine the optimal timing of labour action.

Miners are marched to jail in Ladysmith, BC by troops called out to suppress the strikes at Dunsmuir coal mines on Vancouver Island, 1913. This period saw frequent, often violent clashes between mine owners and newly unionized workers.

Striking miners and their families march through Ladysmith, BC, in 1913. Miners sought better pay and improved safety conditions in the coal mines.

Miners like these Drumheller, Alberta, men turned to increasingly radical unionism, like the syndicalist One Big Union, in their fight for labour rights in Canadian coal mines.

Picture of Quong Lee's store on Vancouver Island, wrecked by strikers. Chinese and other racialized labourers and businesspeople were often targeted for accepting lower wages from owners eager to break labour organizations.

Despite King's efforts to mediate between labour and capital, the battle between the two continued at a fever pitch as owners stubbornly, at times violently, resisted unionization, and workers stepped outside the law to press their case. On Vancouver Island, workers at Canadian Collieries' Cumberland Mine near Comox declared a "public holiday" on September 16, 1912, to press for union recognition and improved mine safety, a job action the company protested was illegal under the Industrial Disputes Investigation Act. The company responded by hiring streak-breakers, especially low-wage Chinese workers, to undercut the strike. Nonetheless, by May 1913 the United Mineworkers decided to expand the strike to companies operating in the Nanaimo and Ladysmith region. One of the smaller operations, the Vancouver and Nanaimo Coal Company, acceded to union recognition and settled with their workers, but Western Fuel and Pacific Coast Coal proceeded with plans to reopen with strike breakers. From August 12–15, riots broke out in Nanaimo, Ladysmith, and South Wellington, culminating in severe property damage, mobilization of the militia, and the arrest of 213 strikers (with 50 of these eventually serving prison terms). The strike continued for another year until a settlement was reached in August 1914, one that included provisions for nondiscrimination against union members but no mandatory recognition of the unions. By 1915 a downturn in coal markets resulted in severe unemployment and the United Mineworkers withdrew from Vancouver Island in almost total defeat.

The intense struggle in the western coalfields continued after the First World War. At Drumheller in May 1919, miners rejected their union, the United Mineworkers of America, because they felt union dues went to head office in the United States. They then struck over the coal companies' refusal to recognize the One Big Union (OBU), a radical Canadian syndicalist organization that was leading the Winnipeg General Strike at the same time the Drumheller action began. Mine owners in the valley banded together and hired special constables who beat and intimidated striking miners, in some cases forcing them back to work or chasing them into the hills. While in some cases the miners resisted, the squads of special constables proved too much. By August the United Mineworkers returned, the workers drifted back to the mines, and the special constables ran the OBU leaders out of town.

Union recognition was also at the core of violent strike in the Souris, Saskatchewan, coal district in September 1931, as management refused any dealings with the miners' choice of the radical left wing Mineworkers' Union of Canada. When the miners marched into Estevan on September 29, the local police chief attempted to arrest striker Martin Day. A shoving match began, and the Estevan police, bolstered by the RCMP, directed fire hoses at the demonstrators and began to fire their weapons in the air, killing three strikers as a full-scale riot ensued. In this case, at least, the miners achieved many of their goals, including an eight-hour day, a minimum daily wage, and independent scale checkers among other demands.

Historians have long debated why the labour battles in the western coal mines were so intense, with owners resorting to violence and miners often flirting with radicalism. David Bercuson's theory of western exceptionalism — that conditions of frontier independence and isolationism pushed miners toward radical labour politics — has held some sway. Of course, labour militancy was not unique to western Canada: Cape Breton coal miners led a veritable war against the British Empire Steel Company with multiple strikes between 1922 and 1926, albeit under the banner of the United Mineworkers of America. Ian McKay has argued persuasively that the centrality of coal as the key energy source of early industrialism contributed to militancy among miners because labour actions had so much potential to cripple the economy. Coal miners, McKay suggests, positioned themselves at the front lines of the battle with management, conscious that their ability to pull the plug on the primary industrial energy source was a powerful means to press for basic rights to union recognition, workplace safety, and fair compensation. By the 1950s coal miners had lost this position at the vanguard of labour radicalism as oil began its ascent to the apex of the industrial energy regime and most of the western collieries were abandoned.

The Northward Course of Mining

Even as the western mining boom was in full swing, boosters and promoters began to turn their eyes to Canada's Far North. With memories of the Klondike gold rush and the "near-north" developments in Ontario's shield country fresh in the mind of government, industry, and the public alike, there was no shortage of rhetoric extolling the mineral potential of the remote territorial and provincial northlands. Especially after the First World War, when famous explorer Vilhjalmur Stefansson's idea of a "Polar Mediterranean" replete with game ranches and industry captured the public imagination, Canada's destiny seemed to lie northward. Fundamental challenges such as extreme distances and lack of infrastructure undermined even the most modest dreams of northern boosters, but, as historian Liza Piper has argued, even the few mining projects to emerge prior to the Second World War provided an initial spark to the industrialization of Canada's northlands. None of these new

Unloading ore sacks from the Keno Hill Silver Mine, one of the earliest large-scale mines in the Yukon Territory, 1934.

mines would replicate the rush of independent alluvial gold miners that dominated the early years of the Klondike; all required the excavation of hard rock and thus significant investments in industrial equipment and wage labour. For northern Indigenous groups who lived primarily by hunting and trapping (and who had not been shunted onto reserves as in southern Canada), the sudden introduction of mining introduced some economic opportunity, but also rapid change in the form of an influx of outsiders, the introduction of wage labour, imported food, and at times severe environmental and health impacts.

The first major hardrock mining development in Canada's territorial north was discovered deep in the Yukon interior. Operating out of Dawson in search of gold, prospector Jacob Davidson staked a claim (he dubbed it Hell's Gate) to rich

silver-lead showing near Duncan Creek, a tributary of the McQuesten River, in 1903. Davidson was skeptical that hardrock mining could be profitable in such a remote region and let the claim lapse. Ten years later Henry McWhorter restaked Davidson's claim and set up the Silver King Mine with several partners, producing impressively rich silver ore at up to three hundred ounces to the ton. Production rates at the Silver King remained low during the war and the mine closed by 1918, but a second major silver discovery on nearby Keno Hill in the fall of that year quickly rekindled interest in the area. The Yukon Gold Company, which operated in Dawson but was a large corporation controlled by the Guggenheim family, decided to invest in the area and development proceeded rapidly. A new boomtown, Keno City, sprang up at the base of the silver hills along with several dispersed mining camps. Further down the valley, Mayo became a base town for shipping ore along the Stewart River, and in 1935 the Treadwell Yukon Company built the new mill and company

Heavy machinery, such as this ten-ton cat transporting silver ore in 1934 from Keno to Mayo in the Yukon, was crucial to the development of large-scale industrial mining in the early twentieth century.

town of Elsa to exploit silver deposits on Galena Hill. Although several companies worked the site over the years, by 1948 most area mines were consolidated under United Keno Hill Mines, which modernized operations and rode the post-war mineral boom to comfortable profits. Between 1914 and closure of the mines in 1989, the Keno Hill area produced 6.8 million kilograms of silver, along with smaller amounts of lead and gold, making it the second-largest silver producer in Canada, next to Cobalt.

The new mines and settlements were also situated in the traditional territory of the Na-Cho Nyäk Dun First Nation. The networks of roads, towns, processing facilities, and mines that spread through the McQuesten River watershed impacted seasonal patterns of summer fishing in local rivers and fall hunting and gathering in the hills through habitat loss and water contamination. Even today, water contaminated with heavy metals, particularly zinc, from old mine adits adversely affects local fish populations. Despite the fact the Na-Cho Nyäk Dun were displaced to a community two miles away from Mayo, a recent oral history study conducted by Alexandra Winton and Joella Hogan suggests that many Indigenous people were able to adapt to the new mining economy, selling meat and fish to the newcomers, cutting

wood, hauling ore, and working steamboats. Later generations would join non-Indigenous miners underground at Keno Hill and other mines. Many Na-Cho Nyäk Dun also kept their ties to the older hunting and trapping economy, harvesting local wildlife when they could as a supplementary form of income and a hedge against periods of unemployment. If mining brought the modern world of the south to the Keno region, it never completely displaced the older hunting and trapping economy that sustained the Na-Cho Nyäk Dun for generations.

Manitoba began a determined push toward northern mineral development in the 1920s as part of a very deliberate strategy to diversify beyond agriculture. Industry and government had known since 1915 of the major copper-zinc deposits near present-day Flin Flon, and the abortive Mandy Mine had exploited a high-grade deposit in the area between 1917 and 1920. To convince the Hudson Bay Mining and Smelting Company (HBM&S, which held rights to the Flin Flon deposits) to develop these deposits the government had to sweeten the pot, agreeing to a royalty holiday, a $500,000 subsidy for railway spur lines to be extended to the mines, and remarkable legislation that granted HBM&S the right to pollute water and air over a 1,036,000 hectare area. As with Sudbury, the area around the Flin Flon Smelter became a moonscape in subsequent decades, while the dumping of tailings severely impacted local fish populations and spread pollution as far away as Lake Athapapuskow, fifteen kilometres to the southeast. As prospectors worked north from Flin Flon they located a second major copper-zinc-nickel deposit in 1922 that would become the Sherridon mine under Sherritt-Gordon, providing additional feedstock to the Flin Flon mill. Although the Cree population living in the region did find economic opportunities, primarily in prospecting and woodcutting, historian Jim Mochoruk has speculated that environmental damage from the mines and smelters impoverished the hunting, fishing, and trapping economies for the Cree who used the area north of the Cranberry Portage leading to Lake Athapapuskow. Across an even broader area of northern Manitoba and Saskatchewan, the prospecting rush of the 1920s brought widespread fires

The Flin Flon Mine in 1930, operated in northern Manitoba by the Hudson Bay Mining and Smelting Company. The smelter attached to the mine emitted sulpher dioxide that denuded local vegetation and caused respiratory issues among local people, and heavy metals that prompted the Winnipeg Free Press to dub Flin Flon as "toxic town."

Two miners in 1934 loading silver from the Keno Hill Mine. The picture was taken by Claude Tidd, a member of the Royal Canadian Mounted Police from 1914-1935 who spent much of his career documenting life in the Yukon through photography.

and consequent destruction of wildlife habitat (particularly for the all-important caribou) as mineral hunters cleared vast areas to expose the Canadian Shield rock below. As Manitoba pushed its mining frontier northward, there were visible environmental and social costs for Indigenous communities, a pattern that reverberated more broadly as the mineral industry began to push further toward the far reaches of Canada's territorial north.

The onset of the Great Depression curtailed the mining industry's ambitions in the North, but for some types of minerals prices remained high enough for miners to stake a foothold in the northern territories. As gold prices remained high, prospectors began to push into new territories in the early 1930s. In 1934 prospector Johnny Baker found gold on the North Arm of Great Slave Lake at Burwash Landing (across the bay from present-day Yellowknife). He established a very small underground mine and camp that never proceeded past the bulk sampling stage, closing in 1936. But Baker's find was enough to attract a much bigger player to the region: BC's Consolidated Mining & Smelting (CM&S) staked extensive claims in 1935 and three years later poured its first gold brick at the newly minted Con Mine. One year later Negus Mine opened on a property adjacent to Con, while several smaller mines such as CM&S's Ptarmigan and Tom and the Thompson-Lundmark Mine began production in the early 1940s. This complex of gold mines supported the new town of Yellowknife, which served as a supply base for existing mines and a float plane base for further exploration in the surrounding countryside. Local histories suggest that Yellowknife was anything but a wild frontier mining town. From the very beginning the mining companies emphasized hiring family men, and supported the establishment of community amenities such as recreation facilities (hockey rinks, recreation halls, and a bowling alley), schools, and churches, making Yellowknife an outpost of small-town Canadian life in the far northern bush country.

As with the Keno Hill mines, the introduction of gold mining proved to be a watershed moment in the history of the Yellowknives Dene (or Weledeh, in their language) who lived in the area.[5] The Yellowknives had traditionally inhabited a series of small camps on the east side of Yellowknife Bay up to the Yellowknife River, moving seasonally between forest and tundra in search of caribou, fish, berries, and fur. Somewhat isolated from the main trade routes along the Slave and Mackenzie rivers, their contact with outsiders was limited compared to Dene who lived near the main fur-trading centres such as Fort Resolution. Nonetheless, an influx of non-Indigenous trappers in the 1920s had depleted local fur populations, prompting the federal government to create the Yellowknife Game Preserve in 1923 as hunting ground reserved for Indigenous people. In 1928 a flu epidemic swept through the region causing sickness and death. According to elder Sophie Potfinger, "Weledeh Yellowknives survivors, fearing a return of disease in Weledeh-Cheh, stayed in the barrenlands year-round for four or five years. When they returned, they discovered newcomers in their traditional lands."

Many Yellowknives objected to the presence of prospectors on their land, particularly in the game preserve. Elders describe how the Yellowknives sometimes learned of the newcomers through the startling and new sound of blasting, and subsequently told them to leave the area. According to Isadore Sangris:

> 1934 was the first time that Weledeh saw non-native people in the area; at first there were 4 non-native men; the Weledeh chief named Sizeh Drygeese (His english name was Joseph) and his Weledeh travelling companions and warriors met with the non-native people at Walsh Lake. One of the Weledeh spoke some English through his work with the trading post. He asked the white men what they were looking for and they said they were looking for rocks. The chief told them that the Weledeh had never seen non-native people before in this area and the chief told them to leave the area and to never come back; so the white men packed and left.

A painting by an unknown artist of the Negus Mine with the northern lights in the background. Negus Mine operated from 1939 to 1952, and was one of three large-scale gold mines adjacent to Yellowknife, Northwest Territories.

Not all of them left, however, and the Yellowknives frequently tell a story claiming that their local knowledge proved critical to the gold strikes in the area. Many elders have spoken about an old woman, Liza Crookedhand, who frequently picked berries in the area that would become the Con Mine. When a prospector visited her tent one day, she showed him a rock from the area and he offered her a stovepipe in exchange for directions to where she found it. Often Yellowknives Dene elders tell this tale to emphasize that the advent of mining in Weledeh was marked by a lack of consultation and unequal terms of exchange between prospectors and the local people.

The gold mines did provide economic opportunities for some Yellowknives Dene such as direct wage labour or the sale of wood and wild meat. A few Dene even worked underground. But most elders remember that the mines had severe impacts on their subsistence practices, particularly since the land occupied by the mines and the city of Yellowknife had been particularly rich for moose hunting, fishing, and berry picking. According to elder Joseph Charlo:

> *Explosions of dynamite by prospectors, air traffic, the development of mines and towns, the building of commercial fish plants, a prison, and roads, and the use of the land and waters for recreation. These developments contributed to the gradual withdrawal of moose and other animals, and to caribou changing their migration route through the area. In spring,*

Dene trapper with a wolverine, 1946. The arrival of the prospectors and mine developers, along with non-Indigenous trappers, disrupted the traditional hunting and trapping economy of the Northwest Territories.

> *Yellowknives Dene used to wait for caribou returning north where the Prince of Wales Northern Heritage Centre now sits on Frame Lake. Although now it is rare to see moose near the Weledeh, these animals used to be common and could be relied on by Weledeh Yellowknives for food and clothing.*

CM&S compounded these environmental issues when it began in 1940 to roast newly discovered ore from arsenopyrite formations, releasing arsenic trioxide from a smokestack into the local atmosphere. Although gold-roasting operations ceased in 1942 with the general shutdown of gold mining in Yellowknife because of wartime restrictions on precious metals production, the problem became acute after the war when Con resumed operations and the new Giant Mine opened in 1948, a story we return to in the next chapter.

The other major mining complex to emerge in the Northwest Territories marked the industry's first foray into both the high technology and ultimately the horrors of the nuclear age. According to the official story, in 1929 prospector Gilbert LaBine discovered pitchblende

A.Y. Jackson, "Radium Mine, Great Bear Lake," 1938. Jackson, a member of the famed Group of Seven Canadian painters, frequently sketched and painted industrial scenes like this one as well as northern landscapes.

on the eastern shores of Great Bear Lake. He returned a year later and staked claims to a rich deposit of radium, then valued on global markets a $75,000 an ounce due to its value for radiation therapy. The Sahtǔot'įnę (Bear Lake Dene) who live in the community of Délįnę (at the mouth of the Great Bear River) claim that LaBine did not happen upon the telltale pitchblende, but learned of it from an elder named Old Beyonnie, either through a direct encounter, or from a rock that Beyonnie had given to a prospector. For all the riches he brought LaBine,

Beyonnie was paid with only a sack of flour, a story that, as with the Liza Crookedhand narrative, emphasizes the idea that the non-Natives pilfered resources from Indigenous lands.

By 1932 the Eldorado Mine had become the first industrial-scale mining operation in the Northwest Territories. The central service community of Cameron Bay (renamed Port Radium in 1937), complete with post office and mounted police detachment, grew to about a hundred residents. The mine closed in 1940 due to poor market conditions, but reopened two years later to produce uranium (which had previously been dumped in the lake as seemingly worthless tailings) for the US atomic bomb project. The federal government secretly took ownership of Eldorado in 1944 due to

Miner pushing an ore cart in 1930 at the Eldorado radium mine at Port Radium, located at the eastern end of Great Bear Lake in the Northwest Territories. While radium was incredibly valuable in the 1910s and 1920s for use in medical therapies, during the Second World War the Canadian government nationalized Eldorado Mining and Refining Ltd. and converted the mine to uranium production for the Manhattan Project.

the strategic importance of uranium, and this Crown corporation continued to ship uranium (refined at Port Hope, Ontario) for nuclear arms production during the Cold War until the US cancelled its uranium contracts with the Canadian government and precipitated another closure in 1960. From 1964, a private company, Echo Bay Mines, produced silver from the site until the mine finally closed for good in 1982.

For the Sahtŭot'ı̨nę, the introduction of mining to the Great Bear Lake region carried profound consequences. From the opening of the mine to 1960, as many as thirty-five Sahtŭot'ı̨nę worked as ore carriers for the Northern Transportation Company (NTCL), carrying burlap sacks of radium or uranium to load on barges for the long journey southwards along what was referred to as the "Highway of the Atom" to the refinery at Port Hope, Ontario. The ore carriers worked without protective clothing, and many in Délı̨nę believe that the ore carriers developed high rates of cancer because of exposure to dust from the ore. By 1999 fourteen of thirty ore carriers had died from cancer and the issue reached a national audience through several media reports and two films.[6] Local people have also worried about the broader exposure to radiation due to the tailings that were

dumped in the mine area. In an oral history produced by the community, elder Alice Mackeinzo recalled that,

> When they handled the ore bags white dust would often spill. The men would come home from work covered with dust . . . The non-Dene people sure were secretive about things and never told us anything and had the Dene people suffer while they worked for them. The Dene people had a right to know but the white people kept things a secret. We worked without knowing the risk involved. Because of that there is so much cancer among our people. . . We ate the caribou that had migrated through the area which probably had been in contact with the contamination. Even that would cause sickness for individuals. We truly believe that people who passed on became sick because of Port Radium.

Despite these concerns, a federal government's collaborative panel set up in 1989 to investigate these claims, the Canada-Délı̨nę Uranium Table (CDUT), concluded that radiation exposure among the ore carriers was unlikely to be the cause of the cancer deaths, a finding that has been disputed in the community.

Even before mining occurred at Great Bear Lake, elders

such as George Blondin maintain that the Sahtűot'įnę recognized the Port Radium area as a place of bad medicine and danger. According to a widely circulated story, when the prophet Ayah camped in the area he had a vision that white people would come one day to take rocks from the ground and build a big stick that a large bird would fly over the ocean and then drop on people who lived in a distant country. When the stick hit the ground it would unleash a huge burst of fire, wreaking havoc and burning many people.

Although the Sahtűot'įnę could never have known about the role they played in the development of the atomic bomb, in 1998 a delegation from Délįnę travelled to Hiroshima to offer an apology. In 1929 the Sahtűot'įnę inhabited one of the more isolated corners of Canada; soon they were drawn into a web of relationships that tied them irrevocably to the defining moment of the global nuclear age.

Mineral Nation

Between the dawn of Canada's industrial boom and the Second World War, mining spread broadly across western and northern Canada, introducing settlers, transportation connections, hydroelectric development, and manufacturing technology to some of the most remote regions of the country. In many ways, the expansion of mining during this period reflected the spreading footprint of Canada's growing cities and the ascension of metropolitan priorities. Minerals from hinterland Canada provided copper for electrical wires and water/sewer piping, iron, and coke to make the steel used in automobiles and new skyscrapers, and precious metals to bolster currency markets. Investment capital flowed out of cities to finance the expansion of mines to the hinterland, the profits flowing back through urban-based financial markets as dividends for investors or to refinance even more expansion in the nation's network of mines. Governments always played a key role as handmaidens to the mining industry, encouraging expansion into new territories along state-funded roadways and railways, frequently deferring taxes and royalties, refusing to create or enforce environmental regulations, suppressing the demands of organized labour, and in some cases permitting industry to process and refine their minerals outside of Canada. The urgency that provincial and

A sign at Port Radium displays fused sand from the first successful atomic bomb test at Alamogordo, New Mexico (a range 210 miles south of Los Alamos) on July 16, 1945, illustrating the link between the uranium mine and the Manhattan Project. The photograph is by Henry Busse, who worked at Eldorado in the mid-1940s and later became an important documentary photographer of life in Yellowknife.

federal governments accorded to mineral development became even more acute when strategic minerals such as nickel and uranium assumed their deadly role in modern warfare. The roads and rail lines out of Canadian mining towns led in many directions, from tiny, remote communities to cities and factories, and ultimately toward some of the most terrible killing grounds of the twentieth century.

Many local historians of remote mining towns have celebrated mining for having brought civilization to the wilderness. Without mining, they suggest, places such as Sudbury, Cobalt, Flin Flon, and Yellowknife would never have come into being. Those towns that survived downturns and the inevitable closure of the mines remain justly proud of their working heritage and the sense of community they carved out of the mining landscape. Of course, histories that emphasize the pioneering spirit and community cohesion of mining towns must rest alongside other stories of violent labour disputes, the displacement of Indigenous communities, and environmental degradation — legacies that remain evident today. While mining in the early industrial era offered an economic rationale for westward and northern expansion, and a material foundation on which to build modern Canada, it also had the potential to tear apart pre-existing landscapes, ecological systems, and Indigenous economies in the areas where it expanded. These immense contradictions between the constructive and destructive aspects of mineral extractions only intensified after World War II as another economic boom spurred a second massive expansion of mining in Canada.

THIS IS OUR STRENGTH

FROM THE PAINTING BY A.Y. JACKSON.

THE *New* NORTH

The doors of the Canadian north open on Asia and Europe. The Alaska Highway, new air fields, oil and mineral developments, make this area a strategic centre both for war needs and the future. Our northern flying routes link the continents together and make Canada a focal point in the new air age.

A propaganda poster issued in 1945 from Canada's Wartime Information Board celebrates the mineral production, transportation, oil, and gas developments in northern Canada as central to the war effort and the future of the nation. The poster presages the strong nationalist tone that tied northern mining to national security and economic development in the post-war period. It is no accident that the poster features a painting by A.Y. Jackson, member of the Group of Seven painters who asserted a Canadian national identity strongly linked to northern landscapes.

CHAPTER 4
New Frontiers and the Post-War Mining Boom

The Second World War and the boom period that followed produced a second rapid and much larger expansion in the Canadian mineral industry. Even more than the 1914–18 conflict, the Second World War demonstrated the principle that modern warfare demands a total commitment in belligerent nations: a complete mobilization not only of soldiers, but also of treasure, labour, industrial capacity, science, and technology to support the war effort. Total warfare relies also, as historian Edmund Russell has argued, on the mass mobilization of nature to support the domestic manufacture of everything from tanks and aircraft to tents and boots, countries marshalled crops, animals, energy, timber, and of course mineral resources on an unprecedented scale. In 1940 Canada created the Department of Munitions and Supply, granting Minister C.D. Howe almost absolute power to regulate and control all aspects of Canadian industry. Howe quickly appointed mining industry insider George Bateman as his metals controller, tasked to pull more and more industrial base metals from the ground to feed expanding smelters and factories. Even as the need for fighting soldiers sapped the strength of the mining labour force, Canada had the potential to be a primary supplier of raw and refined metals for the Allied war effort.

Under Bateman's guiding hand, the Canadian mining industry was extraordinarily successful in answering the call to arms. Canadian mines and smelters provided 95 per cent of the Allies' crucial nickel supply, 75 per cent of asbestos production, and 40 per cent of aluminum, the latter so crucial to aircraft manufacturing that historian Jack Granatstein claims the Royal Air Force would not have been able to fight the war without it. Iron production increased more than tenfold to 1,135,000 tons between 1939 and 1945, while completely new production lines for strategically important minerals such as magnesium and molybdenum emerged during the war. As mentioned in the previous chapter, Howe reserved a special place in his mineral arsenal for uranium, his government buying Eldorado Mining and Refining in 1944, two years after the company had reopened the Port Radium mine, and upgrading the existing uranium processing facility at Port Hope as part of the "highway of the atom" connecting Port Radium to the American atomic bomb project. The Aluminum Company of Canada (later renamed Alcan) managed a remarkable increase in aluminum production at its smelters in Quebec's Saguenay region, from 752,000 to 1,545,400 metric tons between 1939 and 1945 (the bauxite ore was mined and partially processed in South America, primarily Guyana, positioning Canada as a refining hub rather than a primary producer in a global commodity chain). More commonly, however, a figurative line could be traced backwards, following the rails, roads, and shipping lanes from many of the Second World War's key sites of

Two miners work the underground shaft at Burwash gold mine near Yellowknife, Northwest Territories. The Burwash operation only lasted from 1935-36, but set the stage for the development of the town of Yellowknife, and major developments such as the Con, Giant, and Negus gold mines. These mines shut down during the war due to labour shortages and the low priority the Canadian government assigned to gold mining, but expanded production rapidly in the years immediately after the war.

conflict and destruction through factories and smelters to their origins in Canada's metal mines.

As significant as mineral production was for the war effort, military demands did not necessarily result in spectacular production gains across all sectors of the Canadian mining industry. Most conspicuously, Howe's strategic reorientation of the industry left precious metal producers out in the cold. After initially increasing gold production as a hedge against foreign exchange shortages, Canada negotiated the Hyde Park Agreement in 1941 with the United States, substantially increasing war-related purchases by the southern neighbour from Canadian businesses. This new arrangement solved Canada's cash flow problems, and the government subsequently declared gold a low-priority industry. Annual gold production fell by half before the end of the war and silver suffered a similar crash. Some mines, including Yellowknife's

Con and Negus, had to shut their doors as many of their workers headed to the battlefield, an economic shock that nearly devastated the town. Even the more strategic metals were not cushioned from slight downturns. Nickel output, almost all of it from existing Inco and Falconbridge mines, increased only marginally from 113,530 tons in 1939 to 144,008 tons in 1943, falling back to 122,565 tons in 1945. Lead and zinc followed the same pattern of minimal increase followed by decline near the end of the war. As critical as these minerals were to the Allied war effort, the North American military had largely completed the accelerated phase of rearmament by 1943. As Allied troops took the fight to Italy, Japan, and then to Germany in France, labour and materials shortages prevented major expansion into new mineral fields. The US and Canadian governments also controlled supplies and prices tightly for many strategic minerals, severely restricting consumer use of the all-important strategic minerals and ensuring that production did not much exceed actual military requirements. If the war presented some opportunities for the mining industry, matching material output with military need was a much higher priority than industry-wide expansion.

The real mining boom came shortly after the war as Canada ramped up military expenditure in response to Cold War tensions and the lid simultaneously came off of consumer spending. On the military side of the equation, Canadian and US rearmament programs to supply troops fighting the Korean War and prepare for the potential threat of a conventional or nuclear war with the Soviet Union helped stimulate a period of rapid economic expansion from 1951 to 1956 that fuelled strong demand for Canadian natural resources. In 1952 President Truman's special Materials Policy Commission (or the Paley Commission) produced a report, *Resources for Freedom,* that predicted increasing demand and decreasing domestic supply of strategic minerals, creating a dire need for secure foreign sources to support US military preparedness. Almost immediately American military demand sparked the construction of new mines and new transportation pathways in Canada, particularly for iron, uranium, and nickel. In the case of the latter, the US government stockpiled $789 million worth of nickel between 1950 and 1957 as part of a broader plan to build strategic reserves and simultaneously to break Inco's stranglehold on world nickel markets. Although markets for strategic minerals dipped along with an extended recessionary period between 1957 and 1961, the Vietnam War and other Cold War military commitments helped ensure strong demand for strategic minerals during the 1960s.

The race to build weapons was matched by a frenzy to supply North America's post-war economic expansion. The combination of pent-up consumer demand (unleashed from the deprivations of the Depression and the war), rising incomes, and increasing rates of home ownership among a growing middle class created a mass market for new consumer goods. Families bought radios, televisions, and automobiles in unprecedented numbers as

An abandoned pit at the Pine Point lead-zinc mine on the south shore of Great Slave Lake, Northwest Territories. Opened in 1964, the Pine Point Mine was the cornerstone of the Canadian government's plans to develop a modern north through mining development. The government hoped that subsidies for a railroad, highway, and modern mining town would spur a chain reaction of new mine developments in the Northwest Territories. After the mine closed in 1988, the company demolished the town and left forty-three pits behind, many of which filled with water.

Stripping the overburden (or topsoil and loose rock covering the ore deposit) in the N42 pit at the Pine Point Mine in 1964. Mining the open pits at Pine Point relied on heavy machinery to move vast quantities of ore from deposits to the on-site ore concentrator, and then by rail to Cominco's smelter at Trail, British Columbia.

materialism became an article of faith in North American society. Demands for energy and materials skyrocketed as the economy expanded almost continuously (other than the aforementioned 1957–61 recession) between 1951 and the beginning of oil price shocks and economic stagnation in 1973. During this period copper production more than tripled, iron output increased tenfold, lead more than doubled, zinc more than quadrupled, and nickel nearly doubled. The scale of production increases from the end of the first boom in 1914 to the end of the second in 1973 are even more impressive: nickel output increased more than tenfold, lead surged by a factor of twenty, and iron production was two hundred times more than it had been earlier in the century.[7] Some forms of mineral extraction that either did not exist or barely existed in 1914 — uranium, zinc, magnesium, tungsten, molybdenum — had become significant sources of production by 1973. New technologies that emerged in the 1940s and 1950s, such as a field version of the Geiger counter, the scintillometer (a more sensitive radiation detection device), and aerial electromagnetic surveying (which can detect sulphide formations), allowed exploration to occur over vast territories previously inaccessible to individual prospectors. New mines spread to some of the most remote corners of the country, and both government and industry promoted industrial development as the economic salvation of hinterland regions. At many of these new mines, however, the costs of development were thrown into bold relief as environmental, social, and health problems followed the industry in its relentless search for new minerals.

Southern Stories

After the Second World War, mining had largely ceased to be a major spur for territorial expansion in southern Canada. Some of the great mining camps from the first industrial boom continued to thrive: Sudbury, Britannia Mine, Rouyn-Noranda, Val d'Or, and others remained significant producers for decades after the Second World War. In other areas, mines succumbed to market pressure, declining ore grades, or competition from new mines

Miners Cecil Roberts and his brother Charlie eating lunch underground in a Nova Scotia coal mine. The tunnel they are working has put them 2.5 miles from the shoreline of the Atlantic, 800 feet beneath the ocean floor.

in Canada and abroad. Gold production in Timmins declined in the 1950s (though base-metal mining kept the area a mining centre); Kirkland Lake gold mines hung on until the 1960s; and mining finally ceased at Cobalt after a tentative revival in the 1950s. The iron mines of Bell Island, Newfoundland, newly acquired by Canada with Confederation in 1949, ceased production in 1966, largely a victim of the vast (and cheaper to exploit) open-pit iron-mining region that emerged along the Quebec-Labrador border in the 1950s. As petroleum became more important for industrial and transportation use in the 1950s, several of the great nineteenth-century coal mining regions withered and died in the 1950s, especially Nanaimo and Drumheller. The Cape Breton collieries survived until 2001, while other areas, particularly the Crowsnest Pass, Elk Valley, and

A group of men load an injured miner onto a helicopter for transportation to hospital after the Springhill "bump," or minor seismic event, that caused parts of the mine to collapse in 1958. The disaster killed seventy-four men while rescue crews managed to save one hundred miners, several of them after nearly a week trapped underground.

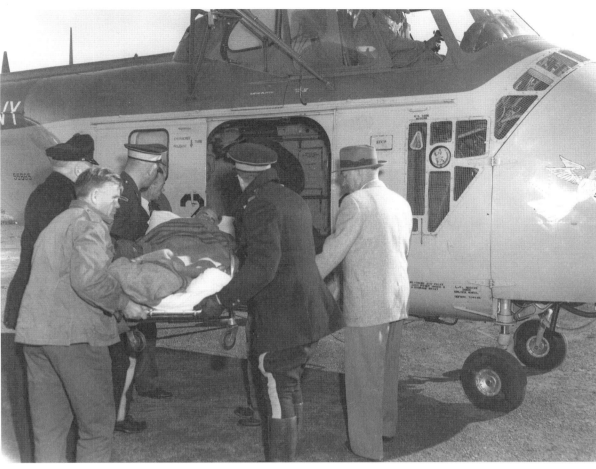

southeastern Saskatchewan regions all converted to cheaper surface strip-mining methods, riding a wave of coal demand for electricity production in the 1970s. Amid the decline of older mining districts at least one new mini-frontier emerged in southern Canada as potash mining in Saskatchewan expanded to a dozen mines between 1962 and 1970. As the mining frontier (and the compelling narratives that go along with industrial expansion to new areas) moved northward after the war, three mining stories from southern Canada — a mine disaster, a strike, and public health crises — gained national, and in some cases international, attention.

Disaster was no stranger to the Cumberland coal mines in Springhill, Nova Scotia. An explosion in 1891 (see Chapter 2) killed 125 miners and a second blast in 1956 took another thirty-nine men. The mine was also subject to frequent "bumps," minor seismic events that occur in underground coal mines when ore is removed from the surrounding rock bed, a severe danger to miners because of the risk of collapse in the mine workings. On October 23, 1958, the Springhill mine experienced the worst bump in the history of North American coal mining. Three shockwaves rippled through the

mine and caused carnage as collapsing chambers and tunnels killed seventy-four workers and sealed in many of the survivors. Fred Hanahan was one of those workers, and testified about his experience underground before a public inquiry:

Our pan line was going and we were shovelling, generally 3 men in a row, and we would put the junks in there and skipped some sometimes, and we were practically in a line, and when the bump occurred I was thrown back and hooked in underneath the conveyor pan. It is up about 2 feet and I was travelling under that, and the chap next to me was thrown up against the pack and the other chap was picked up with it and right up against the roof. He got tangled up in the timber, that was Clyde Murray. The coal came over me and kind of buried me except my face and head, and cut my face pretty bad. The coal filled right up. Then I was absolutely pinned there and I could hear the men above me shouting and moaning,

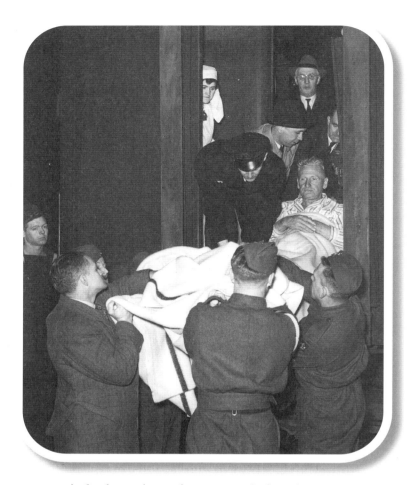

and after being there a few minutes the boys that cleared down below came up and freed me and got me from under the pan, and went to the next man and discovered he was gone, and they had quite a job getting the man above out, he was pinned in timber and they worked with him and got him out, and put us in a travelling road, and Mr. McManaman got them all lined up there at that time.

As Hanahan's harrowing comments suggest, miners already underground and rescue crews reacted quickly, eventually pulling one hundred men from the wreckage. Some endured long waits, as rescue crews found one group of twelve men after six days and another desperate and weakened crew of seven after nine days of hunger and darkness under the ground.

Because the disaster was covered by mobile live television crews, the drama that attended the long days of searching for the missing and the dead captivated the viewing public across

the globe. Indeed, the Springhill mining disaster was the first major Canadian event that the viewing public experienced collectively through live visual media. The Canadian Broadcasting Company and other international media reports from the site (samples of which can be viewed online at the CBC Digital Archives) captured the public imagination when the two groups of "miracle miners" were found days after the disaster. Visits to the disaster from high-profile dignitaries such as Prince Philip (and the more obligatory one by Nova Scotia Premier Robert Stanfield) highlighted the significance of the moment in the public imagination. Some of the rescued miners became minor celebrities in their own right, appearing on *The Ed Sullivan Show* and subsequently receiving a well-publicized offer of an all-expenses paid resort vacation in Georgia from the state governor. As with so many media moments, a scandal erupted when the governor informed one of the miners, Maurice Ruddick, that he would have to stay in segregated accommodation because he was African Canadian. His co-workers balked at the offer, in part because Ruddick was a talented singer who had played a heroic role lifting spirits with song in the underground while suffering the excruciating pain of a broken leg. Ruddick insisted, however, they go ahead with the vacation plan while he accepted his lodging in a trailer.

In addition to this specific injustice, the mine disaster gained widespread notoriety through American folksinger Peggy Seeger's widely recorded song decrying the dangers the coal miners faced as they worked the dark seams. She wrote:

> *In the town of Springhill, you don't sleep easy*
> *Often the earth will tremble and roll*
> *When the earth is restless, miners die*
> *Bone and blood is the price of coal*

Popular song and television ensured that the Springhill bump became the iconic exemplar of the extreme dangers

A female worker handles asbestos fluff in a factory in the town of Asbestos, Quebec in 1944. With no protective equipment, this worker would be exposed to asbestos fibres that can cause chronic, debilitating, and deadly lung diseases including mesothelioma.

coal miners faced in the underground environment.

Slow death rather than sudden disaster marked the history of what is arguably Canada's most notorious mineral: asbestos. By the 1880s Quebec had become the epicentre of Canadian chrysotile asbestos production as mining began in what became Thetford Mines, south of Quebec

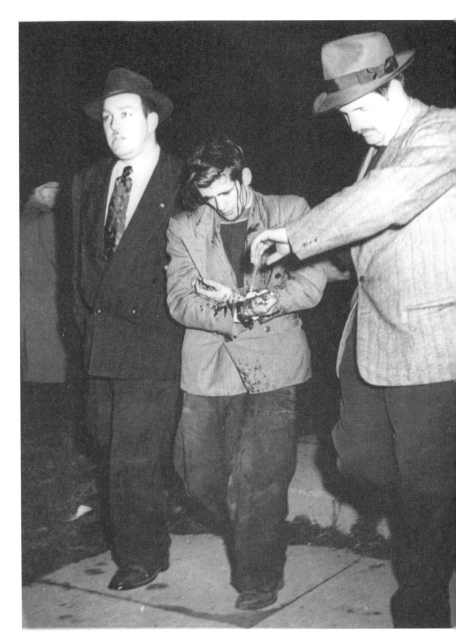

Two provincial police officers with a striking worker, bloodied and handcuffed after being caught in a raid during the strike against Johns-Manville at the Jeffrey Mine, Asbestos, Quebec, 1949.

City, and the town of Asbestos in the Eastern Townships. A mineral fibre that could be used to construct inexpensive fire-resistant material and insulation, asbestos was eventually used widely in building construction. Once associated with progress and safety, the word asbestos now invokes fears of slow, painful death, as it has become widely known that even tiny amounts of asbestos fibres in the air can cause

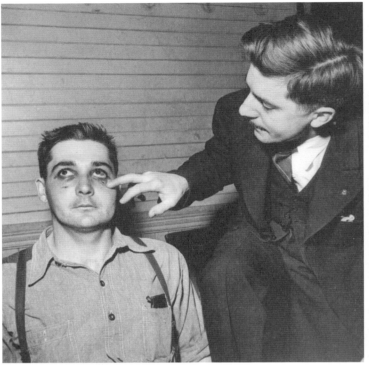

Confédération des Travailleurs Catholique du Canada leader Jean Marchand examines the eye of a worker injured because of strike-related violence in 1949, Asbestos, Quebec.

Police looking through the window of a church, likely surveilling the activities of strikers inside. During the strike at Jeffrey Mine in 1949, the Catholic Church abandoned is usual position of deference to Maurice Duplessis's Union Nationale party, with most priests and Archbishop Joseph Charbonneau supporting the strikers.

fatal lung cancers, asbestosis (a scarring of the lungs causing shortness of breath), and mesothelioma (a cancer that attacks the membrane liner of the lungs and the abdominal area). Canada became a major global producer of asbestos in the twentieth century, mining close to 1.7 million tons of the material annually during the peak period of the early 1970s, a total augmented by the Asbestos Hill Mine in Quebec's far north from 1972 to 1984. The extractive operations at Thetford Mines, owned by Lac d'amiante du Canada (LAC), remained the largest asbestos producer in Canada through much of its history. But it was the Jeffrey Mine, the huge open pit operated by American company Johns-Manville (JM), that occupied a more central position on the historical stage due to a violent and bitter strike in 1949.

The labour dispute at Jeffrey Mine followed several years of deteriorating relationships between JM and its workers, represented by the Confédération des travailleurs catholiques

du Canada (CTCC). A series of short wildcat work stoppages beginning in 1945 presaged the strike vote and subsequent walkout of 2,100 workers after the evening shift on February 13, 1949, an illegal strike (because the vote took place before the establishment of an arbitration board) that CTCC leaders had originally counselled against. The workers had six key demands: a raise from 85 cents to $1 per hour, job security measures in response to new mining technologies, additional holidays, input on promotions, recognition of union legitimacy through the Rand formula (mandatory union dues), and better dust suppression to prevent asbestosis (the one asbestos-related condition that was reasonably well understood by the general public at the time).

Police display rocks and clubs confiscated from striking workers at the Jeffry Mine, Asbestos, Quebec, in February 1949. The confrontation was violent on both sides, with police beating workers with bully clubs, and strikers hitting back at the police and strikebreakers with rocks and makeshift truncheons.

The early days of the strike remained celebratory and conciliatory, as picketers even allowed workers to cross the lines to attend to pit dewatering pumps. On February 18, after JM had printed a message in the local paper declaring the demands of the workers to be excessive, two hundred workers broke into the mining compound to retrieve their final paycheques. Two days later, the avowedly pro-business provincial Premier Maurice Duplessis sent in the provincial police, an action workers perceived as an external invasion of their close-knit community. By mid-March rumours the company would hire strikebreakers

Jean Marchand (holding cigarette) talks with workers during the strike in Asbestos, Quebec.

prompted a group of striking workers to blow up a railway line coming into Asbestos. Despite the damage, replacement workers did arrive by the end of March; subsequent threats from JM to evict strikers and their families from company-owned housing prompted violent attacks against strikebreakers. On May 5, strikers erected barricades on the main routes into town, provoking a standoff with provincial police and intense international media coverage. The next day the provincial police cracked down on the workers, raiding the church where sympathy strikers from Thetford Mines were sleeping, conducting mass arrests, and beating detained workers for further information. The strike continued until June 30, but JM's workers had largely been defeated. A board of arbitration granted what amounted to JM's final contract offer: a 10-cent wage increase, four paid holidays, and a right for strikers to return to work. The broader issues of promotions, job security, and dust abatement remained unaddressed, the latter issue effectively absolving JM of any requirement to admit that asbestos was dangerous for those worked in and lived directly adjacent to the Jeffrey Mine.

The strike at Asbestos has tended to be celebrated and remembered for issues that were only loosely connected to the concerns of the mine workers. Among academic historians and in the public memory, the strike is recognized as a key event heralding the Quiet Revolution of the early 1960s that broke the political stranglehold of Duplessis's conservative Union Nationale party on Quebec politics and ushered in a more modern version of Quebec nationalism. For many Quebeckers, the Asbestos strike pointed to the need to challenge the Anglo elite that owned the levers of industrial production in the province, and to resist the incursions of foreign capitalists such as JM that Duplessis had welcomed to the province with such open arms. The main lesson of the strike was that Quebeckers must become "maîtres chez nous" when it came to the exploitation of natural resources. Supporters of this view often mention the fact that three prominent young anti-Duplessis activists who participated in and wrote about the strike, *Le Devoir* journalist Gérard Pelletier, CTCC

leader Jean Marchand, and the writer and intellectual Pierre Trudeau, became the core of a new Quebec presence in Ottawa as the "three wise men" Prime Minister Lester Pearson recruited to his cabinet in 1965. If the strike had begun with a series of specific demands from workers, many would agree with Trudeau when he later famously argued the dispute constituted "the violent announcement that a new era had begun."

And yet, the tendency of Trudeau and other commentators to subsume the Asbestos strike within broader politics of the Quiet Revolution risks steamrolling over the very specific concerns that the miners brought to the bargaining table. In her recent book-length study of the Jeffrey Mine, historian Jessica Van Horssen has argued convincingly that specific bargaining issues, particularly the health risks associated with asbestos dust, remained the core motivation for the strike. As evidence of asbestos risks continued to mount in the 1940s, JM continued to deny and suppress results from its own internal research program on the risks to workers. The company even engaged in a scandalous program of secret autopsies on workers between 1944 and 1958, illegally shipping lungs across the border to the Saranac Lake Laboratory in New York State, and then suppressing results that showed seventy cases of lung cancer in the bodies of the deceased workers. Had workers known the lengths the company had gone to suppress internal knowledge of asbestos-related diseases even prior to 1949, the strike may have been even more intense than it was. Even so, an extensive public report (published also in *Le Devoir*) by journalist Burton LeDoux in January 1949, on the eve of the labour disruption, largely confirmed for workers that JM had been lying about the risks of asbestos dust and that better dust control was essential to protect their health. Despite the resolve of the strikers, Van Horssen suggests JM's almost total victory required the miners to accept the health risks associated with asbestos as the price of retaining their jobs and their strong ties to the town of Asbestos. In subsequent years, Jeffrey Mine workers actually became an ally of JM in the efforts to deny the risks of asbestos exposure when health regulators around the globe began to ban the use of the

Miners drilling at the face of a tunnel in the Bell Island Mine in the town of Wabana, Newfoundland, near St. John's. The iron deposits on Bell Island were vast, supporting mining activity from 1895 to 1966, primarily to feed the steel mills in Sydney, Nova Scotia.

material beginning in the 1970s. In its latter years, the Jeffrey Mine primarily served developing world markets that had poor handling and health regulations for asbestos, a subject of much criticism and ridicule, even earning harsh satirical treatment from Jon Stewart's *The Daily Show* just prior to the final closure of the mine in 2011. As over 130 years of mineral extraction abruptly came to an end at the Jeffrey Mine, the town of Asbestos was left to wrestle with the economic shock of mine closure and the legacy of its own murky engagement with one of the world's most dangerous minerals.

The dangers of toxic exposure also came to define the experience of workers who toiled in the fluorspar mines of St. Lawrence, Newfoundland. In 1933 Walter Seibert, a New York investor, established the St. Lawrence Corporation of Newfoundland (SLCN) and opened the Black Duck Mine in 1933 (the first of several in the area), an economic lifeline for the Burin Peninsula after a disastrous tidal wave had struck in 1929 and devastated the local fishery, destroying gear, boats, and the productivity

of the fishing grounds. Fluorspar is a mineral important in steel and aluminum smelting processes, and SLCN sensed an opportunity to become a key supplier for the Dominion Steel and Coal Corporation (DOSCO) smelter in Sydney, Nova Scotia. Other small players jumped in to stake claims and conduct exploratory work, development activity that was bought up by the Aluminum Company of Canada (Alcan) in 1939, which then created the Newfoundland Fluorspar Company (Newfluor) as a subsidiary to run a feeder mine for its aluminum smelter at Arvida, Quebec. With only two other mines operating at that time on the island of Newfoundland (the Bell Island iron mines, also a key source of feedstock for the

DOSCO smelter, and the lead-zinc operation at Buchans), the jobs created in the St. Lawrence mines were critical to an economy stalled by the Great Depression (when the Newfoundland government had declared bankruptcy), not to mention the production of strategic metals at the outbreak of global war. But the St. Lawrence mines are remembered more for precipitating a major occupational health crisis surrounding the dangers of dust and radiation exposure that reached national attention by the 1960s.

In the early years much of the mining at St. Lawrence was conducted in open-cast trenches, but health conditions deteriorated markedly when operations moved underground. With few regulations and only the most casual system of mine inspections, poor ventilation and dusty conditions prevailed in the mine environment. Miner Jack Callaghan spoke of his exposure to dust during these early years in anthropologist Elliott Leyton's seminal oral history of the mining operation:

> *In the first eight to ten years they done a cruel lot of dry drilling. No water, see. They were only using a dry hammer and there was nothing, only smoke and dust all the time. Well that going down your throat all day long had to go somewhere. You were all the time blasting, you couldn't hardly live with the smoke down there then, there wasn't much air, see. It used to bother you, but you had to try to do the best you could. You'd just draw back for a spell 'til she'd blow out a bit. You'd turn on your air hose and blow out your drift as clear as you could get it, you'd clear away your chutes, and start mucking again. When you were going ahead with your light, you could see something like a fog, your light was shining through streaks. You'd see circles, you often see the sun shining like that. Outside of that boy she was a beautiful spot to work.*

By the end of the 1930s there were clear indications of widespread health problems among the St. Lawrence miners. In 1939, almost all the SLCN workforce of one hundred had become sick with stomach ailments

The conveyor system used to load iron ore to ships at the Scotia Pier, Bell Island, in 1956. On November 2, 1942, a German submarine badly damaged the pier in a torpedo attack and sunk two ships, killing twenty-eight crew. A previous U-boat attack in September 1942 sunk two other ships anchored off Bell Island, killing twenty-nine people.

from drinking water that was apparently polluted; the Department of Public Health and Welfare had expressed concern about the increasing incidence of unspecified lung disease among the miners in 1940. In 1941 workers at the SLCN and Newfluor staged several walkouts under the auspices of their newly formed St. Lawrence Mine Workers' Protective Union, demanding wage improvements, union recognition from SLCN, and

Miners enjoy a break in the fresh air at the surface of Bell Island Mine in 1956. Ten years later, the mine closed due to competition from open pit operations in Labrador and Latin America. About 3000 people still live in the town of Wabana, many commuting by ferry to work in the St. John's area.

health and safety improvements. A Board of Inquiry established by Newfoundland's colonial Commission of Government generally ignored the health issues, even if oral histories suggest that community members were aware that some kind of chest ailment was taking the lives of miners. Although the lack of medical services in the community made it difficult even to assess what condition afflicted sick miners, the first case of silicosis was confirmed in 1953. When the US government finally provided a small hospital for St. Lawrence in 1955 (a gift for the community's role rescuing 186 sailors from two US destroyers that had run aground in a storm in 1942), medical staff confirmed more cases of silicosis. In 1957 the federal Department of Health and Welfare found dust levels at dangerous levels at various underground locations, renewing calls for better ventilation in the mine.

These new medical facilities revealed that, in addition to silicosis, three new cases of lung cancer had emerged among the St. Lawrence mine workers every year between 1952 and 1959. The federal Department of Health and Welfare immediately conducted more environmental tests in the mine and pinned down the cause as alpha radiation from radon gas that had spread due to the presence of uranium in the surrounding rock. Improved ventilation measures reduced radiation and dust exposure levels in subsequent years, but nothing could be done for those who had already worked underground for long periods of time. By 1967, twenty-five miners had succumbed to silicosis and fifty-one to lung cancer, prompting the establishment of a provincial Royal Commission to investigate all aspects of this industrial epidemic. The commission was highly critical of both companies and the government for lax health and safety standards in the St. Lawrence mines, but the provincial government rejected key findings (such as the link between radon and lung cancer) and offloaded responsibility for radiation monitoring to Newfluor (SLCN had folded in 1957).

In April 1971 a large group of St. Lawrence women picketed the town's loadings docks and halted the shipment of fluorspar for two days as a protest against the harsh poverty the families of sick and deceased miners faced under Workmen's Compensation Board (WCB) programs. The provincial government eventually established a special fund to augment the WCB payouts in 1973, but the miners and their union continually pressed for improvements to compensation programs, hoping to expand the payment amount and eligibility criteria based on years of exposure, place of work, or type of ailment (aboveground workers, for example, were not eligible for compensation until 2011). The issue reached national attention in 1975 through the publication of Elliott Leyton's *Dying Hard*, a subsequent CBC documentary on the issue, and the tour of a play about St. Lawrence put on by The Mummers, a St. John's theatre group. Alcan closed the Newfluor operation in 1978 as it shifted to Mexican supplies of fluorspar. Because so many of the miners remained in the local community, it has been possible to keep an accurate count of the shockingly grim consequences of fluorspar mining at St. Lawrence. By 2001 studies suggested that underground miners at St. Lawrence mines had suffered from 191 cases of lung cancer (plus 15 additional cases among surface workers), 28 cases of abdominal cancers, 11 of bladder cancer, and 64 of silicosis. St. Lawrence had seemed to promise a bright industrial future in the wake of the tsunami and fisheries collapse, but instead became a tragic example of the price some communities have paid for seeking a livelihood underground.

Toward the New North

The end of the Second World War brought renewed interest among successive Canadian governments in the possibility and potential of development in the territorial north. Although one key military megaproject, the Alaska Highway, had proceeded during the war (with devastating consequences for Yukon First Nations), control of that rested with the Americans. As Cold War tensions mounted, American demand for strategic minerals such as nickel and uranium dovetailed with Canada's desire to pursue northern development, maintain Arctic sovereignty, and foster the social welfare of Indigenous people. Prime Minister Louis St. Laurent captured the prevailing

Johnny Baker in 1935 at the site where he and Hugh Muir discovered the 21 gold claims that became Giant Mine. Baker also discovered the gold deposit that led to the development of the short-lived Burwash Mine in 1935. Some Yellowknives Dene have claimed Baker found the gold with the help of elder Liza Crookedhand, knowledge for which Crookedhand was rewarded with a new stovepipe.

enthusiasm for northern development when he spoke in the House of Commons in 1953:

> *Apparently we have administered these vast territories of the north in an almost continuing state of absence of mind. I think all honourable members now feel that the territories are vastly important to Canada and that it is time that more attention was focused upon their possibilities and what they will mean to this nation. We in the southern part of Canada have been so busy in recent years that we have given little close attention to the north country.*

For many politicians and bureaucrats who promoted northern development, price instability and the general decline in the Indigenous fur trade economy in the late 1940s suggested a dire need for northern wage labour opportunities. Reports of declining caribou populations, along with several incidents of starvation among Inuit in the Eastern Arctic interior (which reached a national audience due to the writings of Farley Mowat), reinforced the idea among federal officials that the old hunting and trapping economy of the northern territories was moribund. At the same time, John Diefenbaker galvanized the nation during the 1957 election with his new "northern vision" based on economic expansion and development in the region. For many northern officials, mineral-led development offered the best opportunity to fulfill this vision, the surest way to jumpstart northern industrialization and wage employment opportunities.

The first major mining development after the Second World War resulted less from government planning than new discoveries and rapidly recovering gold markets. As mentioned in the previous chapter, Yellowknife emerged as an important gold mining outpost after Johnny Baker's Burwash Mine began a brief production run on the opposite side of the bay in 1935. After the war, the much bigger Con (operated by Consolidated Mining and Smelting Company, the emerging BC mining giant) and Negus mine (operated by Negus Mines Ltd.)

RIGHT: A worker in the mill at Giant Mine, where ore was crushed and ground, and then put through a flotation circuit to separate gold-bearing sulphide minerals. The sulphide minerals were then roasted to remove arsenic, sulphur and antimony, a precursor to accessing the gold. At the final stage, the roaster byproduct was subject to a cyanide treatment, which dissolved gold that was precipitated out of the solution and refined as gold bricks.

BELOW: Governor General Georges Vanier holds a gold brick from Giant Mine while on a tour of the facility in 1961.

revived operations that had been crippled by wartime restrictions on the production of non-essential metals. Baker's "Giant" find remained merely an exploration site during and immediately after the war, until more evidence of promising deposits and favourable prices created the conditions for the new Giant Mine to open in 1948 under the control of Giant Yellowknife Gold Mines Ltd. (a subsidiary of Ventures Ltd., later acquired by Falconbridge). The mine quickly became a major producer, with workers pulling 8,152 ounces from the ground in the last seven months of 1948 and more than seven million ounces before closure in 2004.

Along with the revived Con and Negus mines, Giant sparked a new staking rush in the region and new interest in northern mining. Most of these new satellite mines in the Yellowknife region remained

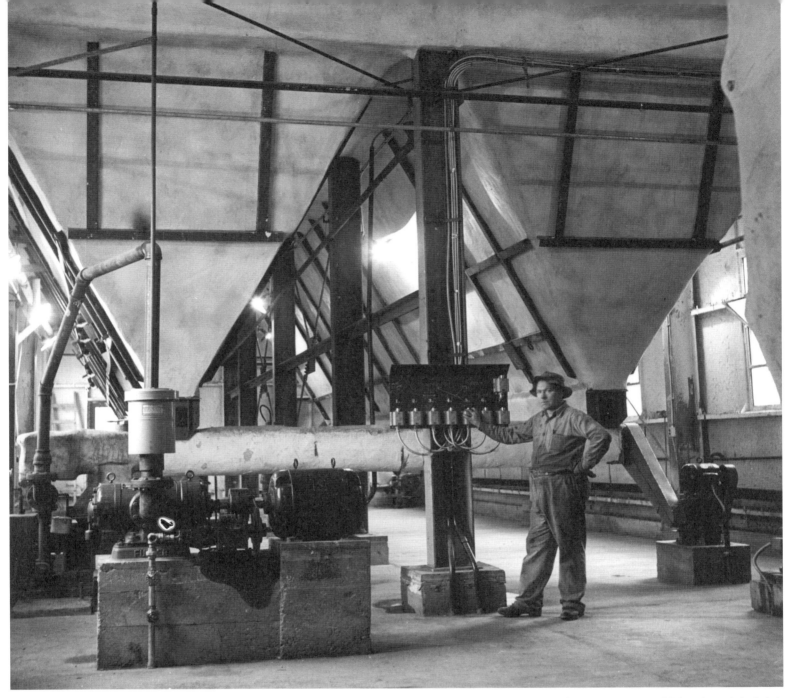

A Giant Mine employee at work in the baghouse facility, likely in the late 1950s. The installation of a baghouse in 1958 reduced, but did not eliminate, the arsenic air pollution that had poisoned the land around Yellowknife, killing a Yellowknives Dene child in 1951. The baghouse complemented a Cottrell electrostatic precipitator, the first pollution control equipment installed in 1951.

small and short-lived, other than the Discovery Mine and town site, which operated from 1950 to 1969 just over eighty kilometres northeast of Yellowknife. Regardless, the economic activity from the big three gold producers directly adjacent to Yellowknife was enough to spark population growth and a building boom, transforming the small mining outpost into a full municipality in 1953 and the territorial capital in 1967. Today, many in

Yellowknife's settler community retain a deep connection to their gold mining heritage, celebrating the work and economic activity that built the modern city of Yellowknife, the place where, as one slogan puts it, "the gold is paved with streets."

For the Yellowknives Dene First Nation, the headframes and smokestack at Giant Mine (only recently torn down) were symbolic of a much darker history. As mentioned

ABOVE: At the last stage of the gold production process at Giant Mine, a bullion furnace pours liquid gold into a brick mold in 1952. The vast majority of Giant Mine's gold output was sold to the Royal Canadian Mint.

RIGHT: The No. 2 Headframe at Giant Mine in December 1949, just six months after the mine officially opened.

in the last chapter, the Yellowknives Dene resented the prospecting boom that began in the 1930s, wary of the newcomers and the impact of blasting and digging on their lands. They could have hardly imagined the severe water and air pollution that accompanied the opening of Giant Mine, however, poisoning their water, their food sources, and their land for decades.

Much of the Giant Mine ore was contained in arsenopyrite formations, a refractory ore that required roasting at extremely high temperatures to burn off sulphur so that the gold could be separated from the ore body in a cyanide solution. One result of the roasting process was air pollution in the form of sulphur dioxide and arsenic trioxide dust. The health and environmental impacts of sulphur dioxide in Yellowknife are poorly documented, though oral history and scientific studies from the 1980s indicate an intermittent

"rotten egg" smell in the air, respiratory problems among local residents, and damaged vegetation in the area. The consequences of releasing large amounts of arsenic trioxide into the local environment were much more severe. Arsenic trioxide is tasteless and odourless, and dissolves in water to become an invisible poison. The main pathway of exposure for humans and other animals is through the ingestion of contaminated food or water, or the direct inhalation of dust. Even relatively small amounts of this contaminant (70 to 180 milligrams) could be fatal to humans, while smaller amounts can cause vomiting, diarrhea, muscle aches, and a variety of skin conditions. Effects from long-term exposure may include impairment of the circulatory system or brain function. Since the 1970s we have also known that long-term exposure to even very small amounts of arsenic trioxide can cause liver, bladder, and lung cancer. There is no safe level of exposure, at least over the long term.

Many of the dangers of arsenic were well-known in the mining industry. In just one high-profile case, arsenic trioxide

A Dene man (surname: Lafferty) drives his dog team through water with Yellowknife's Old Town in the background. The sudden introduction of modern industrial mining, the development of the town of Yellowknife, and the massive arsenic pollution problems at Giant and Con mines, severely diminished the ability of the Yellowknives Dene to hunt, fish and gather berries from the local area.

emissions from the Anaconda Copper Mining Company's Washoe smelter in Montana killed large numbers of farm animals beginning in 1902. Remarkably, Giant Yellowknife Mines neglected to install pollution-control equipment on its roaster stack between 1949 and 1951, while Con Mine also began roasting smaller amounts of ore beginning in 1948 with no pollution abatement until 1949. Between 1949 and 1953 Con and Giant released as much as 22,000 pounds of arsenic trioxide dust from their smokestacks (16,500 pounds of which came from Giant). Testing in the late 1950s revealed that the fallout (and effluent from the mine's tailings ponds) had contaminated Yellowknife Bay, the city's drinking water source, causing frequent spikes in arsenic levels above what was considered safe at the time (0.05 ppm). The Yellowknives Dene who lived on Latham Island (today's Ndilo, near Yellowknife's "Old Town") were particularly vulnerable to the arsenic pollution, not only because prevailing winds frequently placed the Latham Island community in the path of Giant Mine's stack emissions but also because they relied on contaminated snow and ice for drinking water during

the winter months. Through the extremely long and cold Yellowknife winters, arsenic trioxide fallout accumulated in the snow and ice cover with no cleansing rain or water flow to wash it away. By late winter arsenic dust had been accumulating steadily since October, ensuring a spike of toxic material in snowmelt, lakes, and streams when spring finally did come.

In April 1951 disaster struck as a two-year-old Yellowknives Dene boy died from drinking contaminated snowmelt water and federal officials reported widespread sickness in the community. Yellowknives Dene elders insist that up to four children and several older community members died from arsenic poisoning; scattered records suggest two Giant Mine workers and at least two additional Dene people were treated for arsenic poisoning between 1949 and 1958. Various oral history studies and public testimony paint a picture of a heavily contaminated landscape in Yellowknife immediately after the opening of Giant Mine. In a comment that resonates with the descriptions of others, Yellowknives Dene elder

A group of trainees at Con Mine in 1959 participating in an Indigenous prospecting course. While northern Indigenous people did take advantage of employment and market opportunities that accompanied the expansion of the mining economy, it was not until the 1980s that Impact and Benefit Agreements, which generally included training, employment, cash transfers, and some form of environmental monitoring, became standard practice in the northern territories.

Therese Sangris described the wide-ranging impact of arsenic poisoning on her community:

> *The people were never warned about impacts and risks of living near mines. In late December of 1949, a massive emission from the Giant mine dispersed huge amounts of arsenic into the air, settling into the ice and snow. Melting snow in the spring of the following two years was so toxic that notices were printed in Yellowknife newspapers warning people not to drink or use the meltwater. Few*

Weledeh Yellowknives Dene could read the notices. Anyone who washed their hair with arsenic-laden meltwater in the next two springs went bald. A dairy herd, horses, chickens, and dogs were among the domesticated animals that died from drinking meltwater in spring 1950. But the greatest tragedy occurred in spring 1951: four children in family camps in Ndilo died. The mine owners gave their parents some money, as if it could compensate for the loss. Women stopped picking medicine plants and berries, which used to grow thickly in the area of the Giant mine. The people moved away, avoiding the mine area for some years, although it had once been so important to them. To this day, they refuse to use water from Weleh-Cheh for soaking caribou hides or making dryfish.

For decades many Yellowknives Dene elders have similarly described how the heavy arsenic pollution from Giant Mine alienated them from a local landscape that had sustained them for generations.

The federal government and the mining community quickly developed a response plan to the Giant Mine emissions. The company paid $750 to the family of the child who was killed. The federal government arranged for signs warning of arsenic dangers to be placed at local lakes and ran five small advertisements in the back pages of News of the North over the course of 1951. Many Yellowknives Dene would have been unable to read the ads due to barriers of language and literacy. Giant Yellowknife Mines installed pollution control equipment in the form of a Cottrell electrostatic precipitator, which used static charges to recover particles from the roaster effluent. Con had installed a wet scrubber in 1949, which used water to control particulate matter in the roaster stack, but the company dumped the arsenic-contaminated water into local lakes. Between 1954 and 1958, airborne arsenic emissions in Yellowknife fell from 22,000 to 7,250 pounds per day. Further improvements, including the installation of a second Cottrell unit and a "baghouse" filtration system helped achieve further reductions to 695 pounds per day. Nonetheless, ongoing public health monitoring through the 1950s suggested high arsenic levels on local vegetables and berries, while the municipal water supply was above the safe arsenic threshold roughly 15 per cent of the time. In 1969 the city moved the municipal water intake upstream to the cleaner Yellowknife River. The Yellowknives Dene on Latham Island received trucked-in water for which they were charged $5 per month, an amount that many Dene loudly protested was more than they could afford, forcing them to draw from the contaminated bay. It is all the more remarkable that the mining company was never forced to pay for the Yellowknives' water as the barest form of compensation for contaminating a common resource. Today the Yellowknives still resent having to pay for trucked-in water while both communities of Dettah and Ndilo sit directly adjacent to a vast source of what was once clean drinking water.

The arsenic controversy burst onto the national stage in 1975 when CBC's *As It Happens* produced a radio documentary highlighting the impact of arsenic pollution on the Yellowknives Dene. The program accused the Canadian government (using Watergate-era language) of covering up a report that linked arsenic exposure to high cancer rates in the Yellowknife area. In response, the National Indian Brotherhood, an activist group, began to organize hair sample studies measuring arsenic exposure among the Yellowknives, partnering in 1977 with the United Steelworkers and toxicology researchers at the University of Toronto to produce a study showing high rates of arsenic exposure among Giant millworkers and the Yellowknives. The resulting arsenic scare prompted the federal government to contract the independent Canadian Public Health Association (CPHA) to conduct a comprehensive study. The CPHA final report concluded that dangerous exposures to arsenic were confined to workers in the Giant Mine roasting facility, though the risks of long-term, low-dose arsenic exposure were not well understood during the late 1970s.

By 1979 pollution controls improved to the point where the mines only emitted 29 pounds of arsenic per day into the Yellowknife area. Yet all of the thousands of pounds of arsenic collected each day were being stored underground in old mine stopes and purpose-built chambers. Today, 237,000 tons of arsenic trioxide rest underground at Giant Mine, one of the worst-contaminated sites in Canada and currently the focus of an expensive, long-term containment and remediation program. Giant is one of the "zombie mines" profiled in the final chapter. Perhaps better than any other mine in Canada, it symbolizes the dispossession of Indigenous lands that has often accompanied mineral development and the long-term environmental costs of mining that will haunt adjacent communities into the distant future.

The North Rankin Nickel Mine has a more ambiguous legacy. Opened in 1957 as the first industrial mine in the Canadian Arctic, the Rankin Inlet mine landed in the midst of a major economic and ecological crisis for the Inuit of the Eastern Arctic. The collapse of Arctic fox prices in 1947 and periodic caribou shortages through the 1950s prompted the federal Department of Northern Affairs and National Resources to reconsider the long-standing policy of dispersal that had emphasized keeping Inuit as hunters and trappers and discouraged their settlement around missions or trading posts. The federal government's failed attempts to relocate Inuit to Garry Lake and North Henik Lake so they could live off fish resulted in high-profile starvation incidents in 1958 that horrified the Canadian public, especially after Farley Mowat recounted in *Maclean's* magazine the harrowing story of Kikkik, a mother who was tried for abandoning two very young daughters as she struggled across the tundra to escape starvation at Henik Lake. Even before the story reached a national audience, the collapsing subsistence economy of the eastern Arctic reinforced a growing idea among federal officials that the future of the Inuit lay with wage labour and centralization rather than hunting and trapping. The mining company, North Rankin Nickel Mines, Ltd., had already been using Inuit labour seasonally since 1953 during the development phase of the mine; company president W.W. Weber and mine manager J. Andrew Easton actively worked with government

Inuit workers at the North Rankin Nickel Mine in July 1961. When the mine opened in 1957, government and the company recruited Inuit workers, reasoning that mining could provide an alternative to the subsistence economy. While many Inuit feel a sense of pride about their work at the mine, the project was short lived, leaving many workers without employment after the mine closed in 1962.

The Great Slave Lake Railroad reaches its terminus at the Pine Point Mine. Envisioned as a great development railroad, the Canadian government spent millions of dollars to run this line from Waterways, Alberta to Pine Point, Northwest Territories. Today, the section from Hay River to the mine has been torn out and no comparable mining development has been serviced directly by the railway line.

and RCMP officials to recruit Inuit workers away from their "stone age" subsistence economy toward modern wage labour. The government and mine officials also drew on the connections and recommendations of boat pilot Singiituq, efforts that drew eighty Inuit workers to the mine. With Inuit comprising as much as 70 per cent of the mine workforce at its height, federal officials were elated that this "experiment" in Inuit wage labour was proving to be a success.

Inuit recollections of their new life at Rankin Inlet are more ambiguous. An oral history study of former Inuit miners in Rankin Inlet conducted in 2011 revealed a mixture of negative memories combined with pride in the community's mining heritage.[8] Many miners recalled, for instance, that Inuit initially were segregated from the non-Inuit population, hived off into substandard housing and often attending separate social activities in the community, but over time they began to integrate more with their southern counterparts. Peter Ittinuar (a son of one of the early Inuit miners) suggested that, "in a way it was more integration than had ever existed before, even though it was segregated. People took part in the same activities, there was community dances, movies . . . white people and Inuit people went to these things at the same time,

went to church at the same time." In their working lives, many former miners expressed pride at their ability to adjust to their new life as a miners, even as they remember advocating for more flexible work schedules so they could hunt for fresh meat. There was a dark side to Inuit workers becoming so thoroughly incorporated into the mine workforce, as many remember mine closure in 1962 as a period of hardship and economic dislocation. Some workers left Rankin Inlet as the government scrambled to help them find jobs in other mines such as Con in Yellowknife, Lynn Lake in Northern Manitoba, Asbestos Hill in northern Quebec, or as railway construction workers on the line into the new Pine Point Mine on the south shore of Great Slave Lake. Other Inuit workers stayed put, relying on a combination of welfare, hunting, or employment in government-sponsored initiatives such as a fish cannery, sewing enterprise, or the now-famous ceramic and soapstone carving studios, while others returned to their home communities. If the short life of

A survey crew at their camp on the Pine Point property. Although prospector Ed Nagle had staked the first claims at Pine Point in 1898, the mine underwent a lengthy exploration and development phase, particularly in the 1950s, prior to opening in 1964. Survey lines often disrupted the traplines maintained by local Dene and Métis.

the mine pointed to the risks of mineral-led development for Inuit workers, half a century later many former Rankin Inlet miners articulated distinct pride in the community's mining heritage and their own ability to navigate the complex challenges and opportunities that accompanied the advent of the mine.

The relative success of the Inuit employment initiative at Rankin Inlet added weight to the idea that large-scale resource development was the only economic path forward for northern Canada. In 1958 Prime Minister John Diefenbaker made a campaign promise to "aid in projects which, while not self-liquidating, will lead to the development of the national resources for the opening of Canada's northland. We will open that

A portable Sullivan compressor used at the Pine Point site. Although this photograph was taken in the 1950s, this piece of equipment was barged to the site and then hauled by horse from Dawson Landing during an earlier development period in the 1920s. After workers at the site stumbled on the compressor, mechanic Louis Garskie was able to get the motor going using the hand crank.

northland for development by improving transportation and communication and by the development of power, by the building of access roads." Diefenbaker specifically mentioned a rail link to the massive Pine Point lead–zinc deposits on Great Slave Lake as a keystone project that would link northern resources to southern markets.

Prospector and fur trader Ed Nagle had staked the first claims at Pine Point in 1898, though nothing came of this initial prospecting activity. By the 1920s, Consolidated Mining and Smelting (later, Cominco), always hungry for feedstock at its Trail smelter, began staking in the area (led by Ed's son, Ted). In 1948 the federal government showed clear preference for a large corporate actor when it granted the company a five-hundred-square-mile exclusive exploration zone in the area. The government took a further step in the mid-1950s when it began to promote a railroad to Pine Point from Waterways, Alberta, as a catalyst for a succession of

Houses at the Pine Point town site in 1988. After the mine closed that same year, many of the trailer houses were sold to other work camps in the regions, while other buildings were leveled. All that remains today are the old streets and sidewalks. In the eyes of many former residents, Pine Point was an idyllic place to live due to the camaraderie and the high quality of the facilities.

mining developments in the region. In 1955 R. Gordon Robertson, the deputy minister of northern development and commissioner of the Northwest Territories, spoke of the Great Slave Lake Railroad as "one of the great development railroads of the country. . . This railroad is quite different from most of the branch lines constructed in recent years which were destined to serve one mine, or a group of mines; its purpose is to open up a whole new region." By the time the Pine Point Mine opened in 1964, the federal government had poured $99,547,345 into the railroad, a highway extension to the mine, and a dam on the Talston River to power the project. Although CM&S would finance the direct development of the mine, the government was clearly willing to invest public money as stimulus for a project they felt would spark a broader northern development and modernization agenda.

Whether the public investment was worth it depends in some ways on whom you talk to. Undoubtedly the mine was productive and profitable during most of its operational life, shipping over nine million tons of ore concentrate along the Great Slave Lake Railway in a twenty-two-year period. For the miners who moved to the Pine Point, the newly constructed mining town offered unparalleled quality of life for a northern mining town. In keeping with the prevailing practices in the post-war period, CM&S wanted to avoid the chaos and instability associated with frontier mining camps, or the heavy administrative burden associated with running a company town, and to build an "open" town with all the trappings of a modern suburb. With carefully planned subdivisions, modern schools, and first-class recreational facilities (a hockey arena, baseball pitch, golf course, and small ski hill built on a waste-rock pile), many former residents remember the town almost as a paradise. In an award-winning National Film Board web-based documentary, media artists The Goggles documented how many former Pine Pointers remember their town as "the best place to live on earth." Former residents still maintain strong ties to their memories of the place through

An aerial view of Faro in the Yukon, the base town for the Cyprus-Anvil lead-zinc mine. The mine was the largest employer in the Yukon after it opened in 1969, but today thousands of tons of waste rock, a contaminated tailings ponds, and issues with acid mine drainage have left the Canadian government with a complex and expensive cleanup project.

the website "Pine Point Revisited," posting old photos and memories, and sometimes organizing reunions at the town site.[9] For many Pine Pointers, life and work at the mine remain synonymous with the sweet days of youth, a high-water mark in their lives that many would return to in seconds if only they had the opportunity.

The legacy of Pine Point is decidedly more complicated for the largely Chipewyan Dene and Métis community of Fort Resolution just over sixty kilometres to the east. Some residents worked at the mine and lived in Pine Point, sharing the fond memories of their non-Indigenous counterparts. During interviews we conducted as part of an oral history study in 2009, participants described Pine Point as "a picture-perfect town" with "the best of the best of everything," suggesting they had difficulty adjusting to life back in Fort Resolution after the mine closed in 1988. At the same time, many Fort Resolution people regard the mine as something of a lost opportunity and a festering wound. Community elders remember their traplines being destroyed by seismic exploration and ultimately being forced to abandoned hunting and trapping over the large area of the mine. While some Indigenous people did work at the mine, many remember that the numbers were low, a problem compounded by the fact that CM&S and the government did little to develop training opportunities for local people, or even extend the highway from the mine to Fort Resolution until 1972. Employment data shows Indigenous employment peaking at 17 per cent in 1970 but declining to between 7 and 9 per cent in the 1970s.

Fort Resolution thus realized few economic benefits from the mine despite the mine's profitability, a source of local resentment that is compounded by the fact that the mine was only partially cleaned up after closure. The company removed all the town buildings, capped the 570-hectare tailings pond with gravel, and blocked access roads. With no commercial traffic, the rail tracks leading to Pine Point from Hay River were eventually torn up. Left behind were forty-three open pits (many now filled or filling with water), a deteriorating network of haul roads, and numerous massive piles of waste rock and rubble, a landscape reminiscent of the *Mad Max* movies. While some Fort Resolution residents use the roads for hunting and recreation, many fear that heavy metals from the tailings pond and pits have contaminated local fish populations in Great Slave Lake. In 1993 Chief Bernadette Unka summed up a prevalent local sentiment about the mine (one we heard expressed many times during oral history research in 2009) in her testimony before the Royal Commission on Aboriginal People:

Pine Points [sic] Mines nor Canada have never compensated the Dene people that used those areas in their hunting, fishing and trapping. They have never been compensated for their loss or for the land devastation. When I say land devastation, if you are to fly over Pine Point Mines you would look down and you would think you were flying over the moon with the craters and open pits that are left open. The people have never been compensated for the hardships and the heartaches induced by mineral development. While the company creamed the crop at $53 million during their

peak years, we got very little jobs and what we did get
were very low-paying jobs.

Although Pine Point remains an idealized memory
for many, the abandoned streets and mine workings also
challenge the federal government's vision of the mine and
railroad as gateway developments for the South Slave region,
and remain visible reminders of the ephemeral benefits and
long-term legacies of the northern mining economy.

The narrative of unrealized dreams attached to a major
development project was repeated in the Yukon as the
government and private industry worked hand-in-hand
to promote mining at a massive lead-zinc deposit roughly
190 kilometres northwest of Whitehorse. Exploration had
proceeded in the area since 1953 and accelerated in the
mid-1960s, with claims eventually consolidated in a joint
development venture between Cyprus Mines Corporation
and Dynasty Exploration, eventually organized as the new
Anvil Mining Company. Although financed largely through
$42 million in bank loans, the so-called Cyprus-Anvil
mine owners immediately approached the government for
assistance. As with Pine Point, the federal government was
keen to support the company's requests for assistance with
hydroelectric power, all-weather transportation from the
mine to a saltwater port, and development of a town. While
negotiations over government assistance for Pine Point
had been somewhat haphazard, Anvil and federal officials
quickly concluded the more formal "Anvil Agreement" in
August 1967. The agreement followed a similar pattern to
the arrangements at Pine Point: the federal government
furnished the company with a large, exclusive surface
lease in the mine area, provided electric power to the
mine, assisted with the development of the Faro townsite
(through the provision of land, services, and capital costs),
financed telecommunications services through a Crown
corporation, and provided all-important road developments
and upgrades. For a total public contribution of just over
$28 million, Anvil was expected to make efforts to hire local
people and conduct a feasibility study for a smelter in the
Yukon over a five-year period. Five years later the company

and government agreed with a commissioned report that
concluded a smelter was not feasible for the region. Rather,
the company began shipping its ore in 1969 to two Japanese
smelters under a seven-year contract, exporting a partly
finished resource from what became Canada's largest open-
pit lead-zinc operation until it closed in 1998.

As with Pine Point, the Cyprus-Anvil mine was located
sixty-five kilometres west of a First Nations community:
the largely Kaska-speaking Ross River Dena. The Anvil
agreement had stipulated that the company would make
best efforts to hire local residents, "particularly Indians
and Eskimos," at a rate of 5 per cent in the first year of
operation, increasing to 25 per cent in the fifth year of
the mine. Although Indigenous employment did reach 10
per cent of the workforce in year two, it declined to only
1 per cent in subsequent years and Ross River residents
quit due to dissatisfaction with the monotony of unskilled
labour at the mine. At the same time, new roads and growth
in Faro and Ross River brought an influx of outsiders,
along with new types of food, consumer goods, and
competition for local wildlife resources. The new school at
Ross River adopted the British Columbia curriculum and
largely reflected the academic priorities of the southern
white newcomers rather than the Kaska culture. Ross
River became somewhat segregated, with white residents
developing new sections of town with better services. The
newcomers also at times became violent toward members
of the First Nation as the relative social harmony that
characterized life at Pine Point proved elusive in the racially
mixed community of Ross River.

Severe environmental consequences marked all phases of
the Cyprus-Anvil Mine. During the intensive exploration
period of the 1960s, seismic line cutting and digging
disrupted Indigenous traplines, while the digging at the
open-pit and strip mining of the Grum deposit in the 1990s
produced massive landscape-scale changes. The most severe
and ongoing issue has been acid mine drainage (AMD) in
surface water and frequent seepage of acid-bearing water
from the tailings pond, with grave risks for the mobilization
of dangerous heavy metals such as lead, zinc, and arsenic in

A prospector uses a Geiger counter to search for uranium on a high rock outcrop in the Beaverlodge Lake area of northern Saskatchewan in 1952.

the local watershed. Although the government attempted to address the problem collaboratively with the company through the water-licensing provision of the new Northern Inland Waters Act (passed in 1972), very quickly the problem escalated to the point where there was little choice but to prosecute. In March 1975 a breach in the tailings pond resulted in a release of 54,000,000 tons of waste water, yet the company faced only a minimal $5,000 fine under the Fisheries Act. A year later, the company drained its supply of

cyanide from storage tanks into the tailings pond because of fears the tanks would freeze and crack after a failure of the heating system. When the tailings pond water reached levels that threatened a breach, the company released a portion of the highly toxic cyanide effluent directly into Rose Creek, an offense for which it was fined $49,000. Today the acid-generating potential of the 70 million tons of tailings and 320 million tons of waste rock remains a threat to the riparian system, an environmental liability the federal government inherited after the final mine owner went into receivership in 1998. The current remediation plan proposing a $500,000 "stabilize in place" plan will contain rather than repair the toxic threat produced by three decades of lead-zinc mining at Faro. The Cyprus-Anvil mine has become another zombie, behind only Giant Mine as the second-worst contaminated mine site in Canada (see Chapter 6).

Exploiting the "Provincial Norths"

Perhaps not surprisingly, the provinces mimicked their federal counterpart's post-war efforts to spark northern economic development through mining activity. In fact, federal and provincial interests converged at one of the earliest of these projects as Eldorado, a federal Crown corporation since the advent of atomic weapons research during the Second World War, responded to the growing Cold War demand for uranium with expansion into a promising area on Lake Athabasca in northwestern Saskatchewan. Although uranium had been detected on the north shore of Lake Athabasca as early as 1944, prospecting activity exploded during early Cold War years as the US offered a guaranteed price for uranium and Canada eased restrictions on exploration. In 1952 Eldorado opened a mine and mill at Beaverlodge Lake, while satellite mines such as Gunnar (1955–63) and Lorado (a mill operating from 1957–60) formed parts of a complex of fifty-two mines in the region during the 1950s and early 1960s. So enthused was Co-operative Commonwealth Federation (CCF) Premier Tommy Douglas, he declared, "standing as we do on the threshold of the atomic age, uranium is of tremendous importance to our industrial development," regardless of the fact that much of the uranium would be funnelled through the Port Hope, Ontario, refinery and straight into the US atomic weapons stockpile.

As with other mines in the post-war period, government and industry emphasized the creation of well-planned "open" towns that could support a stable workforce in the new mining frontier. Thus Eldorado and the provincial government worked together in 1952 to create a central settlement area dubbed Uranium City nine kilometres from the Eldorado's Beaverlodge Mine site. Construction took some time, and many workers continued to live out at the more remote camps directly adjacent to the mines. Despite glowing press reports in the early 1950s heralding Uranium

City as the harbinger of a "new North" built on technology, industry, and modern settlement, this new "yellowcake town" also attracted exactly what the government hoped to avoid: prospectors and miners built haphazard shacks in the early days and Dene and Métis set up camps near the town, despite the paucity of Indigenous employment opportunities in the mines. By the mid-1950s government and industry began in earnest to implement plans for modern housing subdivisions; the closure of the Beaverlodge camp at the end of the 1950s resulted in a major population influx into Uranium City. Some reports indicate that the town's population reached 5,000 at its zenith, but the brutal nature of uranium markets foreclosed any opportunity for sustained economic development in the Beaverlodge district. After the United States announced in 1959 it would cancel its contracts for Canadian uranium, the situation became grave. By 1965 Lorado and Gunnar were closed; only Eldorado's Beaverlodge operation endured. After a brief revival in the 1970s, due primarily to the energy crisis, Eldorado closed the Beaverlodge mine and mill in 1982. Low prices and deteriorating ore quality signalled the death-knell of uranium mining in the Beaverlodge District.

Thirty years after the bust, the population of Uranium City numbered approximately seventy souls and much of the town had been abandoned. As with some other former mining sites, former residents and outside observers remain fascinated by the skeletal remains. One resident has developed a comprehensive memorial website (uraniumcity-history.com) that includes old photographs, memorabilia, obituaries, and information about reunions. In May 2016 the *Huffington Post* included Uranium City on a list of Canada's abandoned places that are "equally creepy and beautiful." A documentary photographer, Ian Brewster, has created an online display of haunting photographs that document the abandoned buildings (including particularly stunning images of the empty ruins of the Candu High School), along with the lives of the few people who remain.[10] Nor have the abandoned environmental legacies of the site been forgotten: in 2007, the federal and provincial governments launched the multimillion-dollar Project

Miners head home after a shift at the Eldorado Mine in northern Saskatchewan. Eldorado Nuclear Ltd. was made a federal Crown Corporation from 1943-88 because of the strategic importance of uranium for atomic energy and nuclear weapons production.

CLEANS (Cleanup of Abandoned Northern Sites) to remediate radioactive tailings sites, remove buildings, and cover old mine workings. After half a century, the memories and the physical landscape north of Lake Athabasca continue to be worked and reworked as governments and residents cope with the residues of uranium mining.

Canada's unreserved embrace of the Cold War uranium market produced another whirlwind of development in northern Ontario. In 1949 prospector Franc Joubin discovered strong indications of uranium deposits in a geological formation known as the Big Z near Elliot Lake, north of Lake Huron. Four years later Joubin organized a "backdoor staking

An underground train in the Eldorado Mine in 1957. While these trains improved the efficiency of transporting men and ore, they also presented often lethal risks to miners, who could get caught between the train and the mine wall or suffer a blow from any overhanging object while in the roofless passenger cars.

A technician working in the Eldorado Nuclear Plant in Port Hope, Ontario. The Port Hope refinery processed uranium from Eldorado's mines on Great Bear Lake and in northern Saskatchewan, but the plant left a legacy of radioactive soil contamination that the federal government is cleaning up at a cost of more than $1.2 billion as of 2021.

bee" with other independent prospectors, a secret initiative that sparked a broader staking rush when news of the first claims became public knowledge. As more news leaked out about the high quantity and quality of ore at Elliot Lake, major corporations moved in (Rio Algom and Consolidated Denison were the biggest players), developing twelve mines with ten thousand employees by 1958, with the uranium going to fulfill a $1.6 billion contract the Canadian government had signed

with the US Atomic Energy Commission in 1957. Journalist Alan Phillips wrote a celebratory piece in *Maclean's*:

> *Never before in Canada has so much money been spent so quickly in one place, three hundred million dollars, the bulk of it this year and last. The hills swarm with contractors, blasting roads, sinking shafts, raising mills. The amount of money that powers this boom is incredible, till you grasp the extent of the mines.*
>
> *Consolidated Denison, on the top stem of the S-curve, is the biggest uranium mine in the world; its ore reserves are twice those of all the uranium mines in the US Even the Pronto, smallest of the eleven, is surpassed elsewhere on this continent only by two mines, one in New Mexico and the other one in Utah.*

ABOVE: A winter camp near Uranium City in the early days of the town's establishment, circa 1953-54.

RIGHT: An aerial photo of Uranium City, showing how the town was meant to reflect the principles of modern suburban design (grid layout, wide streets, large lots) in vogue during the 1950s.

A small group celebrates the inaugural air mail delivery to Uranium City in 1958. Uranium City's population grew in the late 1950s in response to the hot uranium market during this period.

Amid the euphoria, a local newspaper reported that Foreign Affairs Minister (and member of parliament for the region) Lester B. Pearson spoke at the Blind River Legion hall in October 1956 and noted that "ninety-six percent, perhaps more, of the product of this area, is going to the production of weapons for war — weapons almost too much for the human mind to grasp," though he hoped the peaceful development of nuclear power would create a more lasting need for Elliot Lake's massive uranium deposits. The provincial government and industry shared the sunny prognosis for Elliot Lake's future, sharing the cost of a modern, planned town to ensure workforce stability and lure miners away from the ramshackle camps that had initially mushroomed around the mine headframes. Very quickly Elliot Lake became Canada's most important producer of the uranium that fed the new nuclear age in North America.

The former high school in Uranium City, distinctively named Candu High (after a type of Canadian nuclear reactor), closed in 1993 and sits abandoned at sunset in this photograph from 1997.

The almost utopian technological optimism that surrounded the Canadian nuclear industry provided no defence against the volatility of uranium markets. As with Uranium City, the US cancellation of Canadian uranium contracts in 1962 provided a decisive blow to Elliot Lake's

fortunes; the town that had grown so quickly to thirty thousand people just as quickly emptied, leaving only five thousand behind. By 1965 only two of the original twelve mines remained in operation (Denison Mine and Rio Algom's Nordic Mine), saved only when miners protested to their MP (now Prime Minister Pearson), who arranged for the federal government to stockpile uranium for five years, waiting for the day when demand and prices would be higher. That day came in the early 1970s, when government and industry once again promoted nuclear power as the answer to rising energy prices. In 1976 Ontario Hydro inked long-term supply contracts with Denison and Rio Algom for its nuclear energy program,

Among the many uranium mines in the Elliot Lake area, Rio Algom's Quirke mine (circa 1957) operated from 1956-60 and 1968-90. As with the other mines in the region, this abandoned site has undergone environmental remediation and is currently subject to a monitoring program.

handing an economic lifeline to the town, and the population boomed again to over twenty thousand people. But in 1989, Ontario Hydro looked to new uranium mines in northern Saskatchewan for a lower-cost source of uranium, precipitating a second bust period at Elliot Lake. The last uranium mine in the region, Rio Algom's Stanleigh Mine, closed in 1997, but Elliot Lake managed to survive the steep

Prospectors watch a go-go dancing performance, awaiting the opening of 100,000 acres near Elliot Lake for staking in 1968. While some mining histories have romanticized the sexualization of women as performers and/or sex workers in mining towns, in reality women played diverse roles, providing domestic labour that was critical to maintaining the mining workforce, but also paid labour in the health, education and retail sectors. Work at the mines has tended to be reserved for males, in some provinces by law for periods of time. In 2017 women still only comprised 14 per cent of the mining workforce.

drop of the commodity roller coaster, reinventing itself as a retirement, arts, and tourism destination.

Such a sanguine ending to the Elliot Lake story cannot mask the history of environmental health and justice issues that mark the history of uranium mining in the region. By the early 1970s, some miners had become increasingly concerned with the high rates of silicosis and lung cancer due to dust, radon, and radiation exposure, calling for better ventilation and dust mitigation within the mines. United Steelworkers representatives had earlier attended an Ontario Ministry of Health presentation at a conference in Bordeaux, France, and learned that the Ontario Ministry of Health knew about elevated cancer rates at Elliot Lake, but had not informed workers of the dangers. In April 1974 close to a thousand workers walked off the job at Denison Mine for three weeks as part of a wildcat strike protesting health conditions in the mines. In 1974 Gus Frobel, after six years of repeated applications, rejections, and appeals, became the first worker to persuade the Ontario Workman's Compensation Board that conditions in the mines had caused his cancer. At the same time, United Steelworker officials such as Paul Falkowski began to press the issue with the company and government. The workers managed to present their case in the Ontario legislature via the supportive New Democratic Party leader Stephen Lewis,

who testified in committee hearings that "the mines engineering branch of this ministry is guilty of criminal negligence. I don't know how else to put it." Indeed, Ontario Department of Mines and the federal Atomic Energy Control Board (AECB) had met in 1967 to discuss emerging evidence of health risks in US uranium mines, but failed to enact tougher standards (or even to enforce the existing ones imposed by the AECB).

In July 1974 the Ontario government conducted an epidemiological survey of Elliot Lake miners and confirmed lung cancer rates nearly double that of a control group, because of radon exposure. During the same period Falkowski went so far as to recommend that prospective mine workers avoid positions in the Elliot Lake mines, even as the demand for labour skyrocketed when the Ontario Hydro contracts were signed in 1976. In response to the controversy, the Ontario government appointed a Royal Commission (the Ham Commission) in 1975 to examine health and safety in the Ontario mining industry, a process that produced 117 recommendations and became the basis for the province's Occupational Health and Safety Act (OHSA). The new OHSA provided better regulatory oversight for Ontario mines and a set of workers' rights regarding consultation and the right to refuse unsafe work. The uranium industry, ironically, remained under the oversight of less-stringent AECB rules until 1982. By then it was too late for many Elliot Lake workers: according to the Ham Commission, ninety workers had died of lung cancer between 1955 and 1975 (double the expected rate). Historian Laurel MacDowell has written that more than one thousand miners died of occupational diseases associated with uranium between 1957 and 1995, a staggering death toll for workers who toiled in one of the most deadly of the dangerous trades.

The health impacts from the Elliot Lake mines were not contained solely within the tunnels and drifts of the mine workings, but spread outward to surrounding communities as the mining companies dumped ton after ton of radioactive tailings on the surface. In turn, this material leached radioactive dust, heavy metals, and acids into the surrounding Serpent River watershed, draining south toward Lake Huron. Along this section of the Lake Huron shoreline sits the reserve lands of the Anishinaabe Serpent River First Nation, who were forced to contend with dramatic impacts to their lives and livelihoods. Pollution from the mines rendered local water unfit to drink, killed off local fish populations or made them unfit to eat, and compromised the quality and numbers of aquatic furbearers. Faced with declining returns from the hunting and trapping economy, the federal Department of Indian Affairs gave its blessing to Noranda's proposal to build a sulphuric acid plant on the reserve in the mid-1950s to supply a crucial processing chemical to the mines. Despite the promise of jobs and economic returns, the plant became another pollution point source, with air and water effluent destroying local vegetation, further depleting local fish populations, and causing respiratory problems on the reserve. The plant closed in 1963, but pollution problems persisted into the 1980s, until a study by epidemiologist Rosalie Bertell and vigorous community protests (including the dumping of twenty-six tons of toxic plant waste next to the Trans-Canada Highway) forced the provincial government to spend nearly $6 million on a cleanup program. Nobody has yet figured out how to permanently address the long-term legacy of 170 to 200 million tons of radioactive tailings that have been dumped from the Elliot Lake mines. Currently the tailings are managed through a combination of containment, water treatment, and flooding processes to mitigate radioactivity, curtail the emission of radon gas, and neutralize acid rock drainage, but the long half-lives of thorium, radium, and uranium mean that monitoring and care will be required for thousands of years. However brief the uranium boom in Elliot Lake, its environmental legacy will extend into the unimaginably distant future.

Mining histories across the provincial norths often run parallel to the boom, bust, and environmental devastation that mark the two nuclear mining districts, even if cyclical downturns have not completely decimated many of the mining towns. In the mid-1950s new iron mines along the Quebec and Labrador border created massive open-pit mining districts and new instant towns such as Schefferville, Wabush, and Labrador City. Touted as a new source of iron to replace the fading Lake Superior regions and feed the hungry steel mills of the Great Lakes region, development of the Labrador Trough region provided an important catalyst for the joint Canada–US St. Lawrence Seaway megaproject. Their development was also supported by local infrastructure investments in townsites, the Menihek hydroelectric dam project, and the construction of the Quebec North Shore and Labrador (QNS&L) Railway. In a series of critical papers, geographer John Bradbury has argued that dependency on the Great Lakes industrial heartland prevented even a large mining district such as Quebec-Labrador from developing a stable, diversified economy, locking the region into devastating cyclical downturns that have continued to the present day.

US government nickel stockpiling effectively underwrote the establishment of Sherritt-Gordon's Lynn Lake mine in northern Manitoba in 1953. By 1976 the nickel mine began to collapse and the Lynn Lake town has survived only through a combination of tourism and intermittent gold mining (the fire department had to burn many of the abandoned houses in 2013). Unfortunately, parts of the town, including one subdivision and a playground, were built on top of the 21.8 million tons of tailings Sherritt-

Indigenous trainees work at the Pipe Lake Mine near Thompson, Manitoba in 1985.

Gordon left behind. Many local residents are convinced (based on the numbers of the sick and dead in town) that the tailings have made Lynn Lake a cancer cluster, a claim for which the provincial government suggested (in 2013) there was no evidence, even as its own chief public health officer promised to look into the matter. Though Lynn Lake managed to survive past its original boomtown phase, its history still reveals the environmental and economic vulnerability of remote northern places.

Some northern mining districts did manage to diversify beyond the production of raw or lightly processed ore. At Thompson, Manitoba, the persistently high price for nickel in the early 1950s encouraged Inco to begin building an integrated mining, milling, and smelting operation in 1956. The population of the town — a modern planned community along the lines of others from this period — reached over twenty thousand by the mid-1960s, but even such an integrated operation remained vulnerable to poor nickel markets in the late 1970s, and the town's population declined to roughly thirteen thousand. More recently, Vale announced that the smelter would close in 2018 because of a commodities downturn, though mining and milling operations continued. At remote northern Chibougamau, Quebec, mining began in 1949 and has persisted because

of large and diverse ore bodies containing gold, silver, and copper deposits. The town has also become an important logging and sawmilling centre. The relative stability of the economy did not benefit the Oujé-Bougoumou Cree Nation, however, as government and industry compelled them to relocate their communities several times between the 1950s and 1980s to make way for industrial activity in the region.

Although not a mining town, Kitimat's location on the once-remote deep-port waters of the Douglas Channel on British Columbia's northern Pacific Coast, combined with a ready supply of hydro power from the Nechako River, provided Alcan with an ideal location for an aluminum smelter to serve Asian markets. Opened to much fanfare in 1954 as a northern modernization project (with Prince Philip in attendance), by 2018 the Kitimat smelter was set for a $1.8 billion modernization and retrofit project that would extend its life for at least another half-century. Such mineral processing centres remain rare, however, as the region has largely depended on funnelling raw or concentrated ore for processing to southern Canada or other countries.

Indeed, if the post-war period witnessed an unprecedented expansion of mineral development and settlement in northern Canada, often the grand scale of development was precariously based on an extremely narrow economic foundation. Distant

from markets and often unable to diversify, northern mining communities remained, in essence, houses of cards, vulnerable to shifts in global mineral markets. As the stories of Pine Point, Uranium City, and Faro attest, collapse (or near collapse) was the fate that awaited many northern communities; severe decline from an all-too-brief heyday period characterized many others (e.g., Lynn Lake, Thompson, and Elliot Lake). Obviously, southern mines contributed significantly to mineral production during this period (and sites such as Springhill and Asbestos were implicated in some key moments in Canadian history), but it was the northward expansion of mining that triggered the most comprehensive social, cultural, economic, and ecological changes in the regions where they were built. Northern Indigenous communities were particularly vulnerable at both ends of the mining cycle: the advent of mining is remembered as the central colonial moment in their histories (when land and resources were appropriated without their consent), but the end of mining is often lamented for the loss of employment and economic opportunities. With almost no environmental regulations in place prior to the 1970s, northern Indigenous communities (not to mention northern

The headframe of the Inco Birchtree Mine near Thompson, Manitoba in 1975. Inco's network of nickel mines and smelter spurred growth in the town to 20,000 people in the 1960s. The town also inspired the song "Thompson Girl" by the Tragically Hip, with lyrics evoking images of the nickel stack and juxtaposing mining work with the beauty of the northern landscape.

settler communities and the public treasury) have also had to contend with environmental impacts that compromised human health and the health of lands that had sustained people since time immemorial. Mining brought development and sometimes radical change to northern Canada, as the boosters in government and industry had promised, but it also brought short- and long-term consequences that have, in many cases, brought into doubt the overly confident predictions of the promoters.

Coal mining operations in full swing at Tumbler Ridge, BC in 1983. The town of Tumbler Ridge was the last purpose-built mining town in Canada as the industry shifted to fly-in/fly-out camps beginning in the 1980s.

CHAPTER 5
Rough Terrain, 1973-2016

In 1974 the Canadian government entered into a landmark agreement with Mineral Resources International (MRI) to establish Canada's first mine north of the Arctic Circle. Termed the Strathcona Agreement, the deal committed the government to build the town of Nanisivik (adjacent to the lead-zinc mine site on north Baffin Island), an airport, and a small seaport in return for an 18 per cent equity stake and a seat on the board of directors for the venture. MRI also agreed to abide by several government objectives for northern development, committing to vocational training and skills development for northern workers and promising to work toward a workforce of 60 per cent Inuit drawn largely from the nearby community of Arctic Bay. Meant to advance the mineral-led northern development philosophy the government had been pushing since the 1950s, the agreement repeated the now-familiar pattern of state investment in northern mining operations. At the same time, the agreement was also meant to address some of the weaknesses of previous northern mining projects, by engaging Indigenous people in the workforce and creating the possibility of a bigger return on public investment in the industry. Although the mine remained profitable throughout its relatively long life (1974 to 2002), employment rates for Inuit workers remained stuck between 20 and 25 per cent. Even so, the Nanisivik Mine represented somewhat of a watershed as the first northern mine where government moved beyond mere

Inuk woman at a public hearing in Arctic Bay, Nunavut (then the Northwest Territories) in 1981. Indigenous activism, the settlement of comprehensive land claims, and court rulings defining a "duty to consult" Indigenous communities about development projects have pushed the industry toward broader community consultation and the settlement of Impact and Benefit Agreements.

ABOVE: The ore storage shed and loading facility at the Nanisivik Mine, Baffin Island, in 1982.

RIGHT: Housing at the mining town of Nanisivik, constructed with dome-style roofs used on many of the buildings. Just over 450 people lived at Nanisivik while the mine was open, but the town was completely abandoned by 2006.

rhetoric when promoting the social benefits of mining development. After Nanisivik, Indigenous communities in northern Canada began to demand from mining companies consultation, environmental responsibility, and local economic benefits as a precondition for new mining projects.

Certainly, other key historical moments, such as the famous Berger Inquiry into the proposed Mackenzie Valley natural gas pipeline, helped shaped a debate over Indigenous rights and resource development that has reverberated in Canada to the present day. Nanisivik

signalled, however, that the days where mines such as Giant, Pine Point, Port Radium, and Elliot Lake could be established with no community consultation, few local benefits, and largely uncontrolled environmental impacts were quickly coming to an end.

And yet, if Nanisivik represented a tentative step toward a new approach to mining in Canada, in some ways it also signalled the end of the industry's glory years. The town of Nanisivik was the last of the purpose-built mining communities constructed in northern Canada; subsequent remote operations such as the Asbestos Hill mine in Arctic Quebec (now Nunavik, 1972–84), Polaris Mine on Little Cornwallis Island (1982–2002), and the central Arctic diamond boom of the 1990s would be served exclusively through fly-in/fly-out operations where workers stayed in temporary camps. Across the rest of Canada, Tumbler Ridge, constructed in 1981 to service the Bullmoose and Quintette coal mines in northeastern British Columbia, was the last to be built specifically as a mining town. Gone were the days when government planners and industry leaders carved suburban utopias out of the northern forest as outposts for the advance of civilization. Cheaper air transportation allowed companies to service their operations from regional supply centres such as Yellowknife in the cases of the diamond mines and Fort McMurray, a town synonymous with the vast open-pit mine network in the Alberta oil sands. Always hoping to reduce costs in an intensely competitive global industry, Canadian mining companies (and governments) had been freed of the burden of building, servicing, and ultimately closing remote mining towns. By the 1980s many of the signature mining communities of the post-war era had collapsed from a combination of declining ore grades and plummeting global commodity prices. As highlighted in the last chapter, places such as Pine Point, Schefferville, Faro, and Uranium City either disappeared or were reduced to shadows of their former selves, their unique culture as industrial communities lost amid the decline or disappearance of the towns.

The conditions for a more tentative approach to Canadian mineral development (no longer touted as the vanguard of the expansion of civilization and modernity) had been set in motion the year before the federal government and MRI signed the Strathcona Agreement. The oil price shocks of 1973 signalled the end of post-war economic expansion and ushered in a new era of inflation and slow economic growth (commonly referred to as "stagflation") in Canada and other industrialized nations. Initially, the Canadian mining industry weathered the storm well, with exploration expenditures and prices for copper, zinc, uranium, coal, gold, and silver all rising by the end of the decade. But a second round of oil shocks beginning in 1982, a subsequent severe global recession,

and rapid declines in global mineral prices resulted in a severe slowdown across the Canadian mining industry. Exploration expenditures declined from just over $800 million in 1982 to nearly $640 million in 1983. A federal tax incentive program for exploration helped stabilize expenditures and eventually produced explosive growth to well over $1 billion by the end of the decade. Nonetheless, in the early 1990s yet another recession and crash in global mineral prices further hollowed out exploration expenditures to below $400 million in 1992.[11]

On the development side of the equation, there were no new large-scale mines (those with capital costs over $250 million) built in Canada between 1986 and 1991. Mining was labelled by some as a "sunset industry," doomed to oblivion in the high-tech and services economy. Although the 1980s and 1990s brought some significant projects in the form of the coal developments at Tumbler Ridge, BC, the Hemlo goldfields on the northern shore of Lake Superior, diamonds in the Northwest Territories, and a massive nickel ore body at Voisey's Bay, Labrador, the industry did not really begin to boom again until the commodity upswing in the first decade of the twenty-first century, a period of renewed optimism referred to as the commodities supercyle.[12] The industry had certainly experienced downturns in commodity prices during recessionary periods in the late 1940s and 1950s, but after 1973 the road ahead seemed a particularly rocky one as the cycles of boom and bust occurred with greater frequency and intensity.

The Canadian mining industry responded to this new period of volatility in several ways. The move toward the lower costs and flexible commitments associated with fly-in/fly-out operations was one adjustment. Another was to take advantage of the new global economic framework of deregulation and trade liberalization that arose in response to the economic shocks of the 1980s and move operations to other countries. Canadian mining interests had made forays into foreign jurisdictions since the 1960s: Inco Canada in Guatemala (amid allegations of human rights abuses perpetrated by the government

The Nanisivik mine site was close to the town, and included a docking facility on the Arctic coast from which ore was shipped to processing facilities. The Canadian government is currently converting this port to an Arctic naval station.

against mine opponents), Noranda in Chile (the company was an early investor after the repressive Pinochet regime came to power in 1973 but finally withdrew support for its Andacollo copper project under pressure from Canadian church groups in 1980), and Falconbridge in the Dominican Republic. By the 1990s several factors had opened a window for a new rush of Canadian mining investment in Latin America: the refinement of open-pit mining techniques beginning in the 1960s to allow operations in very low-grade deposits of gold, copper and silver; the final abandonment of monetary exchange rates pegged to the gold standard in the 1970s leading to a general rise in prices; and the liberalization of trade and regulatory policies among Latin American governments eager to attract foreign mining capital as a response to the debt problems of the 1980s. The Canadian industry sensed an opportunity and established over fifteen hundred projects in Latin America by 2007 (many of them hugely profitable open-pit mines), stoking controversy over industry culpability in the repression of mine opponents in

countries with poor human rights records. Barrick Gold, Canada's largest mining company, maintains only one project in Canada (the Hemlo gold mine) but operates globally in countries such as Australia, Papua New Guinea, Zambia, Argentina, Peru, Chile, and the United States (where in some cases it has become a lightning rod for criticism of Canadian mining and human rights abuses overseas). Undoubtedly the most notorious and widely publicized moment in the history of the Canadian mining industry's overseas exploits came in 1997 when the exposure of Bre-X's fraudulent claims of a major gold find in Busang, Indonesia, led to the collapse of the company's inflated share price and angry lawsuits from shareholders who had lost millions. Despite the catastrophe, the Toronto Stock Exchange has remained one of the most important global centres for the transfer of mining capital, a critical source of financing for the expansion of Canadian mining interests at home and abroad.

Even as the industry expanded to distant corners of the globe, foreign investment also poured into the country, making Canada's mining industry less and less Canadian. The strong appetite for foreign investment meant that companies such as Australia's BHP Billiton and Britain's Rio Tinto played a lead role in developing Canada's first forays into diamond mining in the Northwest Territories. Foreign takeovers have meant that very few of the historically important mining giants in Canada remain Canadian-owned. Since 2005, Falconbridge has been swallowed by the Anglo-Swiss multinational Xstrata (which was in turn bought out by another Anglo-Swiss multinational, Glencore), the Iron Ore Company of Canada bought up by Rio Tinto, and Inco Canada absorbed by the Brazilian mining giant Vale. Although the focus of this book is the history of mining activities in Canada, it is crucial to understand that the industry became global in its reach and composition during this period, driven by the growth of transnational corporatism and globalization.

Amid the loosening grip of national commitments and accusations of human rights abuses abroad, the mining industry made a (perhaps somewhat ironic) attempt to respond to growing social, environmental, and economic concerns in Canada, especially those emanating from Indigenous communities and the Canadian environmental movement (including the mining-focused environmental NGO, MiningWatch, created in 1999). Spurred by legal recognitions of Indigenous rights and (especially in the north) the establishment of comprehensive land claim agreements, the industry began in the 1980s to negotiate Impact and Benefit Agreements (IBAs) directly with Indigenous communities in the vicinity of new mining projects. The contents of the IBAs were usually confidential, but often included provisions for guaranteed local employment, training, and cash payments to Indigenous governments. On a broader scale, the industry-wide stagnation in the 1980s and 1990s, combined with the growing public unease over unrealized local economic benefits and poor environmental record associated with mining, pressured industry leaders to consider how they might gain community support for their projects, often described today as a social licence to operate. In 1993 the Mining Association of Canada organized a multi-stakeholder conference, the Whitehorse Mining Initiative (WMI), with government, First Nations, labour, and environmental groups all represented, to develop a consensus approach to community and environmental issues while also promoting new frameworks (taxation, incentives, investment climate, etc.) to enhance the industry's competitiveness. While the WMI's Final Accord represented a remarkable product of consensus decision-making, critics have debated whether the accord was implemented successfully. Regardless, the WMI process highlighted the seeming intractable dilemma of the Canadian mining industry: how to navigate between the seemingly contradictory pressures of hypercompetitive global capitalism and the domestic political demands for a more extensive commitment to local environments and economies.

Expanding the Nuclear North

In the mid-1960s the southeastern side of the Lake Athabasca basin became the epicentre of uranium exploration in Canada. The prize, early results suggested, was an area rich in "unconformity" deposits: extremely high-grade uranium ore that sat on the geological dividing line between layers of newer sandstone and older bedrock. In 1968 two junior companies, Gulf Minerals and the German-owned company Uranerz Exploration, discovered a major uranium deposit at Rabbit Lake, Saskatchewan, close to the western shores of the much larger Wollaston Lake. The Rabbit Lake Mine began open-pit operations in 1975; mindful of the costs and commitments associated with the Uranium City and Gunnar mines, the companies established the mine as a fly-in/fly-out operation. In 1981 Eldorado Nuclear bought the mine, marking its first step toward almost total dominance of the Canadian uranium industry after its subsequent merger with Saskatchewan Mining Development (also a Crown corporation) created the (gradually privatized) behemoth Cameco in 1988. Other discoveries quickly followed throughout the basin: in 1975 Amok Ltd. (a predecessor of the other major mining company operating in northern Saskatchewan, French uranium giant Areva) discovered the Cluff Lake deposit; that same year Uranerz discovered what would become one of the largest high-grade uranium mines in the world at Key Lake.[13] The opening of these two additional (mostly open-pit) mines marked the beginning of an intensive period of exploitation of the world's highest-grade uranium deposits, earning northern Saskatchewan a reputation as the Saudi Arabia of the uranium mining industry.

Northern Saskatchewan is a vast boreal plain punctured by myriad lakes, rivers, and streams. The region is sparsely populated: 80 per cent of the 37,000 people who inhabit the region are Indigenous, primarily Chipewyan Dene (or Denesuline) in the area between Lake Athabasca and Wollaston Lake. Historically, the Denesuline had lived by hunting caribou, fishing, gathering, and trapping over a broad area of northern Saskatchewan and the Northwest Territories from the settlements at Fond du Lac, Stoney Rapids, Camsell Portage, and the Lac La Hache Band in the community of Wollaston Lake. Despite the land-based orientation of their economy (and its supposed protection under Treaties 8 and 10), the Denesuline have contended with the impacts

The McArthur River uranium mine is largest operation in the globally significant uranium production complex in northern Saskatchewan. Cameco opened the mine in 1999. Combined with the nearby Key Lake mine, McArthur River became the largest high-grade uranium producer in the world. As of 2018, however, Cameco has suspended production at the mine due to weakness in global uranium markets.

of mining since a prospecting rush in the 1920s produced widespread fires (a probable cause of caribou decline because of winter-range habitat destruction) and the sudden introduction of uranium mining north of Lake Athabasca in the 1950s (see Chapter 4). The uranium developments of the 1970s and 1980s brought more sustained and widespread environmental, economic, and political change for the Denesuline, irrevocably altering their relationship to the land and prompting a new relationship with the industry giants that came to dominate the region.

At first, many Denesuline resisted the expansion of uranium mining on their traditional territory. Acutely aware of the increased risks of environmental contamination from mining high-grade uranium, some Indigenous groups and several southern environmentalists (many associated with church-based anti-nuclear activist groups) adopted a confrontational stance toward the industry. In 1977 many northern Saskatchewan chiefs boycotted consultations on the Cluff Lake Mine (the Cluff Lake Board of Inquiry) while calling for a moratorium on uranium until unresolved land claims under Treaty 10 could be settled. In 1979 a broad coalition of anti-nuclear and environmental groups also boycotted the Key Lake Board of Inquiry, critical of what they called a pro-industry bias and incensed at revelations that the preparatory drainage of Key Lake had proceeded for the

previous three years prior to the establishment of the inquiry and without the appropriate permits. In 1984 a major spill of one hundred million litres of radioactive water from a reservoir at the Key Lake mine attracted national attention and criticism. In June 1985 the Lac La Hache Band at Wollaston led a four-day blockade of the road leading into Rabbit Lake and the newly developed Collins Bay Mine, an open pit dug out of a dyked-off section of the lake. The protest attracted many supporters from other northern Saskatchewan Indigenous groups, in addition to the anti-nuclear and environmental communities, including Scandinavian author Miles Goldstick, who published an almost scrapbook-like account of the protest (provocatively titled *Wollaston: People Resisting Genocide*) that included interviews, poetry, photographs, pamphlets, and posters. Lac La Hache Band Councillor Thomas Sha'oulle's comments are representative of many in the book:

The concerns that are being raised about Rabbit Lake are coming from all of us. We oppose the mining because of the problems. When we had the meeting with the government officials they said they won't stop mining until all the fish are destroyed. What is the sense of stopping the mining then? You can see that the older people here have always lived off the land. What will the children live on if they don't have fish? . . . We rely on the fish and caribou. Now we have to go quite a ways to get at the caribou; they used to come closer

Another tactic the mining company is using now that we are protesting is they're just hiring left and right, even young boys. We the people of Wollaston Lake oppose uranium development.

The Wollaston protest collapsed under threats of arrest and rumours that social assistance cheques might be cut off from those in need. In 1989, however, a major spill of two million litres of radioactive water occurred at the Rabbit Lake Mine, once again attracting national attention to the risks, and prompting loud cries for a public inquiry into the industry.

Amid all of this conflict, Saskatchewan's uranium industry came to the realization it would have to reach out to Saskatchewan's Indigenous communities to defuse the criticisms from the environmental and human rights movements and to develop mutually beneficial relationships. From the beginning of this second wave of uranium development in the province, the industry took steps to avoid the pitfalls of previous northern mining projects that had combined limited economic opportunities with major environmental problems. Among many innovations on the safety and environmental fronts, the industry touted new extraction and containment methods such as remote-control mining operations (that protected workers from exposure to radioactive gases and material), and freezing around orebodies and around the perimeter of tailings ponds to prevent the escape of contaminated water. By the late 1970s employment agreements for new uranium mines included quotas for Indigenous workers; over time Cameco CEO Bernard Michel adopted a "best efforts" policy that exceeded the mandated targets and achieved a 51 per cent employment rate of northern Indigenous people by 1997. Cameco also began to consult regularly with regional chiefs and worked with government and community representatives to develop comprehensive northern training programs. Even

during the Wollaston Lake protests, it was clear that some Indigenous representatives saw more opportunity than risk in uranium mining. At a meeting held on June 20, 1995, in the wake of the blockade, Sol Sanderson of the Federation of Saskatchewan Indian Nations criticized government and industry for a breakdown in communications, but also claimed that environmentalists had misunderstood the protest's purpose. He claimed that the Indigenous protestors were not dogmatically anti-nuclear, but wanted proper environmental safeguards and more economic benefits to flow to communities that could no longer rely solely on hunting and trapping to address the poverty in their midst. Sanderson told a reporter that:

We told industry and governments that we want to sit down and discuss it formally but we do not want anyone exempting themselves when it comes to the bottom line of accessing money towards Indian development. At the Band and community we want to know what the benefits are going to be in real terms to the Indian people. So that's the stage it is at, at this moment. We are not going to be preoccupied with protestors because these same protestors from the outside, like I say, are also protesting in Europe and across the country right now with Greenpeace opposing our traditional livelihood in terms of fur, hunting, trapping, that includes the Wildlife Federation. They might be wise to get on our side pretty quick.

As Sanderson anticipated, the Wollaston protests proved to be the last gasp for joint activism between environmentalists and Indigenous communities in northern Saskatchewan, the latter adopting a strategy of direct engagement with the industry on issues of environmental protection and economic benefits.

In 1991 Roy Romanow's New Democratic Party returned to power in Saskatchewan. With the party having recently abandoned its policy position advocating a phase-out of uranium mining in northern Saskatchewan, the new government was eager to show that industry could balance environmental and social development concerns with the expansion of uranium mining in the Athabasca Basin. In 1991 the government established the Joint Federal-Provincial Panel on Uranium Developments in Northern Saskatchewan to review major new mining proposals at McArthur River, Cigar Lake, McClean Lake, and South Mahon Lake (the Midwest project), as well as expansions at some of the older mines. Over the next seven years, the panel held consultations across northern Saskatchewan, considering the cumulative social and environmental impacts of multiple projects in the region. The process was not always free from controversy: the epidemiologist on the panel, Dr. Annalee Yassi, resigned in 1996 over the failure to consider the long-term impacts of low-dose radiation exposure; another panel member, Chief John Dantouze, quickly followed over the issue of direct royalty revenue sharing between government and local communities. The leadership of four northern communities (including Wollaston Lake) refused to allow public hearings on the McArthur River and Cigar Lake projects to proceed in October 1996 because of community distrust over the process.

Despite such setbacks, the Joint Panel did show that it was not simply a pawn of the industry. The panel rejected the Midwest mine proposal because of the environmental risks (though a new version of the project was approved in 2012). In 1993 the panel's more general calls for increased transparency and community involvement in environmental monitoring resulted in the creation of environmental quality committees in three regions of northern Saskatchewan. The industry also proactively engaged with communities outside of the government processes, establishing the Athabasca Working Group in 1993 as a forum for discussion and information exchange between uranium companies and community leaders. Although the issue of royalty sharing was never resolved, the uranium industry, especially Cameco, often invested directly in community infrastructure, health training, and education initiatives. The spirit of reconciliation was so far advanced by 1999 that Cameco, COGEMA (subsequently named Areva and then

Orano), and the Cigar Lake Mining Corporation negotiated a comprehensive Impact Management Agreement with the Athabasca region communities covering benefits sharing, training, environmental monitoring, cultural issues, and economic development.

Certainly Indigenous attitudes to uranium mining in Saskatchewan are not unanimous. Recent alternative press articles document ongoing concerns among the Denesuline about uranium mining, and ethnographic research has suggested that mechanisms for community consultation and the incorporation of traditional knowledge into decision-making processes are not as robust as industry, government, and some community representatives suggest. The anti-nuclear activist Jim Harding has argued that uranium industry investments in northern Saskatchewan are nothing more than a strategy to buy off former critics of nuclear colonialism, paper over lingering concerns about the long-term health and environmental impacts of uranium mining, and sever the tenuous ties between anti-nuclear activists and Indigenous communities. At the same time, the uranium companies' new approach represented a massive transformation from the old days of government and mining industry indifference toward northern Indigenous communities, even as Indigenous people themselves worked to place the issue of community impacts and benefits at the very core of all future discussions of mining development in northern Canada.

Disaster Underground

The more progressive approach in Saskatchewan did not spread to all mining operations in Canada. In some cases the early 1990s brought disaster, death, and labour strife that harkened back to the industrial mayhem of the pre-Second World War era. The first of two major tragedies was the harrowing coal mine explosion at Curragh Resources' Westray Mine in Pictou County, Nova Scotia. On the morning of May 9, 1992, crews in the Southwest 2 area of Westray worked with a continuous miner, a bulldozer-like machine with a rotating drum and picks used to dig out the coal from the working face of the mine. As the miners pressed forward, a torrent of sparks burst outwards as the machine's picks struck rock, igniting layers of methane gas that had not been properly ventilated. The initial explosion of methane blew into the air the large amounts of coal dust that had accumulated on the walls and floor of the mine tunnels, providing fuel for a much larger coal-dust explosion that spread throughout the entire mine, causing nearly instant death among those working that day. A full mine rescue operation ensued, but the crews could find only the dead bodies of fifteen men, killed variously by carbon monoxide poisoning, burns, or the shock wave of the explosion. Eleven others who died could not be found; the mine was their final tomb.

The Westray explosion was the worst mining disaster in Canada since the Springhill bump in 1958 (see Chapter 4). In the immediate aftermath families of the victims were left wondering how their loved ones could have been killed by coal-mining hazards that had been common knowledge for decades. In 1995 a public inquiry led by Justice K. Peter Richard answered this question with a stinging rebuke of the company and the provincial government, emphasizing there was nothing accidental about the explosion and plenty of blame to be spread around. Richard's final report used unusually harsh (but nonetheless fitting) language to describe the Westray explosion as "a story of deceit, of ruthlessness, of cover-up, of apathy, of expediency, and of cynical indifference," that "in all good common sense, ought not to have occurred." Richard assigned primary responsibility for the disaster with the mine managers who were fully aware of the immediate hazards from coal dust, methane gas, and poor roof conditions in the mine. He went on to describe a litany of startling failures on the part of a Curragh management team that promoted an "unsafe mentality" in the mine, an object lesson in how not to run a coal mine. Just some of their willful acts of negligence included the illegal imposition of twelve-hour shifts, failure to set up a tagging system to keep track of miners underground, allowing the use of acetylene torches underground,

permitting the shutdown of a main ventilation fan for maintenance while the mine was operating, and actually tampering with methane detection equipment to promote production. To make matters worse, mine managers refused to hear any feedback about safety issues: as one worker declared, "if you refused unsafe work, you were threatened with your job or intimidated into submission."

In addition to rebuking Curragh, Richard levelled sharp criticism at the provincial Department of Labour's Mine Inspectorate, demonstrating that it had been "demonstrably apathetic and incompetent," and "markedly derelict in meeting its statutory responsibilities at the Westray Mine." Richard suggested that Nova Scotia's Department of Natural Resources had also been negligent during the approval stage for Westray, failing

The ribbon cutting ceremony to officially open the Westray coal mine in Pictou County, Nova Scotia, on September 11, 1991. Left to right: Gerald Phillips, Westray General Manager and VP; Nova Scotia Premier Donald Cameron; Clifford Frame, CEO, Curragh Resources; Central Nova MP Elmer MacKay; Marvin Pelley, Curragh VP.

A group of draegerman (a mining industry term for rescue crew members) don breathing equipment as they prepare to go underground in the aftermath of the Westray explosion in 1992.

to demand a clear operational plan for the mine and adequate safety provisions to operate in Pictou, a coal mining region known for problems with methane, where as many as 650 miners had died since the industry began in 1866. Finally, Justice Richard pointed to the urgency with which the provincial government pushed the project, particularly Donald Cameron, the local MLA and minister of industry, trade and technology. Cameron's government arranged a loan guarantee and Cameron himself negotiated an unauthorized agreement with Curragh to purchase 275,000 tons of coal annually for fifteen years, contextual factors that, while not directly responsible for the disaster, contributed to the sense of haste surrounding a poorly planned mine.

In spite of Richard's hard-hitting report, grief at the loss of family members and co-workers was compounded by the fact nobody was ever held criminally responsible for the disaster. Although the RCMP charged two mine managers, Gerald Phillips and Roger Perry, with criminal negligence and manslaughter, the trial fell apart when the prosecution team failed to disclose key pieces of

evidence. After several appeals and the Supreme Court of Canada's order for a new trial, Crown attorneys decided to drop the case. A lawsuit filed by the Westray families against the provincial government also failed. Along with a lingering feeling of injustice, the families were left to endure the economic insecurity the disaster had created with only the vagaries of insurance payouts and private donations. To make matters worse still, the remaining Westray workers lost their jobs as Curragh went into receivership in 1993 and the mine remained closed for good. Westray workers and families were determined to mark the tragedy, however, raising money for the creation of a memorial park in New Glasgow positioned over the tunnel where the eleven buried miners are thought to have been killed. In 2002 the Westray families could take some comfort in the federal government's Bill C-45, legislation that enshrined the obligation of management to ensure workplace safety and strengthened criminal liability provisions for negligence.

Across Canada, Westray stayed in the public eye as the subject of innumerable feature articles and television stories as well as a full-length National Film Board documentary directed by Paul Cowan and released in 2001. For many the Westray disaster symbolized the industry's sometimes callous disregard for workplace safety and the need for tighter regulations in Canada. In an era when the mining industry was trying to shake its poor image, Westray served as a horrific reminder of the extreme danger of underground coal mining in an environment where a corporation placed profits and production ahead of the lives of its workers.

The seeds of Canada's second great mining tragedy of the 1990s were sown only thirteen days after the Westray explosion, when the new owner of Yellowknife's Giant Mine, Royal Oak Mines, locked out its workers the day before they had planned to go on strike. Royal Oak was an upstart company that had purchased its first two mines, Giant along with Pamour Mine in Timmins, in 1990 for $35 million. These were properties that nobody wanted because they had become money losers in a low-gold-price environment. Royal Oak's founding CEO was Peggy Witte, a metallurgical engineer from Nevada who set about restructuring her new acquisitions so they were profitable. Witte immediately laid off 120 administrative, exploration, and mining sector staff to squeeze a profit out of Royal Oak in only its second year, a feat that prompted the *Northern Miner* newspaper to name her as the first female recipient of the "mining man of the year" award. Witte's and new manager Mike Werner's tough-as-nails cost-cutting style brought changes to local operations at Giant Mine as well: a purge of management staff, indifference to union grievances, and a new disciplinary system that assigned steps for even the most minor infractions, with four steps leading to dismissal. Royal Oak's relationship with the mine's union, Local 4 of the Canadian Association of Smelter and Allied Workers (CASAW), began a downward spiral toward the mining

A rescue team descends into the mine to attempt to locate any co-workers who might have survived the blast.

industry's worst labour dispute since the 1940s.

Remarkably, the company and the union did manage to come to a tentative agreement during contract negotiations in April 1992. Sensing they would not gain much at the negotiating table, the CASAW bargaining committee agreed to a wage freeze, provided that wages could be renegotiated after three years if the price of gold went up. This, combined with reductions in benefits, the removal of overtime premiums for working weekends, and changes to the frequency of safety inspection proved too much for CASAW's membership, who were well aware Royal Oak had turned a $4 million profit in the final quarter of 1991. Apparently Local 4's Vice President Harry Seeton called the proposed deal "a piece of shit" at a meeting and on April 28 the union membership voted down the tentative contract. In the wake of the vote, Royal Oak refused to budge on its contract demands. On May 22, the day before CASAW was in a legal strike

Aerial view of modern Yellowknife. The 1990s saw the gradual
decline of gold mining in the territorial capital, but the
city experienced rejuvenation with the advent of diamond
exploration in the years around the millennium.

position, the company locked out its workers, refusing
a union proposal for last-minute negotiations unless the
CASAW membership voted a second time on the existing
tentative agreement. Security guards shouted at workers
to get off the property even though the company was not
entitled to do so until the next day, setting the stage for
the pitched battle that was to come.

The rising tension of the previous weeks almost
immediately came to a boil. In a provocative move, Royal
Oak decided to use replacement workers to keep the
mine open, a tactic that had not been employed in a legal
Canadian mining strike since Kirkland Lake in 1941–42.[14]
Many picketing workers watched helplessly as helicopters

ferried workers and supplies into the mine. Almost from
the beginning some picketers decided that if they were
to maintain the only weapon they had — shutting down
the mine — they would have to take matters into their
own hands. They threw rocks at security guards, lit fires
on the Giant Mine property, and refused to let buses full
of replacement workers pass. One picketer practiced his
golf swing using the windows of mine buildings for target
practice. A few days into the strike, Giant Mine's security
contractor (Cambrian) abandoned ship after its chief was
injured when a striker's pickup truck rammed his vehicle.
In a confrontational move, Royal Oak replaced Cambrian
with Pinkerton, an American security firm with a well-
earned reputation for brutal strikebreaking in labour
disputes throughout North America dating all the way
back to the industrial conflicts of the nineteenth century.
Fearful of escalating violence, the Northwest Territories
government called for and received additional policing

help from the Royal Canadian Mounted Police.

The presence of an aggressive security force and the constant police patrols near the mine served only to heighten tensions. On June 14, the seemingly inevitable confrontation erupted as picketers broke through a fence and stormed the mine site, precipitating a full-scale riot with Pinkerton guards and the hastily summoned RCMP riot and tactical squads. Each side blamed the other for the chaos; the police arrested twenty-four picketers and the company announced the firing of thirty-eight workers they claimed had committed acts of violence and/or vandalism both before and during the riot. The list of workers Royal Oak wanted dismissed eventually swelled to fifty-two names and became a major stumbling block to settling the strike as Witte refused even to consider binding arbitration until the union agreed that those named would not be allowed back to work. Witte's intransigence ultimately reinforced the notion that the company was out to break the union rather than settle the strike.

With negotiations at an impasse and the community (and union) divided, escalating acts of sabotage by strikers culminated in a bloody act of vengeance against replacement workers. On the morning of September 18 an explosion ripped through a tunnel at the 750-foot level of the mine. Blasting was a regular part of the morning routine at Giant Mine, but the strength and location of this particular detonation seemed unusual to the miners who heard it. Those who inspected found carnage beyond their wildest imaginings: the explosion had destroyed a man-car carrying nine strikebreaking workers. There were no survivors. As news of the disaster leaked out to the town, CASAW members thought the blast must have been the result of lax safety measures they had complained about since Royal Oak took over the mine, with one rumour speculating that the deceased men had been travelling with a load of explosives. But an RCMP investigation quickly revealed that the explosion was no accident. The police had found a trip wire and a detonator indicating that the deceased miners — Chris Neill, Joe Pandev, Norm Hourie, David Vodnoski, Shane Riggs,

Vern Fullowka, Robert Rowsell, Malcolm Sawler, and Arnold Russell — had been murdered. The fact the deaths were intentional killings served only to further divide the city; some strikebreakers and their family members branded all CASAW members as murderers. Out of respect for grieving families, no striking workers (other than a very close friend of Chris Neill's) attended a memorial service for the nine victims on October 3. The RCMP investigation zeroed in on strikers who were involved in picket line violence and vandalism. After thirteen weeks of unbearable local tension, striking worker Roger Warren, originally not on the prime suspect list, confessed to the murder during an RCMP interview. Warren later recanted his confession, but in 1995 was convicted of nine counts of second-degree murder. In 2003 Warren confessed again that he had committed the crime, maintaining that he had never intended to kill anyone. In 2014 Warren was granted day parole after serving twenty-one years in prison. He died in 2019.

Remarkably, CASAW managed to persist with the strike until December 1993 despite the massive cloud of suspicion the murders had placed over the union. In the aftermath of the bombing, CASAW received financial support from the broader Canadian labour movement and critical legal and logistical help from the Canadian Auto Workers (with which CASAW later merged). CASAW resisted attempts by some workers to form a rival union and endured ever-more confrontational tactics from Witte, including legally questionable demands for more mass firings of CASAW members, the dismissal of all pre-strike grievances, and the institution of a one-year probationary period where returning strikers could not challenge firings through the grievance process. Ironically, these hardline tactics paved the way for a resolution after the Canadian Labour Relations Board (CLRB) imposed a settlement requiring Royal Oak to table the original tentative contract and mandating arbitration for the strikers who had been fired. By April 1994, arbitration hearings reinstated all but two of the forty-nine workers fired during the strike, a major victory for CASAW. Never one to accede control over her company easily, Witte fanned the flames of discontent among union loyalists by challenging a CLRB bad-faith bargaining decision critical of Royal Oak all the way to the Supreme Court of Canada. Witte lost this appeal in 1996, exhausting any further avenues for prolonging a labour dispute that had exacted such a heavy toll on the people of Yellowknife.

Any gains made by either side of the Giant Mine strike ultimately proved pyrrhic, as declining ore grades and crumbling infrastructure meant that the aging mine's days were numbered. In 1999 Royal Oak went into receivership and the federal government took control of the site. Although the Department of Indian and Northern Affairs did manage to lease mining rights to Miramar to remove more gold ore for processing at nearby Con Mine, the responsibility for cleaning up the mine site — including the 237,000 tons of arsenic stored underground — now fell to the federal government (see Chapter 6). Neither the painful memories of the strike nor the environmental and health issues associated with Giant Mine would prove easy to erase. And yet, even as the final closure of Con Mine in 2003 and Giant Mine in 2004 brought an end to the gold mining era in Yellowknife, the city had already turned its attention to a promise of a new mining bonanza on the tundra to the east.

Canada's Diamond Boom

Marketed for over a century as a symbol of eternal love and commitment, diamonds arguably carry the most cultural currency of any of the materials humans dig from the ground. Their extreme hardness provides for some industrial utility in cutting and polishing instruments, but their high value is determined almost entirely by their use in wedding bands and other expensive jewellery. Diamonds are also exceedingly difficult to find. Most diamonds large enough to use as gemstones are composed of carbon atoms crystallized under intense heat and pressure in the earth's mantle approximately 150 kilometres below the surface of the earth. Diamond prospectors search for elusive kimberlite pipes, cone-shaped deposits of diamonds that have been transported to the earth's surface by volcanic activity. Strongly associated with older, geologically stable portions of the earth's crust and mantle (termed cratons), commercially viable diamond pipes are concentrated in just a few distinct zones that have become the diamond-rich areas of the world: southern Africa, Russia, Australia, and northern Canada. Although subject now to periodic market dips, large diamond mines that produce high-quality gems consistently generate enormous revenue in the hundreds of millions of dollars annually.

It was the lure of such riches that brought Chuck Fipke and his partner Stewart Blusson to the Northwest Territories in the early 1980s in a search for North America's first diamond mine. Throughout the 1970s, Fipke toiled in the field of mineral exploration for Cominco and Kennecott, his adventures taking him to Papua New Guinea, Brazil, and southern Africa. In 1977 he returned to Canada and formed an exploration company, C.F. Minerals. A year later Superior Oil contracted Fipke to search for kimberlite pipes in Colorado, and then near Blackwater Lake in the Richardson Mountains area of northern Canada. Here Fipke and Blusson began to apply geochemist John Gurney's cutting-edge ideas about the use of indicator minerals, particularly G-10 garnet, as a sure-fire predictor for diamond pipes. Blusson and Fipke found plenty of signs of diamonds at Blackwater Lake, but reckoned they were deposited by glacial forces, compelling them to trace the trail of retreating ice backwards to find the origin point for the actual kimberlite formations. In 1984 Mobil Oil bought Superior and dismantled the diamond exploration program; that same year Fipke started another company, DiaMet Minerals, to raise capital from investors so he and Blusson could continue their search. By 1989 Fipke and Blusson had narrowed their hunt to an area near Lac de Gras on the Arctic tundra east of Great Slave Lake. Fieldwork from that summer revealed lots of diamond indicator minerals. Two years later DiaMet formally announced it had discovered the most promising

diamond deposits in the world, forming a partnership with Australian mining giant Broken Hill Proprietary (BHP) to build and open the Ekati Mine.

Although it took seven years of further exploration and construction before the mine could begin operations, the announcement ushered in the largest staking rush in Canadian history. Almost inevitably new major diamond projects mushroomed across northern Canada: Rio Tinto's and Dominion Diamond Corporation's Diavik Mine in 2004; De Beers's Snap Lake project, which opened in 2008 and closed in 2013; De Beers's and Mountain Province Diamonds's recently opened Gahcho Kué project; DeBeer's Victor Mine, which opened near Attawapiskat, northern Ontario, in 2008; and Tahera Diamond Corporation's ill-fated Jericho Mine, which opened in 2006 as Nunavut's first diamond operation only to close six years later due to the high cost of such a remote operation. The timing of the boom could not have been better for Yellowknife, which became the major air and ice-road supply hub for the mines just as local gold mining operations began to falter. The sudden eruption of diamond mining activity in Canada also was opportune because the end-product could be marketed as an ethical alternative to the blood (or conflict) diamonds that media reports and NGO campaigns had revealed as a fuel for

Opened in 1998, the Ekati Mine was the first diamond mine in Canada. The discovery of kimberlite on the arctic tundra 300 km northeast of Yellowknife sparked the biggest staking rush in Canadian history.

civil wars in countries such as Angola, Sierra Leone, Liberia, and the Congo. Finally, the diamond boom also cemented Fipke's place in the pantheon of Canadian prospectors, a latter-day George Carmack who ushered in a new era of mineral wealth in northern Canada.

What did this new wave of northern mining activity mean for the Indigenous inhabitants of the Northwest Territories and Nunavut? To the eyes of outsiders, the region surrounding Lac de Gras might seem a cold, uninhabited, and nearly lifeless barren. No Indigenous or other community is located directly adjacent to the mines. Indeed, prior to diamond mining the area was roadless, accessible from the nearest communities only by a journey of a couple of hundred kilometres by boat, snowmobile, or in the old days, by dogsled. But for the Dene communities who lived on the north and east arms of Great Slave Lake, and the communities of the Kitikmeot Inuit Association to the north, the land beyond the treeline had for generations been used as a source of fur, fish, and most importantly, caribou meat. With memories of Giant Mine's arsenic and Pine Point's ghost town fresh in everybody's mind, it is little wonder the potential environmental impacts of major new mining developments on the tundra brought apprehension. The geology of the kimberlite pipes ensured that diamond mining did not represent the same kind of toxic threat as Yellowknife's gold mining complex, but Indigenous communities remained concerned that BHP would have to fish out and drain five lakes to access the diamond ore. The potential impact of major industrial activity on the Bathurst caribou, at that time the largest in the Northwest Territories with 350,000 animals, was also unknown and a major source of unease about the project. BHP's poor environmental record at its Ok Tedi copper and gold mine in Papua New Guinea was also well known in the Northwest Territories. One affected landowner at Ok Tedi, Alex Munn, spoke passionately at the federal Environmental Assessment and Review Process (EARP) about how a failure in the poorly managed tailings containment pond in 1984 had severely polluted the water sources of downstream (mostly Indigenous) communities. And yet, with many Dene communities facing severe unemployment, anticipation began to build that northern Indigenous communities might realize some direct economic benefit from the new developments.

The approval process for the Ekati Mine reflected the sometimes contradictory impulse to demonstrate the tangible benefits of industrial development to northern Indigenous communities and the federal government's desire to reassure potential investors that Canada was ready to become a major player in the global diamond industry. The federal EARP process conducted between 1994 and 1996 has been heavily criticized by participants for imposing rushed timelines, for refusing to consider the cumulative impacts of multiple potential diamond projects that might arise from the staking rush on the tundra, and for providing only limited funding for participants. The federal government also limited the bargaining position of Indigenous groups, refusing to consider the diamond mine in light of the two major groups with unresolved land claims in the area: the Tlicho communities north of Great

Slave Lake and the Akaitcho Treaty 8 group, composed of the Yellowknives Dene communities (Ndilo and Dettah), Deninu Ku'e First Nation (Fort Resolution), and Lutsel K'e on the East Arm of Great Slave Lake. As many critics have pointed out, the government's position privileged the "free entry" system of claim staking over any potential Indigenous claims in the region, reducing the Indigenous communities to mere participants in the process rather than the holders of distinct rights to the land. The Dene communities and a coalition of environmental groups were so dissatisfied with what they saw as the superficial nature of the EARP hearings that on several occasions they considered court action. Not for one minute did anybody think that the EARP process would do anything other than rubber-stamp the Ekati mine.

In July 1996 the Environmental Assessment Panel did indeed approve the project with twenty-eight specific recommendations. Some of the more general proposals, such as the completion of a protected-areas strategy for the Northwest Territories, have never been fulfilled. Nonetheless, Ron Irwin, federal Minister of Indian Affairs and Northern Development, set off a flurry of activity when he imposed a sixty-day deadline for implementation of three key panel recommendations: an environmental agreement, a social impact monitoring agreement, and impact and benefit agreements with the Tlicho and Akaitcho communities. All of these deals were meant to counter the historical experience of mining in northern Canada as an activity that siphoned money south while leaving severe environmental damage in its wake. The environmental agreement (negotiated between BHP and the federal government with the participation of Indigenous and environmental groups) established an independent oversight and monitoring board funded by BHP, mandated the inclusion of Indigenous traditional knowledge in environmental planning, and required the company to develop a closure plan with a security deposit of $11 million (with another $20 million promised) to cover the cost of any incomplete remediation of the mine site. The socio-economic agreement was meant primarily to ensure distribution of economic benefits widely throughout the Northwest Territories through such measures as training programs, support for local business, and employment targets for northern residents of 62 per cent of the total workforce at the operational phase of the mine (with 50 per cent being Indigenous northerners). BHP also concluded separate impact and benefit agreements (IBAs) with the Tlicho, Akaitcho Treaty 8 group, the North Slave Métis Alliance, and the Kitikmeot Inuit Association, the contents of which are private, but which generally contain provision for annual cash payments to local governments, employment agreements, and commitments to ongoing community consultation. Clearly, the mining industry, governments, and northern communities had taken huge steps forward from the days when the only constraint on the companies was their own willingness to start digging.

How successful were attempts of government and industry to shake off the colonial past and pursue northern diamond mining under the aegis of corporate social responsibility? As with any complex question, you are likely to get a variety of answers if you ask a random selection of people on a stroll down Yellowknife's Franklin Avenue. Government and industry reports on Northwest Territories diamond mining typically paint a picture of an unqualified success story, a growing industry attentive to social and environmental issues. With the opening of the Diavik Mine in 2004, a joint venture of Rio Tinto and Canadian company Aber Resources, and De Beers's Snap Lake Mine in 2008, the industry repeated the pattern of negotiating environmental, socio-economic, and community benefit agreements as had occurred with the Ekati project. Industry and government reports justly celebrated northern employment rates of just over 50 per cent of the workforce at the diamond mines, with northern Indigenous people comprising 28 per cent of the 3,038 employees at Ekati, Diavik, and Snap Lake in 2007. Environmental projects, such as Diavik's wind farm of four turbines, have helped buttress industry claims that it is moving toward a sustainable approach to mining. The

A heavy drill rig at the Ekati Mine. The tundra diamond mines provided a critical economic lifeline to Yellowknife just as the local gold mining industry was dying out.

Northwest Territories diamond industry also points to its award-winning workplace safety practices, support for local businesses (including millions spent on contracts with Indigenous-owned companies), the success of its training programs, and charitable contributions to community initiatives ranging from folk festivals to school breakfast programs. By many measures the diamond industry has become a community pillar in the Northwest Territories, a good corporate citizen that thinks beyond the narrow confines of the bottom line.

A community report from Lutsel K'e tells a somewhat different story about diamond mining, at least in the early days. It emphasizes how the community felt extremely rushed, unprepared, and often unable to understand the technical reports presented at community hearings. One of the community negotiators reflected that, "we didn't know anything about mining companies, their influence and powers. When they first came and found diamonds, the federal government proposed an IBA. We had sixty days to come up with an IBA. That wasn't sufficient time."

Although the IBAs typically stipulate that the communities will not oppose the mine, a common refrain from Lutsel K'e was that the community never granted their consent to the project because the federal government had already made the decision to go ahead. One community member reflected on the process in this way:

> *I don't think I'd call it consent. . . I mean they [the Dene negotiators] did the best they could to respond to it, but everything was so rushed through. . . and you look at the agreement. . . the EA and the IBA and they're horrible! If you look at some of the stuff that's been done since then and compare it to that, obviously people didn't understand what they should be asking for, or monitoring, or keeping an eye on, just because it had never been done before. . . Consent is when you have all the information, you understand it and you make decisions based on that. With it being rushed through and people not having the understanding. I don't see that as consent at all.*

The report also highlights major worries over the environmental impacts of the mine, citing oil spills, dust, noise pollution, and an increasing prevalence of deformed fish in the area. Of particular concern is the status of the barren-ground caribou, with community members citing frequent injuries to the animals when their legs are caught in the rocks at the side of mine access roads, increased road access for non-Indigenous hunters to take caribou, and the fact that their migratory routes have been "screwed up." Finally, Lutsel K'e community members underscored social impacts such as family stress due to the fly-in/fly-out work schedule, increased access to drugs and alcohol, the loss of traditional skills and knowledge, and increased gambling in the community. For all the negotiated benefits, nothing could hide the fact that mining development often brings enormous and sometimes disruptive change to the human and ecological communities that lie in its pathway.

Negotiators from the Indigenous communities have managed to make some gains from the newer mines (securing, for example, designated seats on environmental and social monitoring agencies), but some of this work has been undermined by the economic instability that remains inherent to the industry. For instance, the diamond-cutting plant in Yellowknife, touted when it opened in 2000 as a source of skilled jobs and a means to keep diamond money in the North, closed in 2009 due to slackening demand associated with the Great Recession of 2008. Similarly, all of the anticipated community benefits associated with the Snap Lake Mine dissipated in December 2015 when De Beers temporarily shut down the mine, a closure that became permanent seven months later when the company announced that the mine was for sale and it would soon be flooding the underground workings. Some of the Snap Lake workforce (96 in total) were able to transfer to De Beers's new Gahcho Kué mine, though this was a far cry from the 678 people who had worked at Snap Lake in 2011. Similarly, the fanfare surrounding the opening of Tahera's Jericho Mine in 2008 was such that Prime Minister Stephen Harper attended the opening ceremonies. Four years later a new owner, Shear Minerals, suddenly abandoned the site, leaving its employees without work and forcing the federal government to address issues surrounding the containment of contaminated water, tailings, and hazardous materials (especially abandoned fuel drums). While the government had collected $8.3 million dollars as a security deposit for environmental remediation of the site, $2.3 million was still owing and Shear faced potential charges for environmental mismanagement under the Nunavut Waters and Nunavut Surface Rights Tribunal Act, with possible fines of up to $100,000 and/or a one-year prison term. At this point, however, there was nobody to charge as company board members had resigned *en masse* and Shear became the vanishing mining company of the diamond fields. For all that some players in northern Canada's diamond fields have tried to dispel the idea that mining brings ephemeral benefits and long-term liabilities, the new northern diamond industry could not completely escape the hit-and-run reputation associated with older mining operations in the region.

Big Nickel in Labrador

Canada's second major mineral discovery of the 1990s came about almost by accident. On September 9, 1993, while flying back to base camp after yet another bleak day in a disappointing summer of mineral exploration, Newfoundland prospectors Albert Chislett and Chris Verbiski spotted a large area of gossan, or reddish oxidized iron, on the Labrador Coast at Voisey's Bay, a possible indication of a large base metal ore body. Initially Chislett and Verbiski thought they had found a copper mine, but further surveying on behalf of their backers, Diamond Fields Resources Inc., confirmed they had found a colossal nickel deposit with thirty-one million tons of ore (2.9 per cent nickel, 1.69 per cent copper, 1.14 per cent cobalt) located near the surface (thus suitable for open-pit mining) and conveniently adjacent to a viable tidewater port. In Canada it was the biggest nickel find in a generation; globally it was one of the largest of the late twentieth century. Along with the diamond strikes in the Northwest Territories, Voisey's Bay ignited the enthusiasm of an industry mired in a funk of low prices and the poor public image that came with the disasters and disputes at Westray and Giant Mine. The discovery also sparked a battle among corporate players, Indigenous groups, and the Newfoundland and Labrador government over who would control the new nickel bonanza and how the spoils of the new mine would be distributed.

In the wake of the Voisey's Bay discovery the co-chair of Diamond Fields, Robert Friedland, was seemingly in a weak position as the major mining companies turned hungry eyes toward Labrador. Not only was his company suffering from severe cash flow problems, Friedland had also earned the moniker "toxic Bob" in 1992 after a Colorado mine he operated with former company Galactic Resources spilled cyanide in the Alamosa River, destroying all aquatic life along a seventeen-mile stretch of the waterway. Generally Friedland had developed a reputation for flamboyant and reckless

The M/V *Umiak* is an ice-breaking ore carrier used to carry ore from the Voisey's Bay nickel mine in Labrador. Indigenous groups and the province of Newfoundland and Labrador all lobbied for a better share of Inco's nickel revenue in the 1990s.

behaviour throughout his career, a character assessment the business press reinforced in the wake of the Voisey's Bay discovery by dredging up his past incarnations as a convicted drug dealer at the age of nineteen and cohabitant of a hippie commune with Steve Jobs.

Nonetheless, Friedland ably fended off a hostile takeover bid from Falconbridge, inking a deal with Teck Cominco in April 1994 that saw the larger company buy 10 per cent of Diamond Fields for $108 million while surrendering voting rights on the shares to Friedland. Perhaps not surprisingly, Inco CEO Mike Sopko also wanted at least a cut of Voisey's Bay as a means to develop new Canadian feedstock for its Sudbury mills. After tenacious negotiations, in May 1995 Inco bought a 25 per cent stake in Voisey's Bay and an 8 per cent share in Diamond Fields for a cost of $386.7 million, sparking a doubling of Diamond Fields' share value to $80. By November 1994 further exploration at the site revealed large, high-grade nickel deposits beyond the original deposit; Diamond Fields' suitors began to line up in earnest through the early months of 1996. During the ensuing bidding war Friedland rejected Inco's initial takeover offer of $3.5 billion, Falconbridge's counter offer of $4 billion, and a joint Inco and Falconbridge offer of $4 billion. In March Inco announced it would up its bid to $4.3 billion, an amount that most in the business community felt was a triumph for Friedland, who took home $500 million when the deal was finally signed in April 1996.

Along with a nickel deposit, Inco (now operating the Voisey's Bay Nickel Company as a subsidiary) inherited a brewing conflict with Labrador's two main Indigenous groups, the Innu and the Inuit, over the costs and benefits associated with the new development. The Voisey's Bay deposit is located just thirty-six kilometres south of the largely Inuit hamlet of Nain and roughly eighty kilometres north of the Mushuau Innu First Nation village of Natuashish, a community that had voluntarily relocated from the nearby island settlement of Davis Inlet in 2002. Both the Innu and Inuit had used the Voisey's Bay area for hunting and had never ceded the territory to Newfoundland or Canada. Thus the issue of who actually owned the land on which the Voisey's Bay claims were located was very much in question: the Labrador Inuit Association (LIA) had actively pursued land claims since 1977 and the Innu Nation since 1978. Of the two groups, the Innu were the most vehement with their objections, drawing on the experience of their ongoing fight against the impacts of low-level NATO military training flights from the Goose Bay air force base on the nearby community of Sheshatshui, and the memory of another development project, the Churchill Falls dam, that flooded huge areas of their former hunting grounds without their consent or any compensation. Closer to Voisey's Bay, the community of Davis Inlet had experienced dire social problems since they had been relocated to the Iluikoyak Island site in 1969, cut off from the caribou herds that were their main source of food. As the Voisey's Bay strike was announced, Davis Inlet residents still maintained extremely raw emotions from a horrific house fire that had taken the lives of six unattended children in February 1992 and a videotaped instance of youth gas sniffing that shocked Canadians when it was released on national television (an incident that prompted the relocation to Natuashish in 2002).

In 1995, a group of Innu led by Chief Tshakapesh travelled to the exploration camp and issued an eviction order to the Diamond Fields exploration crew for drilling without permission. When the Diamond Fields crew refused to leave the protestors returned, destroyed the landing strip, encircled drill sites, and triggered an intense twelve-day standoff with the police. Although they did not, in the end, disrupt the drilling effort in the short term, they did serve notice that in the long run they would not tolerate development at Voisey's Bay without their consent. The Labrador Inuit Association did not participate in the protests and remained supportive of exploration, acutely aware there was much to be gained from nickel mining due to the fact their Inuit "neighbours" in Arctic Quebec had signed Canada's first comprehensive Impact and Benefit Agreement for Falconbridge's Raglan nickel mine in January 1995. By the time Inco finally took control of Voisey's Bay in 1996 there could be no doubt that the Indigenous people of Labrador would fight the mine every step of the way if the company and government refused to address the issues surrounding land claims and local impacts and benefits.

Relations between Inco and the two Indigenous groups started out well enough with a Memorandum of Understanding in January 1997 (signed also by provincial and federal governments) agreeing to a single environmental assessment of the project rather than separate federal and provincial reviews. But the new cooperative spirit quickly dissipated when the province issued a permit to begin infrastructure development at the mine before the environmental assessment. In July Innu attempts to obtain a court injunction to stop the work fell on deaf ears, prompting the Innu Nation and the LIA to plan a second occupation of the Voisey's Bay camp. On August 20 the first group of Inuit protestors arrived by barge and set up a blockade and camp that shut down road construction. Four days later the Innu contingent moved in on the main Inco camp, occupying trailers with so many people that the floor fell out of three units. Later the RCMP played an unwanted game of cat and mouse with groups of children who climbed up on top of the trailer roofs. Innu Nation

President Katie Rich was arrested and later released while tensions built throughout the day. Inuit and Innu leaders halted the second Voisey's Bay occupation after the astonishing announcement that the provincial Supreme Court had issued an injunction to cease construction at the camp until the outcome of the LIA-Innu appeal of the case could be heard. In September the Court ruled that the province's Minister of the Environment had gone beyond his rightful authority in issuing construction permits and ordered all work at the site to stop until the completion of the environmental assessment. This, combined with Premier Brian Tobin's vow that "not one teaspoon of ore will leave the province for processing," raised fears for many in the business community that the massive Voisey's Bay nickel deposit would be delayed for years or possibly never developed at all.

Delays there certainly were as the various stakeholders jockeyed with Inco for a cut of Canada's most anticipated mining project. In March 1999 the environmental assessment final report added weight to the concerns of the Indigenous communities, approving the project with 107 conditions, most notably the unique requirement that environmental and social sustainability be placed at the core of the project. To ensure more lasting local economic benefits, for example, the panel recommended that the project life be increased through a reduction in daily production capacity at the mine (Inco eventually agreed to reduce the capacity of the ore concentrator from twenty thousand to six thousand tons per day). To address environmental concerns, the report urged the creation of an environmental agreement and co-management with Indigenous communities of key issues such as tailings and waste rock disposal. Key social and environmental issues should also be addressed, the panel recommended, through the completion of IBAs and the settlement of land claims with the Innu and Inuit prior to the development of the mine.

The environmental assessment was widely lauded as a solid way forward for the Voisey's Bay project. The federal and provincial governments accepted most recommendations, but crucially rejected the idea of settling land claims, likely terrified the process might hold up the Voisey's Project for years, if not decades. The Innu and Inuit continued to press the point, however, through negotiations and court action in 1999, while at the same time the province and the company reached an impasse on negotiations over the smelter issue. It was not until May 2002 that the logjam broke, when both the LIA and Innu Nation announced the successful negotiation of an environmental co-management agreement and IBAs that included provisions for revenue sharing, contracting, employment, training, and ongoing community consultation. These agreements also paved the way for the conclusion of the historic Labrador Inuit Land Claims Agreement and the creation of the Nunatsiavut Government.

The provincial government also reached an agreement with Inco for the company to construct a hydrometallurgical plant at Argentia so that all of the Voisey's Bay ore would be processed on the island of Newfoundland. After the mine opened in 2005, however, Inco (owned by Brazilian mining giant Vale after 2006) shipped more than a few teaspoons of Labrador ore concentrate out of the province: the Long Harbour Nickel Processing Plant received its first Voisey's Bay ore only in 2015 (although the provincial government allowed the ore to be smelted in Manitoba and Ontario only after Inco agreed to process in Newfoundland an equal amount of nickel ore from other sources).

In 2015, Vale announced plans to construct a new underground mine that would extend the life of Voisey's Bay (and add a massive boost to the Labrador economy), and in 2017, roughly five hundred people worked at the mine site and concentrator with just over 50 per cent of the workforce made up of Indigenous people. Despite all the acrimony and conflict surrounding its origins, Voisey's Bay represented a major pivot in the Canada's mining history as Indigenous groups and government were able to wring major concessions from one of the oldest and arguably most intransigent companies in the business.

Courting Controversy in the Environmental Era

The mining industry was not always successful in its attempts to accommodate First Nations and environmental concerns as it pushed major projects through the regulatory process from the 1980s to the 2000s. Prior to the 1970s, there was almost no chance that government would stop or delay a major mining project. But tighter environmental regulation and growing legal recognition of Indigenous rights meant that mining companies sometimes had a difficult time jumping over the higher bar that had been set for them. Some companies fought back, challenging environmental assessment decisions in the courts and relentlessly pursuing new projects despite significant objections from First Nations and the general public. Although the industry had attempted to foster a more cooperative and environmentally responsible image with the Whitehorse Mining Initiative in 1993 and the Toward Sustainable Mining program in 2004, new mining projects in Canada continued to be a front line in the battles over Indigenous land rights and ecological issues in the 1990s and 2000s.

One of the most prominent skirmishes erupted over Geddes Resources' proposed Windy Craggy copper mine in the Tatshenshini-Alsek region of southwestern Yukon/northwestern British Columbia. By the time the Windy Craggy proposal was subject to environmental assessment in 1990, it was clear that Geddes had no solid answers to issues such as containing acid rock drainage, impounding tailings safely, or mitigating the impact of hundreds of kilometres of new road construction on fish and wildlife. Very quickly fifty leading conservation groups formed a consortium called Tatshenshini Wild to actively oppose the mine, citing the unique natural beauty of the mountainous and glaciated Tatshenshini-Alsek River, the value of existing ecotourism ventures such as river rafting in the area, and especially the potential destruction of some of the best grizzly bear habitat in Canada. The dispute took on an international dimension as US Vice President Al Gore voiced opposition to the project, which raised the spectre of cross-border disputes over pollution and habitat destruction under the provisions of the Boundary Water Treaty, the Migratory Birds Treaty, and the Pacific Salmon Treaty. In 1993 BC Premier Mike Harcourt rejected the mine proposal and announced the creation of the Tatshenshini-Alsek Provincial Park, commenting that "we came to the conclusion that the preservation of wilderness and the proposed mining activities could not coexist." The new park added to a complex of contiguous international protected areas (including Canada's Kluane National Park, and Wrangell–St. Elias and Glacier National Parks in the United States) that now comprises nearly 58,000 square kilometres, one that the United Nations Educational, Scientific and Cultural Organization (UNESCO) has recognized as a World Heritage Site. An interesting footnote to the story is that Peggy Witte's Royal Oak Resources swooped in and bought Geddes Resources only two months before the rejection of the mine proposal. Never shy of a dispute, Royal Oak then promptly threatened to sue the BC government for hundreds of millions of dollars of damages due to lost revenues and exploration costs. The province eventually settled out of court, compensating Royal Oak with $29 million in cash and $138 million to support the development Royal Oak's Kemess Mine in northern British Columbia. Aside from the bizarre spectacle of a government having to compensate a private company for exercising its regulatory duties over publicly owned lands, one can't help noticing the irony of government providing recompense to a company that would soon saddle the public with a billion-dollar problem of arsenic contamination at Giant Mine (see Chapter 6). Regardless, many would likely consider the compensation package a small price to pay for the preservation of one Canada's most breathtaking and ecologically significant natural areas.

The Tatshenshini controversy environmentalists have achieved only mixed success in stopping controversial mining projects, as the industry became more persistent with its use of court action and the resubmission of project applications that had been rejected on environmental grounds. For instance, environmental groups fought a pitched but ultimately futile battle against the Cheviot Coal

Remediation work at Imperial Metals' Mt. Polley Mine in 2019, five years after the collapse of a tailings pond dam at the site allowed 24 million cubic meters of contaminated tailings and wastewater to flood into Quesnel Lake.

Mine, a project that inspired broad public opposition to a development project located in prime grizzly bear habitat directly adjacent to Jasper National Park. A federal environmental review panel approved the mine in 1997, but a consortium of five environmental groups argued successfully in court that the review process had been flawed for failing to adequately address the impact on migratory birds, for neglecting to incorporate evidence submitted by environmental groups, and for ignoring the cumulative impacts of coal mining and forestry in the region. The court ordered a second panel review that finally recommended approval of the mine; a last-ditch court challenge by the environmental groups using the habitat protection provisions of the Migratory Birds Treaty failed. By 2005 the Cheviot coal mine was up and running despite widespread public opposition to the project.

More recently the industry has successfully challenged environmental and Indigenous opposition to Imperial Metals' Red Chris copper and gold mine in northern British Columbia. In 2007, the NGO MiningWatch challenged in court the federal approval of the Red Chris mine based on the fact it had been subject only to a screening rather than a comprehensive environmental assessment. After an appeal sent the case all the way to the Supreme Court of Canada in 2010, the court ruled that developers could not split the project proposal into smaller-scale subprojects to avoid triggering

comprehensive environmental assessments. The court did not, however, overturn the approval of the mine, raising alarm among environmentalists, the Tahltan First Nation, and the state government of Alaska about the potential for a leaky tailings dam to contaminate the so-called Sacred Headwaters area, the source of the Skeena, Stikine, and Nass Rivers. The issue came to a head in August 2014 when a disastrous spill at Mt. Polley Mine (also an Imperial Metals property) near Quesnel Lake, BC, raised fears about the Red Chris mine's tailings facility. Four days after the spill, Tahltan First Nation members (who had forced a coal company to back down voluntarily from a mine proposal in the Sacred Headwaters the previous summer) blockaded the Red Chris site, demanding improvements to the tailings area. One of the protest leaders, Rhoda Quock, told the media, "when we talked to them they told us the tailings pond is the same design as Mount Polley and that it works fine. Look at it now. We can't have that happen here." The controversy over the mine (documented in Nettie Wild's critically acclaimed film *Koneline*) abated somewhat after Imperial agreed to respond to the recommendations of an independent review of the tailings facility. By the time the mine

In April 1995, the Secwepemc Women Warriors' Society organized the "Evict Imperial Now" protest in Vancouver in response to the Mt. Polley disaster. The Mt. Polley spill undermined trust in another Imperial Metals project, the Red Chris Mine.

opened in 2015, Imperial had also signed an agreement with the Tahltan First Nation granting them a partnership role in the environmental oversight of the mine. If the Tahltan could not prevent development in the Sacred Headwaters (and in fact the First Nation's government and many members welcomed the jobs brought by the mine), they could at least have a role managing the environmental risks that inevitably accompany large-scale mining projects.

Environmentalists had more success with Taseko Mines over its proposal for the Prosperity gold and copper mine southwest of Williams Lake, British Columbia. In 2010 a federal review panel rejected the Prosperity proposal, responding to environmentalists' and the Tsilhqot'in First Nation's concerns about the loss of fish habitat. One year later Taseko applied for federal approval a second time, but the environmental panel rebuffed the proposal once again, reiterating concerns that the tailings dam and containment area were likely to destroy trout habitat and contaminate nearby Fish Lake. Taseko responded by suing The Wilderness Committee (one of the environmental groups that had opposed the project) for defamation, a case the BC Supreme Court dismissed with a terse ruling that suggested the court action was meant to stifle criticism of the company. The company subsequently

repackaged and resubmitted the project as "New Prosperity," only to have it rejected again by the federal government in 2014, a decision backed by a federal court judge in late 2017. Taseko subsequently lost an appeal against the environmental assessment and federal court decisions, leaving its New Prosperity claims in limbo.

In Arctic Canada Indigenous activists have had some success stopping mining projects that threaten local livelihoods. The Baker Lake Inuit, for instance, have since the 1970s managed to fight off recurring proposals to dig large open-pit uranium mines on the tundra eighty kilometres west of the community. Their first victory came with a court injunction in 1978 to stop exploration in the area, a ruling that recognized Inuit use and occupancy rights to the land (though the ruling stopped short of granting Inuit the right to control mineral exploration) and helped set the stage for the Inuit Land Claims agreement and the creation of Nunavut. Inuit opposition also flared up in response to a uranium mining proposal from a West German firm, Urangesellschaft, in 1989. Two groups — the Baker Lake Concerned Citizens Committee (the BLCCC) led by Joan Scottie and the Northern Anti-Uranium Coalition, a small group of public health and local government officials organized by Tagak Curley — mobilized local, national, and international opposition to the proposal, concerned about the environmental health impacts and the potential negative effects of open-pit mining on the migratory routes and calving grounds of the Beverly-Quamanjuriaq caribou herd. In March 1990 the BLCCC organized a plebiscite and Baker Lake voted 90.2 per cent against the uranium proposal. Six months later Urangesellschaft asked for an "indefinite delay" to the federal environmental assessment of the project, effectively withdrawing the mine proposal in response to a request for extensive information from the panel and due to widespread public concern. In 2006 French uranium giant Areva revived the Kiggavik proposal, hoping to cash in on high uranium prices and a political climate more conducive to mining now that the Nunavut Land Claims Agreement (NLCA) had guaranteed Inuit rights to consultation and benefits from mining projects. Inuit advocacy groups such as the Kivalliq Inuit Association and Nunavut Tunngavik Incorporated, which had opposed uranium mining in 1989, now supported (and stood to benefit from) the new proposal. Local opposition to Areva's proposal remained strong, however, as a new local grassroots opposition group, Nunavummiut Makitagunarningit (or, simply, Makita) arose in the wake of the BLCCC and became an important source of information about the mine through its website and social media feeds. In 2015, after a five-year review process, the Nunavut Impact Review Board rejected Areva's proposed uranium mine because, in the face of low uranium prices, the company refused to specify project start dates or timelines. The board reasoned that it would be impossible to determine project impacts when ecological conditions (especially caribou numbers) and the cumulative impacts of other developments remained glaring unknowns if the mine opened ten or twenty years in the future. As of 2020, a combination of grassroots activism and careful regulatory oversight had held the line in the long battle over uranium mining in the Baker Lake region.

All of these cases suggest that, in spite of the fact some projects have been rejected for environmental deficiencies, at least some players in the mining industry were willing to play hardball to push forward controversial mining proposals. Certainly the industry has radically transformed the way that it approaches communities in the past three decades, offering opportunities for consultation and economic benefits that were unheard of in earlier decades. The development of more comprehensive approaches to environmental assessment and government regulation — practices that were nearly non-existent in the freewheeling days prior to the 1970s — add weight to the idea that industry and government have turned a new leaf in terms of their responsibility to community and environmental interests. Mining projects can also be a significant economic boon to the remote and economically isolated communities where mineral activity usually takes place, so any analysis of communities resisting this type of development must acknowledge that specific environmental and social concerns often exist alongside strong advocacy for well-paying jobs, training opportunities, and, in the case of Indigenous communities, royalty sharing and other benefits.

On the other hand, the playing field remains uneven between heavily financed multinationals and small communities. Companies are most often in a much better position to navigate complex legal and regulatory processes than communities whose resources are often taxed by multiple development processes, not to mention a host of other social, economic, and environmental challenges. Even with a concerted industry-wide campaign promoting the increasing environmental sustainability of mining, the industry has not been able to shed completely its reputation as an environmental laggard. Ongoing environmental battles over specific projects, international concern over the impacts of extensive oil sands mining in northern Alberta, and public shock over the 2014 Mount Polley tailings dam breach in BC that released millions of litres of contaminated water and tailings into Quesnel Lake, suggest the industry has a long way to go to allay public apprehension over its activities. In the new millennium, stories of conflict, confrontation, and the ballooning environmental costs of remediating older, abandoned mining sites continued to dominate news coverage of the industry, raising questions about how

The restored Wake Up Jake Saloon in Barkerville, BC, circa 1976. The former gold rush town remains a popular heritage tourism attraction featuring gold panning, theatre shows, and historical re-enactments.

CHAPTER 6
Heritage, History, and Zombie Mines

In a 1976 CBC television program, the renowned literary critic Northrop Frye observed that "Canada is full of ghost towns: visible ruins unparalleled in Europe." His touchstone for the comment was the full panoply of historical boom and bust resource rushes in Canada — the chase after lumber, fish, and minerals — that constituted Europe's "ransacking of the colonies." While more recent conservationist ideas present models for stable and sustainable communities based on renewable resource exploitation, nobody disputes the fact that the defining feature of mineral production is its transitory nature, a sudden eruption of intense development and an often equally abrupt collapse of human activity. At their inception, mines may symbolize progress, modernization, and expansionism; in many cases, their aftermath — the piles of rubble, the abandoned buildings, and the empty open pits — can serve as evocative metaphors for instability and societal collapse. Under pressure from regulators and changing public attitudes, in recent decades, companies and governments have attempted to clean up or "remediate" some of these problems. But in many cases, mineral development has left behind abandoned mines and towns with complicated and contested social and environmental legacies.

After a century and more of intensive industrial-scale mineral exploitation, the manifold environmental problems associated with abandoned mines have come into bold relief. In their hunt for the tiny fractions of valuable minerals contained in an ore body, mining companies produce enormous amounts of waste. At any given closed or abandoned mine, one may find massive waste rock piles and tailings ponds that leach toxic substances such as cadmium, arsenic, mercury, and lead through the air as dust or into surrounding waterways, often with significant impacts downstream of the mine site. Extensive landscape disturbance may prevent significant revegetation, while water filling open pits may also contain toxicants. Add to all of this significant safety concerns about old mine workings, particularly large-scale underground mines that are slowly collapsing, threatening human communities on the surface, and it is easy to see why some historians, ourselves included, use the term "zombie mines" to describe the malevolent afterlife associated with mine abandonment.

The zombie mine problem is global in scale, with hundreds of thousands of sites spread throughout the historic mining districts that emerged in the late nineteenth and early twentieth centuries. In Australia (a mining-dependent nation if there ever was one) there are an estimated 50,000 abandoned mines; more than ten times that number (550,000) dot the landscapes of the United States. In Canada an industry-government partnership, the National Orphaned and Abandoned Mines Initiative, estimates there are ten thousand

S.S. *Keno* National Historic Site, Dawson City, Yukon. While the *Keno* was mainly used to haul silver ore on the Stewart River near Mayo, sternwheelers like it plied the Yukon River during the Klondike Gold Rush. It was refloated and moored on Dawson's Front Street as part of historic commemoration activities in the 1960s.

abandoned mines in Canada (defined as closed sites that require some kind of remediation but have reverted to government control). The cost of cleaning up these sites is enormous. In 1994 one environmental advocacy group, the Mineral Policy Group, placed a price tag of $32 billion to $72 billion on cleanup of abandoned mines in the United States, all of it to be borne by the public. In Canada a federal auditor general's report from 2002 estimated a $555 million cleanup for abandoned mines in the territorial north, an appraisal that has proven far too low considering the more than $1 billion it will take just to address the arsenic problem at Giant Mine (discussed later in this chapter). In so many of the world's mining regions, the historical lack of environmental regulations and the ease with which mining companies could walk away from their problem sites has created a massive public liability that retrospectively subsidizes the private wealth accumulation generated by mining activity.

There is, moreover, no easy technological fix for many of the chemical and physical threats associated with abandoned mines. In too many cases, the environmental risks and financial costs associated with mobilizing and removing toxic waste means that containment is the only viable, if imperfect, option for the short term. At other sites, however, it is nearly impossible to shield humans and animals from the toxic legacies of mining. Underneath the city of Johannesburg, South Africa, for example, toxic groundwater poses a public health threat as it slowly rises from the extensive mine works under the city, while on the surface tailings piles at the edges of the city present a public health threat as they spread toxic dust into residential areas. At the bottom of the infamous Berkeley Pit adjacent to Butte, Montana, sits a 900-foot-deep lake of acidic water laden with heavy metals, a toxic stew that defies a permanent cleanup solution and that recently resulted in the death of hundreds of snow geese seeking refuge from a storm during migration. In Canada and throughout the globe, we live with the environmental consequences and costs of decades of poorly regulated mining development.

But not everyone sees waste and destruction when they look at abandoned mining landscapes. For many communities, abandoned mines evoke their history and heritage of working the land, an expression of affinity to a place that is far from "ruined" in their view. Government agencies charged with remediating mine sites often face pushback from communities that want to preserve rock piles, headframes, and other visible signs of their labour. In Yellowknife, for instance, mining heritage advocates and the city government recently campaigned to save Con Mine's Robertson shaft headframe, only to watch as the local landmark was blown up in October 2016. At former mine sites that do escape the wrecking crews, local heritage advocates have developed museums and mine tours as a way to mark their community's labour history and also develop tourism as a post-mining economic opportunity. Popular publications, such as Peter Goin and C. Elizabeth Raymond's *Changing Mines in America* or the UK-based Eden Project's *101 Things to do with a Hole in the Ground*, survey many examples where environmental and heritage values have been preserved in post-mining landscapes, even while new uses for these sites (as movie sets, cheese cellars, experimental physics labs, and radium health spas) are developed. Obviously, the mining industry relishes stories of renewal and repair at abandoned mine sites (the Eden Project book was an industry-funded publication). But the question of how to reconcile these heritage values with the environmental legacies of the zombie mines is key to understanding the legacies Canada's mining past has bequeathed to the present — and the future.

Mining Heritage

Hiking the Chilkoot Trail from Dyea, Alaska, to its terminus at Lake Bennett offers a chance to trace the path of the most famous gold rush stampede in Canadian history. The trail is a national historic site commemorating the Klondike rush on both sides of the Canada–US border, offering hikers the chance to experience what the US Park Service describes as "the world's longest [fifty-four kilometre] museum." When author Sandlos and his spouse, Yolanda, hiked the trail in 1998 it certainly lived up to this billing, with rusted tin cans, tangled tram cables, and many old tools carefully demarcated in "no touch" zones along the way — this was heritage trash! As that year was the one-hundredth anniversary of the Klondike Gold Rush, special wall-tent museums had been set up along the way, replete with photographs and artifacts from a century ago. The Klondike centennial also meant there was no shortage of people from all walks of life and from all over the world seeking some connection with this mining heritage landscape. Just as in the famous images from a century ago, a veritable herd of outsiders struggled over the gruelling and iconic Chilkoot Pass's Golden Staircase, albeit with far less than the thousand pounds of supplies the stampeders needed as a precondition for crossing over to the Canadian side of the border. With local centenary celebrations in full swing, hikers who reached Lake Bennett were treated to free pancakes from a local heritage society, their outdoor kitchen protected from bears by a spiderweb of electrical wiring. Some hikers spotted a group celebrating the trail's centennial anniversary in a novel way: running its entire length in the nude. Those hikers with enough money could travel back in time (and more practically, back to Skagway) along the White Pass and Yukon Railway in vintage rail cars (my spouse and I caught a ride in the back of a pickup truck, with no questions asked in those days by US Border Services). That evening many of us completed our journey to the past with a screening of Charlie Chaplin's *The Gold Rush* (1925) at the Klondike National Historic Park visitor centre.

Further north, Dawson City, the terminus of the Klondike route and base town for gold mining in the area, is known worldwide for its nineteenth-century storefronts, dance halls, and the houses of authors Jack London and Pierre Berton. As one of Parks Canada's network of

Canadian border post at the summit of the Chilkoot Pass between Alaska and Yukon. Today, thousands of tourists reproduce the grueling Chilkoot Trail used by stampeders during the Klondike Gold Rush-though without the once-required thousand pounds of supplies!

National Historic Sites, visitors to Dawson experience an elaborate re-creation (complete with costumed interpreters) of the frontier experience in a northern boomtown. Keen observers will also notice evidence of the destructive power of the bucket-line dredges used to scour the local riverbed in search of gold, the effects still visible in the landscape as sinuous, human-made moraines.

If the Klondike remains Canada's most famous mining district, the desire to walk in the footsteps of yesterday's miners remains a popular tourist draw at other former mine sites across Canada. At Britannia Mine, an award-winning National Historic Site just a forty-five-minute drive north of Vancouver, visitors are treated to a heritage museum centre, a mineral gallery, an old machine shop, and the obsolete mill. For those who prefer more hands-on experiences, a gold-panning station has been set up at the surface, a kids' play centre has been built complete with a giant sand pit, and ore trains take visitors on guided tours into the heart of the mine. As one of the biggest copper mines in Canada over its seventy-four-year history (1900–74), the site's industrial heritage lives on as an interpretive centre for a large public audience. Because Britannia was also a major polluter, with acid rock drainage and heavy metals flowing for decades into Howe Sound adjacent to Britannia Beach, the museum also teaches about the environmental costs of mining. But Britannia's recent history also provides museum visitors with a story of hope: a site remediation project begun in 2003 successfully removed toxic soil from area and ongoing water treatment stemmed the flow of pollution from the mine, eventually allowing salmon to return to Britannia Creek and marine mammals such as dolphins and orcas to return to the surrounding waters.

As in the case of Dawson, many abandoned mine sites focus as much on the heritage of old town sites as they do on the industrial heritage and environmental legacies of the industry. Cobalt, Ontario, for instance, has billed itself as "Ontario's most historic town," featuring a driving tour (the Heritage Silver Trail) that takes visitors to a mining history park, a museum, old headframes, monuments, and representative geological formations. The National Historic Site at Barkerville, BC, preserves a rich heritage of wooden buildings from the province's mid-nineteenth-century gold rush, accentuating the historic nature of the town with period theatre, a museum, and even a winter tubing hill. From a later period, Quebec's Val d'Or hosts the historic Lamaque mine and Bourlamaque mining village, part of the "Cité de l'Or" tourist attraction, which boasts the deepest underground mine tour (ninety-one metres) in Canada. While all of these towns were founded because of major mineral rushes, today they mine their own history both as a point of local pride and as a draw for tourist dollars. Whether solemn or whimsical, at its best mining heritage interpretation connects the experience of mining communities and landscapes to wider issues in local and national history.

Of course, for many history buffs, there is nothing more exciting than a mining ghost town. The sudden collapse of mining boomtowns often results in their hasty abandonment, leaving behind mine workings, town buildings, and residences. These sites hold a particular fascination for their states of suspended animation or dereliction, the absence of restoration and preservation efforts contributing to the idea that these places represent history in the raw. The fact that a few hardy souls sometimes persist in these places adds to their allure as relict landscapes. Sandon, BC, is a classic Canadian mining ghost town. One of several such towns in the picturesque Slocan Valley, especially along the "Valley of the Ghosts," Highway 31A, Sandon boomed in the 1880s as the hub of the Idaho Peak-area silver rush, at one point supporting a population of over four thousand. An extension of the western American mining frontier, it resembled the stereotypical Western town, with its bars, brothels, and false-fronted buildings. By the 1920s, after repeated fires and floods and with mining in decline, Sandon went

Former Lamaque Mine National Historic Site, Val d'Or, Quebec. Dating to the 1930s, the mine site and neighbouring Bourlamaque village exemplify a classic mining company town, preserved thanks to the efforts of local citizens in the 1960s and 1970s.

Restored building in Sandon, BC Like many mining boomtowns, Sandon became a ghost town for decades after the mines closed. After being looted, burned, and hosting squatters, it has re-emerged as a quirky and popular tourist spot in the picturesque Slocan Highway "Valley of Ghosts."

bankrupt and the town was largely abandoned. Used briefly as an internment camp for Japanese-Canadians during the Second World War, the town was looted in the 1950s and occupied by squatters for a while. Though the town hosted a population of only six as of 2016, thousands visit Sandon annually to see mining artifacts and take in the broken-down boomtown landscape.

The story of Keno City, a picturesque former silver-mining town high in the mountains of the central Yukon, illustrates how "ghost towns" can become reawakened "zombies" through the redevelopment of an abandoned mine. A mining boomtown in the 1920s, Keno City thrived for years as a kind of satellite to the nearby United Keno Hill Mining Company town of Elsa, which was itself shuttered with the end of mining in the district in 1989 (see Chapter 3). While a handful of Keno residents hung on in the years after closure, living among the town's picturesque false-fronted buildings and developing modest tourism opportunities along the Yukon's "Silver Trail," more recently a combination of remediation activities and renewed silver mining has brought sudden upheaval to the town. Some residents voiced concerns about noise, dust and water pollution, and changes to their quiet lifestyle; others saw economic opportunity in the renewed developments. The up-and-down fortunes of the company conducting both the remediation and redevelopment, Alexco Corporation, have only contributed to the uncertainty around the town's future.

Not all ghost towns are artifacts of the romantic boomtown past. Kitsault, BC, is a remarkable example of the "cyclonic" effect of mining busts on even the most modern towns. Built in 1979 to service the AMAX molybdenum mine on the central BC coast, Kitsault was an "instant town" that boasted all the modern amenities: suburban-style homes and apartments, a mall, hospital, community centre, and curling rink. Yet by November 1982 the mine failed, a victim of crashing "moly" prices. The town closed and was completely abandoned by its nearly twelve hundred residents the following year. Remarkably, in 2004 the town was sold for $7 million — lock, stock, and abandoned buildings — to Canadian businessman Krishnan Suthanthiran, who began remediation and restoration work. Suthanthiran hoped to revive the abandoned town as a liquid natural gas facility and/or retreat for researchers. As of 2018, media reports suggest Suthanthiran was still struggling to find a viable use for Kitsault. The town did find a new life as a musical (simply titled *Kitsault*) that staged a first public

reading of the score at Toronto's Al Green Theatre in February 2019. Documenting the dying days of the mine and the close attachment of residents to the town, the musical markets itself as the story of a "town [that] was abandoned, but no one really left."

Other sites promoting mining heritage rely as much on the inner workings and built features of former mine sites as the attraction of a heritage or ghost town. Mine headframes, the iconic symbol of underground mining, are often the focus of historic preservation and identity-making activities — even in cases such as Rankin Inlet, Nunavut, where the headframe was destroyed by fire in 1978 but remains a representative symbol used in marketing material for the town. In Wabana, on Newfoundland's Bell Island, it is the heritage value of the underground mine rather than the town that attracts visitors. Mine tours begin in a small museum displaying stunning historical photographs of town residents and miners taken by the world famous photographer Yousef Karsh, and proceed underground with compelling stories and songs about life, work, and danger in the depths of the iron mine. Even in cases such as Pine Point, NWT, where the remains of the mine attract little interest and the town has been removed, virtual commemorative sites, such as former resident Richard Cloutier's *Pine Point Revisited* website, have preserved the collective memories of those who lived and worked at the mine.

Many mines offer their most compelling historical narrative as landscapes of labour. The toil and danger of life underground hold a fascination for visitors and former mine workers alike, and danger and conflict always accompany the histories of coal mining districts. While the tragic stories of Springhill and Westray, Nova Scotia, have been amply documented in song, film, and popular books, commemorative sites for lesser-known abandoned coal mines are spread throughout the country. In Alberta's badlands, the coal mining towns of Wayne and East Coulee have been mostly abandoned, while Drumheller is much more famous for the dinosaur collections at the Royal Tyrrell Museum than for its mining heritage. Nonetheless,

Atlas Coal Mine National Historic Site, Drumheller, Alberta. Many historic sites commemorate the dangers of mining and sacrifice of workers in this most dangerous of industrial professions.

Underground mine tours, like this one at Newfoundland's Bell Island Mine, are enormously popular tourist attractions, often engaging former mine workers and community members in heritage preservation and interpretation.

the abandoned Atlas Coal Mine, yet another National Historic Site, is well known regionally as the site of the last wooden coal tipple in Canada and for apparent sightings of the ghosts of former workers in the mine tunnels. The Atlas mine museum's interpretive programs focus on the difficult and dangerous working life of the miners, including an annual May Day march and festival to honour those who died in the mines. At the other end of the *gravitas* spectrum, an annual Halloween celebration evokes the spirits that both staff and psychics claim to have seen repeatedly on the site. Similarly, on Vancouver Island the Cumberland Museum and Archives commemorates the conflictual nature of coal mining through its collections of artifacts belonging to Chinese workers and its tributes to the socialist labour organizer Ginger Goodwin, shot by police while on the lam in 1918.

No doubt such places attract visitors and former residents (in person and on the internet) in part due to the irresistible lure of nostalgia, along with the cultural fascination with industrial ruins and other abandoned places as small-scale measures of what a postapocalyptic world might look like, in television shows such as the *Forgotten Planet* series and books such as Alan Weisman's *The World Without Us*. Such places also represent an affectionate attempt on the part of the children and grandchildren of mine workers to document their community's history of work underground and spare moments of leisure at the surface.

Dangerous Places

For all these efforts to venerate and memorialize the human history of mining, in too many cases former mines also carry a darker legacy of physical and environmental risk, the long-term legacies of hazard and contamination. Only since the latter decades of the twentieth century were companies required to plan for environmental reclamation activities when mining ended. Though mining may have ended and the miners moved on, former mine sites are far from dead: malevolent zombie landscapes often pose ongoing and future environmental and public health hazards that threaten to betray the very communities that built and sustained the mines.

In some cases, the physical instability of abandoned underground mines presents the greatest threat. At Newfoundland's Bell Island, for instance, tidal water moving in and out of the mine tunnels threatens to cause instability among the pillars holding up the roof of the mine. In the event of a massive collapse of the tunnel roofs, one local engineer has suggested, the underground shock waves could cause an earthquake, flooding in the town of Wabana because of the gush of water forced out of the ground, and possibly a drop in the water level of Conception Bay, which could in turn produce a tsunami as water rushes in from the open ocean. In a different case, surface hazards and safety issues associated with underground subsidence at the massive Hollinger mine in Timmins have prompted the local and provincial governments to approve a reclamation project engineered by the company Goldcorp. The plan is to neutralize the surface and underground hazards by digging them up, creating a huge open-pit mine within the urban area of Timmins that will eventually be transformed into a park and recreational lake. The project has proved controversial, with local residents voicing apprehension about dust and noise, both during public consultations in 2012 and through a "Concerned Residents of Timmins" Facebook page. Goldcorp, which began work on the site in late 2013, has constructed a huge berm to shield the community from the mining operation, though noise remained a

major concern. One could argue that the community had few choices: the hazardous ghost tunnels of a previous mining development could be repaired (ironically) only through the application of more mining activity.

At many abandoned mines hazards stem from the massive waste left behind as rock piles, gravel, and tailings. Often the fine wastes from mineral processing are stored aboveground in tailings ponds, which require careful engineering and structural maintenance to contain the contaminated water. The Mount Polley disaster in 2014, where a large tailings dam failed at an operating mine and sent contaminated wastes down a local creek into Quesnel Lake and the Cariboo River (see Chapter 5), brought the potential hazards of such facilities to the public though national media attention. Efforts to contain waste at abandoned mines can also fail, as did Newfoundland's Gullbridge dam in 2012, the resulting tailings spill threatening the nearby community of South Brook's water supply. For communities and environments downstream, such failures present both physical dangers from the sudden, potentially massive spills of water and fine sediment, as well as chemical hazards in cases where acid-forming rock, trace heavy metals, or other contaminants are present in the tailings.

While such disasters capture headlines, perhaps of greater concern are the long-term or "slow" toxic legacies of zombie mines. In many cases, the chemical and/or radioactive hazards produced by mines and mineral processing facilities may persist for decades, centuries, or even indefinitely after the end of mining. If the companies responsible have not cleaned up the site, the effects of these wastes may pose a threat long after mine closure and abandonment, requiring long-term care and maintenance. For instance, uranium mining in the 1950s and '60s at Port Radium in the Northwest Territories and around Uranium City in northern Saskatchewan left behind a hazardous legacy of millions of tons of radioactive tailings waste that polluted local waterways for decades after the end of mining (see Chapter 4). As mentioned briefly in Chapter 3, a more common problem is acid rock drainage:

Main street of Uranium City, Saskatchewan, 1997. Once hailed as a modern industrial settlement, Uranium City suffered the fate of many remote, single-industry mining towns in the 1980s: abandonment and decline. Only a handful of residents remained, while the town itself became an object of fascination for "ruin" enthusiasts and photographers.

at abandoned mines sulphide-bearing rock, complex processes of oxidation often produce very low pH water that wreaks havoc with aquatic life and in turn leaches heavy metals from the mine workings and waste rock — a condition that can persist for decades or longer.

Remediation and Reclamation: Successes and Challenges

Cleaning up these toxic zombie mines — and avoiding their creation in the first place — is a major focus of contemporary mineral regulation. Since the 1970s the regulatory environment surrounding mine establishment and closure has changed a great deal from the days when companies simply operated mines without planning for future closure and abandonment. Today mining companies and consulting firms loudly proclaim their successes with sites that have been restored (where the mine environs are

returned to something resembling the ecosystem that existed prior to the mine), reclaimed (where the land is returned to some sort of purpose), or remediated (where all contaminants and other hazards are contained or removed from the site). While standards vary across the provinces and territories, most governments require some sort of abandonment and reclamation plan before the approval of a mine, and many require annual financial security deposits to offset the cost of site reclamation should the mining company become insolvent. Critics have noted that the amounts set for annual financial security payments often fail to account for the costs of inflation and reclamation monitoring over time, that words such as "reclamation" are vague and can result in the creation of industrial-grade lands that incorporate many of the environmental ills of the original mine, that remediation efforts tend to focus on containing contaminants in situ rather than on adopting the more expensive option of removing them from the site, and that restoring abandoned

Once notorious for its "moonscape" denuded of vegetation due to smelter pollution, Sudbury became famous for community-led "regreening" efforts in the 1980s. Though the local environment is improved, considerable historic pollution of local water and soil remain.

mine sites can be a form of "greenwashing" because re-creating infinitely complex ecosystems out of vastly degraded mine lands is nearly impossible. While creative reclamation projects over the past several decades suggest that the afterlife of a mine can be marked by regeneration rather than environmental havoc, at some sites environmental remediation poses deep, possibly intractable, challenges.

Within the industry, the Island Copper Mine on the remote west coast of Vancouver Island stands as a celebrated and pioneering case of successful mine reclamation. This open-pit copper-molybdenum mine operated from 1971–95, producing over a billion tons of ore from a massive, 400-metre-deep open pit located right on the shoreline of Quatsino Sound. The site also included mine infrastructure and extensive waste rock and tailings dumps (although much of the tailings were deposited in the inlet during the mine's operations), the disturbed area totalling near 800 hundred hectares. The major environmental concern, aside from physical stability of the extremely deep pit, was acid rock drainage from the site, which threatened the aquatic environment and commercial salmon fisheries of Quatsino Sound and Rupert Inlet. At many open-cast mines, mined-out pits are allowed to fill with water naturally; at Island Copper, a trench was dug to fill the pit with ocean water from the inlet — temporarily creating the world's largest marine waterfall! Once the pit filled with seawater, the mine's process water was re-routed to the pit to create a freshwater cap over the seawater. The pit water was subsequently used to contain the acid-laden wastewater, by injecting the latter into the lower reaches of the pit lake where saline conditions and sulphate-reducing bacteria keep contaminants at the bottom. This strategy, along with almost complete revegetation of waste rock and other disturbed surface areas, earned Island Copper a series of industry awards for reclamation.

The most well-known case of reclamation in Canada is the greening of the nearly barren landscapes produced by decades of sulphur dioxide pollution and tailings deposits in the Sudbury area. As discussed in Chapter 3, by the 1970s sulphur dioxide from roasting and especially smelting activities, combined with extensive woodcutting for fuel, pulp, and timber, had produced large swaths of "moonscape" in the greater Sudbury area. Despite the improvements in air quality that came with Inco's construction of the "superstack" in 1972, persistent acidification and heavy metal contamination of soils (primarily with copper and nickel) continued to prevent natural regeneration of a barren landscape that stretched over 10,000 hectares and 36,000 hectares of additional semi-barren lands. After several years of experimental revegetation work, in 1978 the Regional Municipality of Sudbury launched a program to revegetate the area through a process involving liming soil, fertilization, seeding, tree planting, and natural revegetation. Funding from industry and government partners meant that students and those on unemployment benefits performed much of the labour through summer work terms and other temporary employment programs. Over the next three decades the regreening program produced some major successes, including 3,435 hectares of land limed, more than nine million trees planted by 2011, and multiple awards from conservation and land reclamation organizations. With intermittent media attention making the public aware of the regreening project, Sudbury came to symbolize the regenerative potential that can be cultivated within even the most degraded mining landscapes.

The project also illustrates the high cost and long-term work commitments often associated with mine reclamation. Between 1978 and 2015, the regreening of Sudbury cost more than $30 million dollars, 77 per cent of that total coming from the federal, provincial, and municipal governments and only 8 per cent from Vale/Inco (though in 2015 Vale contributed nearly $600,000 to the project, well over half the annual budget). For all the money spent, the amount of land reclaimed represents less than half of the most heavily impacted lands and none of the much larger semi-barren areas within the development area. Moreover, the environmental impacts of Sudbury's mining history extend beyond the issue of local land degradation. For instance, approximately seven thousand lakes in a 17,000-square-kilometre area around Sudbury were subject to heavy-metal contamination and acidification to the point of causing significant ecological damage, a condition that has gradually improved with emissions reductions. The lakes closest to the old smelters

have exhibited only chemical recovery, however, and not a full restoration of the former biological community. In 2012 a local resident reported green-coloured seepage leaking from a slag heap into nearby Nolin Creek. A subsequent Environment Canada investigation suggested that Vale/Inco had been knowingly permitting the seepage of acutely toxic wastewater from the slag heaps since 1997. The company denied any wrongdoing and has co-operated with government to address the impact of the pollution on aquatic life, but residents of the surrounding neighbourhood remained concerned about the possible health impacts of seepage into soil from a slag heap that had been used since 1929. No doubt the regreening of Sudbury has resulted in vast improvements to environmental quality in the region, but the pollution from historic mining activities continues to haunt the community to the present day.

In many cases senior levels of government are forced to manage reclamation and remediation activities at some of Canada's largest and most expensive toxic sites because the companies responsible for the contamination no longer exist. At the northern Saskatchewan uranium mines, the Saskatchewan Research Council (SRC) Project CLEANS (Cleanup of Abandoned Northern Sites) began work in 2008 to assess and remediate thirty-seven abandoned uranium mine and mine waste sites in the Uranium City area. These range from small adits (surface openings) that require sealing to massive, complex remediation projects like the Gunnar mine, dealing with contaminated mine buildings, a small open pit, and millions of tons of radioactive tailings on the shore of Lake Athabasca. After years of study, regulatory reviews, and community consultations, SRC began major remediation activities at Gunnar, including capping the tailings to prevent contaminant flows into the lake. But, as at many abandoned mine sites, the costs of remediation have soared, from an original estimate of $24.6 million to more than a quarter billion dollars for the Gunnar site alone, and federal and provincial governments disputed how much of the tab each should pick up.

As eye-popping as those costs are, they are dwarfed by

At Yellowknife's abandoned Giant Mine, these fork-like thermosyphons will use air exchange technology to freeze underground rock chambers containing arsenic wastes, the byproduct of fifty years of gold ore roasting.

Canada's two most notorious abandoned mines: Cyprus-Anvil (Faro, Yukon) and Giant (Yellowknife, Northwest Territories). As noted in Chapter 5, the owners of these mines went bankrupt in the late 1990s, victims of low mineral prices and declining ore grades. Now they account for two of the biggest cleanup bills for abandoned mines in Canada, in the neighbourhood of $1 billion each merely to contain, let alone remove, the toxic material at the sites. Aside from these high costs, the Giant and Faro sites illustrate the often controversial strategies for dealing with mine wastes, raising the thorny question of how to manage the very long-term challenges posed by such complex wastes.

At the Faro mine complex, the main concern is the hundreds of millions of tons of acid-producing waste rock and tailings. These mine wastes and associated contamination affect approximately 2,500 hectares, and include 70 million tons of tailings and 320 million tons of waste rock. Obviously the lingering presence of such a large-scale contaminated site represents a grave concern to local communities such as the Kaska Dena people of Ross River, the Liard First Nation, and the former mining town of Faro. The mine is part of the federal contaminated sites program, but the Yukon Government assumed responsibility for care and maintenance of the site in 2003 while the governments devised an initial remediation plan. Although general closure objectives were established, and some remediation work has been undertaken, a detailed remediation plan had yet to be established by 2017 — in spite of expenditures of over $350 million at the site. After the federal government again took

over the site, a new plan was developed. The final bill for the Faro mine remediation is forecast to come in at over a billion dollars, not including the costs for the perpetual care, maintenance, and water treatment that will be required.

Like Faro, Giant Mine illustrates the often very long-term environmental legacies. As detailed in Chapter 4, decades of gold roasting produced more than 237,000 tons of arsenic trioxide as a byproduct. This material was stored in mined-out underground chambers under the misguided assumption that it would be encased in permafrost. Instead, with the mine's bankruptcy and eventual closure in 2004 the problem of arsenic management fell to the federal Department of Indian and Northern Affairs (which became Crown—Indigenous Relations and Northern Affairs in 2017). Located right across Yellowknife's Back Bay from the city's Old Town and the Dene community of Ndilo, the potential mobilization of this highly toxic and easily water-soluble material poses a grave environmental threat. To address this problem, the government proposed a controversial solution: to freeze the arsenic in its underground chambers using thermosyphons, an air-exchange technology intended to re-establish permafrost and contain the poison "in perpetuity." In addition, the government proposed to remediate the vast tailings sites and surface contamination around the former mine site.

For many in Yellowknife, the prospect of living on a permanent toxic site did not sit well. For the Yellowknives Dene in particular, the toxic mine site had become a symbol of their exclusion from the benefits of mining and the poisoning they suffered during the mine's operation. The community voiced deep concerns with the proposal to permanently store arsenic underground. Public concern led to an unprecedented four-year environmental assessment of the proposal, including public hearings and major technical reviews. When the Mackenzie

Valley Review Board handed down its decision in 2013, it recommended the project be licensed for only one hundred years, and mandated significant safeguards such as independent oversight, project reviews, research into alternative solutions, and a human health risk assessment.

Still, the sheer scope and severity of the toxicity at Giant raises difficult questions about the mine's past, present, and future. Although many in Yellowknife are proud of the city's mining heritage (and the region's ongoing engagement with mining), the catastrophe at Giant has led to some reckoning with mining's dark side. In 2016, new research documented how historical arsenic contamination from the mine's smokestack is still detectable in lakes more than seventeen kilometres from the mine site, prompting new warnings about drinking local lake water. The billion dollar cost of the Giant Mine Remediation Project does not account for the costs of long-term water treatment, maintenance, and monitoring of the site for decades or more after completion. And although the remediation project is licensed for only a hundred years, the prospect of long-term arsenic storage at the site raises hard questions around how funding, management, and knowledge of the site can be maintained into the distant future. How do we keep people in the future from entering the arsenic chambers? How can we explain to them what must be done to keep the arsenic contained? From 2013–17, the question of how to communicate these hazards to future generations was the focus of research involving the authors and community members in Yellowknife, including officials from the remediation project team. While no concrete strategies have been developed as of writing, the participants have increasingly recognized the importance of commemorating the mine site and undertaking deliberate strategies of "remembering" and communication to ensure a continuity of knowledge and the protection of future generations from what some Yellowknives Dene members describe as a toxic underground "monster."

Perhaps more than any other example, Giant Mine reminds us that abandoned mines too often cannot be confined to the realm of heritage and memory. Many forsaken mines continue to exert a detrimental material influence on landscapes of the present. Barring major breakthroughs in remediation technology, the toxic zombie mines demand that we think about issues of care and responsibility across the unimaginable span of deep time (ironically, the same timespans over which these ore bodies formed). Even at sites where a cleanup program is possible, the price tag (often borne by the public purse) is often large and the risks to nearby residents are significant as toxic material is mobilized (or contained) at the site.

In recent years historians and geographers have described contaminated sites more broadly as sacrifice zones, spaces designated as expendable when faced with the relentless expansion of modern industrial development. In Canada, a country with huge expanses of land unsuitable for agriculture, the mining industry has produced large numbers of these sacrificial wastelands, a process that has only accelerated since the early 2000s as the oil industry pursued a vast and unprecedented expansion of open-pit bitumen mining in the Athabasca region of northern Alberta. As with mineral mining projects, oil sands development has raised concerns about the destruction of wildlife habitat, water pollution, and landscape scarring, as well as whether the problem of containing toxic wastes (bitumen, naphthenic acids, cyanide, and heavy metals) in enormous tailings ponds will come to haunt future generations. Environmental remediation and restoration of landscapes degraded by decades of oil sands extraction has barely begun. As in Canada's earlier periods of mineral development, short-term thinking and a development-at-all-costs mentality tend to overwhelm cautionary approaches to mining. Absent a radical shift toward extensive metal recycling, alternative energy, and a much less material-intensive economy, we will continue to see more zombie mines produced across Canada, sites that future historians will see as markers not only of our industrial heritage and labour, but also as symbols of our immoderate and sometimes indifferent attitude toward the natural world.

The closed and partially flooded Jeffrey Mine pit, Asbestos, Quebec. Open pit mining exemplifies the often permanent landscape scars that accompany large-scale mining development.

CONCLUSION

The History and Future of Mining in Canada

The mining industry is everywhere in Canada. The industry's products — metals, gems, hydrocarbons, radiological material, rare earth elements, and even construction aggregate — are implicated in every aspect of our daily lives, from small things such as sending a text message on a cellphone to much larger objects such as the vehicles we drive and the massive buildings and infrastructure where urban dwellers live and work. Some might argue that the mining industry is no longer central to the Canadian economy, with many iconic Canadian companies sold off to foreign owners and mining activity accounting for only a small share (about 5 per cent) of the country's GDP in 2019. But the industry remains important in many parts of the country and, as this book has made clear, mining was woven into key periods in Canada's history: the rise of Indigenous copper cultures, European exploration, national expansion, industrialization, military conflict, and the colonial displacement of Indigenous people. Often hidden from view have been the industry's unwanted byproducts — pollution, landscape change, and waste sites — that have accumulated and may persist for unimaginably long periods of time at some abandoned mine sites. If mining has provided Canada with jobs, economic growth, foreign capital investment, and energy sources, many examples in this book demonstrate that the industry carried often-unacknowledged costs that may stretch into the distant future.

It is no exaggeration, however, to suggest that the mining industry in Canada (as in many other areas of the globe) provided the material base for modern society. Life as we know it in the industrialized world simply would not be possible if Canadians relied solely on organic materials such as wood and cotton fabric. If we could go back in time to the nineteenth century and subtract the mining industry's marquee energy product, namely coal, then Canada would have been hard pressed to find a cheap substitute to fuel urbanization and industrialization (at least until petroleum came on stream). Canadians owe a great deal to the mining industry for furnishing so many of our needs and desires, not least to the miners who drew all this material from the ground, often at great risk to their health and their lives. From this vantage point, it is easy to understand why so many communities have gone to such great lengths to commemorate and celebrate their heritage of labour and ingenuity in wresting ore from the Earth and transforming it into useful material and energy for human use.

But to view Canada's mining history only through the frame of material prosperity and technological progress obscures fundamental questions about whether such minerals-fed materialism can be sustained. Even a cursory assessment of mining history in Canada (and elsewhere) suggests that the environmental impacts and social injustices associated with mineral exploitation are far from trivial, exacting a significant cost for the relative affluence the industry has helped generate — costs that are often left for the public to bear. Too often money set aside to offset eventual cleanup costs is inadequate, failing to account for

Wind power installations (like this site on Prince Edward Island) and other sustainable energy developments are likely to increase demand for "green" minerals. Meeting this demand while addressing mining's social obligations and toxic legacies is a central sustainability challenge for the industry.

rising project costs over time and doing little to address the issue of mining companies that abandon ship after only a few years into the expected life of a project, before cleanup funds have sufficiently accumulated. If a mining project collapses suddenly, whether because of falling commodity prices or ore depletion, communities may lose their economic foundations, and the remaining population is left to navigate the complicated and sometimes risky prospect of mine remediation. Obviously many remote communities in Canada have benefited immensely from mining, particularly in recent decades as mining companies have begun to negotiate impacts and benefits agreements prior to development. Too often, however, local and particularly Indigenous communities have borne the brunt of environmental and health impacts from mining, becoming frontline witnesses to the profound unsustainability of many of Canada's biggest mining operations. In this sense, remote mining regions have indeed become the "sacrifice zones" of the modern economy, places where the dirty work of extraction occurs far from the sites of consumption and wealth accumulation in distant cities.

Consider Pine Point. As described in Chapter 4, the community was established on the south shore of Great Slave Lake in the Northwest Territories around a major lead-zinc mine, founded on a vision of modern prosperity and amenities to be unlocked by large-scale mining. And for about a quarter century, this vision held — at least for those able to access the jobs and modern housing offered by the company. But when ore prices collapsed in the late 1980s, so did the community: the mine works were dismantled, the town's buildings were sold off or bulldozed, and the residents dispersed. Today, all that remains are the eerie streets and sidewalks of the town, being slowly reclaimed by fireweed and other local vegetation. A few curious explorers find Pine Point and drive its streets and haul roads, to wonder at the azure waters of the open pits, tour the bizarre open-air archive of drill-core boxes, or to race around its spacious roads on recreational vehicles. Nearby Dene and Métis communities, who benefited only marginally from the mine's operation, express concern about the degraded landscape left behind, while eyeing contemporary redevelopment discussions targeting Pine Point with a mixture of hope and uncertainty. If there was ever a landscape that embodied the fickle promise of mineral development, especially in remote regions, Pine Point is it.

In recent decades there has been a push toward more environmental responsibility in the Canadian mining sector. The Toward Sustainable Mining (TSM) initiative was launched in 2004 as an industry-led voluntary program in

Canada that promotes practices such as energy efficiency, pollution control, community outreach, and greenhouse-gas reductions. While the TSM represents considerable progress when measured against the industry's historical tendency to ignore environmental and community concerns, it is unlikely that large-scale mining can ever become a truly sustainable activity. The problem is less one of the absolute supply of minerals — though this is unquestionably finite over time — but with the declining quality of mineral deposits. As engineer Gavin Mudd's research makes clear, ore grades (the percentage of valuable minerals within the surrounding rock) have declined markedly over time all over the globe, even as annual production rates for many minerals have increased. As high-grade deposits disappeared, the industry adopted open-pit mining as the prevailing method of extraction, moving vast amounts of earth to obtain relatively small amounts of minerals. As a result, more fossil-fuel energy is required per ton of minerals extracted, more greenhouse gases are generated, and more waste (crushed rock, tailings, and chemical runoff) is produced. Northern Alberta's bitumen mines are an extreme example of this downward trend. As the province's easily obtainable crude oil reserves declined, industry has pursued hydrocarbon mining operations that require large energy inputs, eliminating large tracts of boreal forest environments in northern Alberta, producing large amounts of greenhouse gases, and generating immense amounts of toxic waste in the form of contaminated tailings and water. For many, Alberta's oil sands operations have become the hallmark of an unsustainable economy, a key driver of climate change and biodiversity loss at the very historical moment human beings have little choice but to make the transition to renewable energy.

While there has been much public debate about sustainable energy, discussions about a renewable materials regime have only recently begun to gain traction, mostly in the form of the growing movements to refuse or at least reuse harmful plastics. Recycling initiatives for plastics and metals have been with us for decades, but they have done little to dent the endless production of petroleum-based plastics or the continual push of mining companies into new frontiers and ever-higher production rates for raw metals. In the case of metals, the problem is partly economic: it remains cheaper to process raw ore and/or concentrates from a few large-scale mines at a centralized smelter than it is to collect and process recycled metal from all of the literally millions of disaggregated sources throughout the globe. Green taxes on new metals (already proving a hard sell politically in Canada in the case of carbon taxes on fossil energy) and waste recovery in the form of mining landfills might alleviate some need for new mines. A truly sustainable mineral regime will, however, inevitably require a slackening of demand for the vast amounts of metal that are now required to manufacture everything from soda cans to military hardware. Nothing short of a transformation to a much less material-intensive economy will be required to reduce the unsustainable demand for mineral products.

If such a transformation seems impossible, or even vaguely utopian, consider how quickly the transition to new mineral and energy regimes occurred in Canada during the late nineteenth and the twentieth centuries. This transition to a mineral-intensive economy was not simply a natural one, a product of supply and demand; rather, industrial technologies and economies were deliberately introduced and fostered to generate markets and applications for minerals. In just a few short decades during the late nineteenth and early twentieth centuries, Canada's material and energy base changed radically as iron, coal, copper, and nickel ascended to pre-eminence. In theory, at least, a rapid transition to a more sustainable materials and energy regime is possible in the near future given the right combination of political will and technological change. In any event, alternative proposals to address future supply and ore quality crunches from some mining promoters range from the unappealing to the seemingly unrealistic. According to many predictions, within a decade humans will be mining commercially on the ocean floor, seeking in particular the rare-earth metals that are essential to the production of smartphones and (ironically) low-carbon technologies such as electric cars and wind turbines. Even more fanciful is the idea that the mining frontier will expand into space, relentlessly scouring nearby asteroids or even the moon for untold trillions of dollars' worth of valuable minerals. Some popular and academic debate has occurred about how to reconcile such new mining initiatives with potential ecological damage in new environments or the astronomical costs of impossibly long supply chains. Perhaps the image of spaceships ferrying ore across vast distances, or massive remotely operated vehicles scraping the ocean floor suggest the path of less material and energy use is the more viable one.

We completed this book amidst the global coronavirus pandemic of 2020, when calls to "build back better" suggested an accelerated energy transitions away from fossil fuels and the embrace of remote work with digital technologies. For some in the mining industry, these developments heralded a massive increase in mineral production, particularly nickel and the rare earth minerals so essential for the production of green energy and digital technologies. But as the environmental scientist Barry Commoner reminded us decades ago, "there is no free lunch." Re-organizing workplaces and energy production in an attempt to restrict carbon emissions and the risk of future pandemics may carry costs in the form of massive mineral extraction, power-sucking server farms, and toxic e-waste disposal. The material impacts of energy systems in the "virtual" world, while often out of sight, remain vast and unevenly distributed.

How one views the future of the mining industry revolves in part around whether one thinks its history is indicative of technological triumph or environmental disaster. In case of the latter, one need not stretch the imagination too far in Canada to see the physical manifestation of abandoned mines and ghost towns — places such as Giant Mine, Pine Point, and Faro — as emblems of broader environmental and societal collapse that can occur after resource exhaustion. These places carry wide symbolic currency in Canada and beyond, whether in the form of Northrop Frye's ghost towns, Jared Diamond's invocation of mining as a central metaphor for the

unsustainability and environmental decline of civilizations (in the popular book *Collapse)*, or the frequent use of underground mines as sources of evil in cultural products such as the *Lord of the Rings* or the dreadful Canadian horror flick *My Bloody Valentine* (featuring the deranged survivor of a coal mining accident, complete with a mining gear costume, as the slasher). Canadian photographer Edward Burtynsky, who has gained a large audience for his stark photographs of industrial resource landscapes, suggests his mining images are symbolic of a societal moral failing: "What this civilization leaves in the wake of its progress may be the opened and emptied earth, but in performing these incursions we also participate in the unwitting creation of gigantic monuments to our way of life."

Mining heritage enthusiasts might protest, with some justification, that abandoned mines are also monuments to the labour, technology, and ingenuity that miners applied to landscapes. Important histories of sacrifice and struggle are etched into these landscapes (and especially in the underground spaces less readily observed by visitors), and it is not in disrespect to these histories and communities that we highlight mining's post-industrial landscape scars. In places such as Sudbury, where mining caused extensive environmental degradation, the further application of technology and creativity has at least partially repaired the landscape. Nonetheless, the history of mining in Canada and other nations suggests we are far from inhabiting a world where energy and materials can be pulled from the ground without severe deleterious impacts. From the moment Frobisher arrived to seek gold near Baffin Island, the story of mining in Canada has been persistent growth in the amount of material that the industry digs from the ground and the unending (if at times uneven) expansion of the mineral frontier into new, often Indigenous, spaces. Canadians must at some point decide whether such endless growth of mineral extraction can be maintained much further into the future.

REFERENCES

1. With the possible exception of Basque whalers working on the Labrador coast in the mid-sixteenth century.

2. The later emergence of the Cape Breton and Nova Scotia coal industry is taken up in Chapter 2.

3. Although on a global scale Canada has never been a major producer of coal, and much coal was imported from the United States to meet domestic demand in Canada during the boom years.

4. After the Second World War French Canadians became the most populous ethnic group in both towns, which finally merged in 1986.

5. The Yellowknives also use the term *Weledeh* to describe their language and their area of traditional occupancy around the Yellowknife River.

6. Peter Blow's *Village of Widows* and David Henningson's *Somba Ke: The Money Place.*

7. The latter figure distorted somewhat by the fact that Newfoundland's Bell Island mine would have only been counted as part of Canadian production figures after Confederation in 1949. Gold was the notable laggard, declining by more than half during the 1951–73 period.

8. This study was conducted by author Keeling and master's student Patricia Boulter.

9. See pinepointrevisited.homestead.com.

10. See www.ianbrewsterphotography.com.

11. All figures are in 1993 dollars.

12. According to the Mining Association of Canada, the value of Canadian mineral production increased from roughly $20 billion to $43 billion between 2003 and 2013.

13. Uranerz eventually sold a 50 per cent stake in the mine to the Saskatchewan Mining Development Corporation, which then gained majority control after it became Cameco.

14. Of course, as outlined in Chapter 4, the use of replacement workers was a major issue in the Jeffrey Mine strike in 1949, but the premier of Quebec had declared labour action to be illegal.

BIBLIOGRAPHY

Abel, Kerry M. *Changing Places: History, Community, and Identity in Northeastern Ontario*. Montreal: McGill-Queen's University Press, 2006.

Aho, Aaro. *Hills of Silver: The Yukon's Mighty Keno Hill Mine*. Madeira Park, BC: Harbour Publishing, 2006.

Ali, Saleem H. (Saleem Hassan). *Mining, the Environment, and Indigenous Development Conflicts*. University of Arizona Press, 2003.

Andrews, Thomas G. *Killing for Coal: America's Deadliest Labor War*. Cambridge: Harvard University Press, 2010.

Angus, Charlie, and Brit Griffin. *We Lived a Life and Then Some: The Life, Death, and Life of a Mining Town*. Toronto: Between the Lines, 1996.

Archibald, Linda, Mary Crnkovich, and Status of Women Canada. *If Gender Mattered: A Case Study of Inuit Women, Land Claims and the Voisey's Bay Nickel Project*. Ottawa: Status of Women Canada, 1999. publications.gc.ca/site/eng/293449/publication.html.

Baird, Moira. "Uranium Exploration Heats Up: Aurora and Crosshair Spending Millions in Labrador." *The St. John's Telegram*, June 15, 2007: D1.

Baker, William M. "The Miners and the Mediator: The 1906 Lethbridge Strike and Mackenzie King." *Labour/Le Travail* 11 (1983): 89–117.

Baldwin, Doug. "A Study in Social Control: The Life of the Silver Miner in Northern Ontario." *Labour/Le Travail* 2 (1977): 79–106.

Baldwin, Douglas O., and David F. Duke. "'A Grey Wee Town': An Environmental History of Early Silver Mining at Cobalt, Ontario." *Urban History Review/Revue d'histoire urbaine* 34, no. 1 (2005): 71–87.

Barman, Jean. *The West Beyond the West: A history of British Columbia*. Toronto: University of Toronto Press, 1991.

Barnes, Michael. *Fortunes in the Ground: Cobalt, Porcupine and Kirkland Lake*. Erin, Ont.: Boston Mills Press, 1986.

Basque, Garnet. *Ghost Towns and Mining Camps of the Boundary Country*. Victoria: Heritage House Publishing, 1999.

Belshaw, John Douglas. *Colonization and Community: The Vancouver Island Coalfield and the Making of the British Columbian Working Class. Montreal and Kingston*: McGill-Queen's University Press, 2014.

Bercuson, David. "Labour Radicalism and the Western Industrial Frontier: 1897–1919." *Canadian Historical Review* 58, no. 2 (1977): 154-175.

Bernauer, Warren. "Mining in Caribou Calving Grounds: Can Nunavut Beat the Status Quo?" *Northern Public Affairs* 2, no. 3 (2014). www.northernpublicaffairs.ca/index/volume-2-issue-3-arctic-search-rescue/mining-in-caribou-calving-grounds-can-nunavut-beat-the-status-quo.

Bickis, Ian. "Troubled Cigar Lake Uranium Mine Gets Official Launch." *The Globe and Mail*, September 23, 2015. www.theglobeandmail.com/report-on-business/industry-news/energy-and-resources/troubled-cigar-lake-uranium-mine-gets-official-launch/article26494526/.

Bielawski, Ellen. *Rogue Diamonds: Northern Riches on Dene Land*. Seattle: University of Washington Press, 2004.

Bothwell, Robert. *Eldorado: Canada's National Uranium Company*. Toronto: University of Toronto Press, 1984.

Boutet, Jean-Sébastien. "Opening Ungava to Industry: a Decentering Approach to Indigenous History in Subarctic Québec, 1937–1954." *Cultural Geographies* 21, no. 1 (2014): 79–97.

Bowes-Lyon, Léa Marie, Jeremy P. Richards, and Tara M. McGee. "Socio-Economic Impacts of the Nanisivik and Polaris Mines, Nunavut, Canada." In *Mining, Society, and a Sustainable World*, 2009, 371–96. doi:10.1007/978-3-642-01103-0_13.

Bradbury, John H. "The Rise and Fall of the 'Fourth Empire of the St. Lawrence': The Quebec-Labrador Iron Ore Mining Region." *Cahiers de Géographie Du Québec* 29, no. 78 (1985): 351–64.

Bridge, Gavin and Phil McManus. "Sticks and Stones: Environmental Narratives and Discursive Regulation in the Forestry and Mining Sectors," JOUR, Antipode [Great Britain] 32, no. 1 (2000): 10–47.

Bridge, Gavin, "Resource Triumphalism: Postindustrial Narratives of Primary Commodity Production," *Environment and Planning* A 33, no. 12 (2001): 2149–73, doi:10.1068/a33190.

Brown, David Roger. *Blood on the Coal: The Story of the Springhill Mining Disaster*. Halifax: Nimbus, 2002.

Bryce, Robert. *Canada and the Cost of World War II: The International Operations of Canada's Department of Finance, 1939–1947*. Montreal: McGill-Queen's University Press, 2005.

Buckingham, Graham. *Thompson: A City and Its People*. Thompson, MN: Thompson Historical Society, 1988. http://manitoba.ca/resources/books/local_histories/107.pdf (last accessed 15 May 2016)

Buik, William A. "Noranda Mines Limited: A Study in Business and Economic History." M.A. Thesis. University of Toronto, 1958.

Bullen, Warwick, and Malcolm Robb. "Socio-Economic Impact of Gold Mining in the Yellowknife Mining District." 2002. www.miningnorth.com/_rsc/site-content/library/Socio-Economic%20Impacts%20of%20Gold%20Mining%20in%20Yellowknife%202002.pdf (last accessed on 20 June 2016).

Cameron, Emilie. "Copper stories: Imaginative Geographies and Material Orderings of the Central Canadian Arctic. In Baldwin, A., Cameron L., and Kobayashi A. (eds) *Rethinking the Great White North: Race, Nature, and Whiteness in Canada* (Vancouver: UBC Press, 2011) 169–190.

Cameron, Emilie. *Far Off Metal River: Inuit Lands, Settler Stories, and the Making of the Contemporary Arctic*. Vancouver: UBC Press, 2015.

Canada-Déline Uranium Table. *Final Report Concerning Health and Environmental Issues Related to the Port Radium Mine*. Ottawa: Indian and Northern Affairs Canada, 2005.

Canadian Broadcasting Corporation (CBC) News. "Lynn Lake Burns Abandoned Homes Littering Town." Nov. 28, 2013. www.cbc.ca/news/canada/manitoba/lynn-lake-burns-abandoned-homes-littering-town-1.2441906 (accessed April 15, 2016).

Canadian Broadcasting Corporation. "Manitoba Responds to Lynn Lake Residents' Cancer Concerns: Residents Believe Toxic Mine Waste Under Community is Making them Sick." Nov. 28, 2013. www.cbc.ca/news/canada/manitoba/manitoba-responds-to-lynn-lake-residents-cancer-concerns-1.2444398 (accessed April 15, 2016).

Canadian Broadcasting Corporation. "Camecon Puts Northern Sask. Mellenium Mine on Hold." May 17, 2014. www.cbc.ca/news/canada/saskatchewan/cameco-puts-northern-sask-millennium-uranium-mine-on-hold-1.2646313.

Canadian Broadcasting Corporation. "Government now Maintaining Jericho Diamond Mine, Company Says." December 15, 2008. www.cbc.ca/news/business/government-now-maintaining-jericho-diamond-mine-company-says-1.728402

Canadian Broadcasting Corporation. "Mount Polley Mine Spill Fallout: Neskonlith Deliver Ruddock Eviction Notice, Red Chris Blockade Continues." August 14, 2014. www.cbc.ca/news/canada/british-columbia/mount-polley-mine-spill-fallout-neskonlith-deliver-ruddock-eviction-notice-red-chris-blockade-continues-1.2736711.

Canadian Broadcasting Corporation. "Yellowknife Diamond-Cutting Plant's Future in Limbo." June 11, 2009. www.cbc.ca/news/canada/north/yellowknife-diamond-cutting-plant-s-future-in-limbo-1.800202.

Canadian Environmental Assessment Agency. *Report of the EUB-CEAA Joint Panel, Cheviot Coal Project*. August 2000. www.ceaa.gc.ca/D9BC55EE-docs/report-eng.pdf.

Canadian Nuclear Safety Commission. *History of Uranium Mining in the Elliot Lake Region of Ontario and Associated Effects on Water Quality and Fish Intended for Human Consumption*. January 2015. www.bape.gouv.qc.ca/sections/mandats/uranium-enjeux/documents/NAT32_VA.pdf.

Canadian Press. "Red Chris Mine Gets Green Light from BC" June 19, 2015. www.cbc.ca/news/canada/british-columbia/red-chris-mine-gets-green-light-from-b-c-government-1.3121297.

Canadian Press. "Taseko Mines Sues over Blocked New Prosperity Proposal." February 12, 2016. www.cbc.ca/news/canada/british-columbia/taseko-mine-new-prosperity-bc-supreme-court-1.3446271.

Canadian Press."Panel sees BC Mine as Environmental Threat." July 2, 2010. www.cbc.ca/news/canada/british-columbia/panel-sees-b-c-mine-as-environmental-threat-1.922239.

Canadian Public Health Association, Task Force on Arsenic. *Final Report: Yellowknife, Northwest Territories*. Ottawa: CPHA, 1977.

Careless, James M.S. *The Rise of Cities in Canada before 1914*. Ottawa: Canadian Historical Association, 1978.

Casdorph, Herman Richard and Morton Walker. *Toxic Metal Syndrome*. Penguin, 1995.

Cater, Tara, and Arn Keeling. "'That's Where Our Future Came from': Mining, Landscape, and Memory in Rankin Inlet, Nunavut." *Études/Inuit/Studies* 37, no. 2 (June 23, 2014): 59–82.

Clement, Wallace. *Hardrock Mining: Industrial Relations and Technological Changes at Inco*. Toronto: McClelland & Stewart, 1981.

Coates, Ken, and William Morrison. *Land of the Midnight Sun: A History of the Yukon*. Montreal and Kingston: McGill-Queen's University Press, 2005.

Coates, Ken. "The Klondike Gold Rush in World History: Putting the Stampede in Perspective," *Northern Review* 19 (Winter 1988): 21–35.

Collins, Paul. "No Other Choice: Industrial Disease and the St. Lawrence Fluorspar Mines, 1933–2011." Paper prepared for Provincial Historic Commemorations Board, Government of Newfoundland and Labrador, September 1, 2014. http://commemorations.ca/wp-content/uploads/2014/11/St-Lawrence-Miners-Commemorations-Paper-by-Paul-W-Collins-PhD.pdf (accessed June 18, 2016).

Commito, Mike, and Kaleigh Bradley, "It's History, Like it or Not: The Significance of Sudbury's Superstack." ActiveHistory.ca Blog (November 17, 2014) http://activehistory.ca/2014/11/its-history-like-it-or-not-the-significance-of-sudburys-superstack/.

Condon, Richard G. *The Northern Copper Inuit: a History*. Toronto: University of Toronto Press, 1996.

Cooper, H. Kory. "Copper and Social Complexity: Frederica de Laguna's Contribution to Our Understanding of the Role of Metals in Native Alaskan Society." *Arctic Anthropology* 43, no. 2 (2006): 148–63.

———. "Innovation and Prestige Among Northern Hunter-Gatherers: Late Prehistoric Native Copper Use in Alaska and Yukon." *American Antiquity* 77, no. 3 (2012): 565–90.

Cooper, H. Kory, John M. Duke, Antonio Simonetti, and GuangCheng Chen. 2008. "Trace Element and Pb Isotope Provenance Analyses of Native Copper in Northwestern North America: Results of a Recent Pilot Study Using INAA, ICP-MS, and LA-MC-ICP-MS." *Journal of Archaeological Science* 35 (6): 1732–47.

Cordier, S., G. Theriault, and H. Iturra. "Mortality Patterns in a Population Living Near a Copper Smelter." *Environmental Research* 31, no. 2 (1983): 311–322.

Cowan, Paul. *Westray*. Ottawa: National Film Board of Canada, 2001.

Cox, David J. "Environmental Impact Assessments and Impact Benefits Agreements: The Participation of Aboriginal Women at Voisey's Bay Mine." Thesis. McMaster University, 2013.

Cranstone, Donald A. *A History of Mining and Mineral Exploration in Canada and Outlook for the Future*. Ottawa: Natural Resources Canada, 2002. publications.gc.ca/collections/Collection/M37-51-2002E.pdf.

Cross, L.D. *Treasure under the Tundra: Canada's Arctic Diamonds*. Victoria: Heritage House Publishing, 2011.

Cuffe, Sandra. "Uranium Debate Heats up in Northern Saskatchewan." *The Media Coop*, October 26, 2012. www.mediacoop.ca/story/uranium-debate-heats-saskatchewan/13907.

Cuffe, Sandra. "Uranium's Chilling Effects." *The Media Coop*, November 21, 2013. www.mediacoop.ca/index.php?q=story/uraniums-chilling-effects/19083.

Danielson, Vivian and James Whyte. *Bre-X: Gold Today, Gone Tomorrow: Anatomy of the Busang Swindle*. Toronto: Northern Miner, 1997.

De Villiers, A.J. and J.P. Windish. "Lung Cancer in a Fluorspar Mining Community," *British Journal of Industrial Medicine* 21, no. 94 (1964): 94–109.

De Villiers, A.J. and P.M. Baker. *An Investigation of the Health Status of Inhabitants of Yellowknife, Northwest Territories*. Ottawa: Occupational Health Division, Environmental Health Directorate, Department of Health and Welfare, 1970.

Délı̨nę Uranium Team. *If Only We Had Known: The History of Port Radium as Told by the Sahtúot'ı̨nę*. Délı̨nę, NWT: Délı̨nę Uranium Team, 2005.

DeMont, John. *Coal Black Heart: The Story of Coal and the Lives It Ruled*. Doubleday. 1990.

Denny, J.J., W.D. Robson, and Dudley A. Irwin. "The Prevention of Silicosis by Metallic Aluminum. I. A Preliminary

Report." *Canadian Medical Association Journal* 37.1 (1937): 1–11.

Deprez, Paul. *The Pine Point Mine and the Development of the Area South of Great Slave Lake.* Winnipeg, MB: Center for Settlement Studies, 1973.

Diefenbaker, John. "A New Vision." www. canadahistory.com/sections/documents/ Primeministers/diefenbaker/docs-thenorthernvision.htm.

Dominion Bureau of Statistics. *Chronological Record of Canadian Mining Events from 1604 to 1943 and Historical Tables of the Mineral Production of Canada.* Ottawa: King's Printer, 1945. www.empr.gov.bc.ca/Mining/ Geoscience/PublicationsCatalogue/ MiscellaneousPublications/ Documents/1604_1943tablesBC.pdf.

Dominion Government of Canada, Department of the Interior. Natural Resources of Quebec. Ottawa: King's Printer, 1923.

Dominion Government of Canada, Department of the Interior. Natural Resources of Quebec. Ottawa: King's Printer, 1929.

Dow, Alexander C. "Metal Mining and Canadian Economic Development to 1939." *Business History* 32, no. 3 (1990): 146-161.

Dumaresq, Charles. *Cobalt Mining Legacy.* www. cobaltmininglegacy.ca/index.php.

Dunn, A.R. "The Marmora Ironworks in Upper Canada: The first phase 1819 to 1826." *Historical Metallurgy* 14:2 (1980): 74–79.

Ehrhardt, Kathleen L. 2009. "Copper Working Technologies, Contexts of Use, and Social Complexity in the Eastern Woodlands of Native North America." *Journal of World Prehistory* 22: 213–35.

Evenden, Matthew. "Aluminum, Commodity Chains, and the Environmental History of the Second World War." *Environmental History* 16, no. 1 (2011): 69–93.

Falcon-Lang, Howard. "Earliest History of Coal Mining and Grindstone Quarrying at Joggins, Nova Scotia, and its Implications for the Meaning of the Place Name 'Joggins.'" *Atlantic Geology* 45 (2009), doi:10.4132/ atlgeol.2009.001.

Fetherling, Douglas. *The Gold Crusades: A Social History of Gold Rushes, 1849–1929,* rev. ed. Toronto: University of Toronto Press, 1997.

Ficken, Robert E. *Unsettled Boundaries: Fraser Gold and the British-American Northwest.* Pullman: Washington State University Press, 2003.

Fitzpatrick, Patricia, Alberto Fonseca, and Mary Louise McAllister. "From the Whitehorse Mining Initiative towards Sustainable Mining: Lessons Learned." *Journal of Cleaner Production* 19, no. 4 (2011): 376–84, doi:10.1016/j.jclepro.2010.10.013.

Forestell, Nancy M. "'And I Feel Like I'm Dying from Mining for Gold': Disability, Gender, and the Mining Community." *Labor: Studies in Working-Class History of the Americas* 3, no. 3 (2006): 77.

Gagné, Daniel. "Blood Lead Levels in Noranda Children Following Removal of Smelter-Contaminated Yard Soil." *Canadian Journal of Public Health / Revue canadienne de santé publique* 85, no. 3 (1993): 163–166.

Gardner, S.L. Coal Resources and Coal Mining on Vancouver Island. Ministry of Energy and Mines, Government of British Columbia, Geological Survey Branch, 1999 http:// www.empr.gov.bc.ca/Mining/Geoscience/ PublicationsCatalogue/OpenFiles/1999/ Documents/OF1999-08_report.pdf.

Gerriets, Marilyn. "The Impact of the General Mining Association on the Nova Scotia Coal Industry, 1826-1850." *Acadiensis* 21, 1 (Autumn 1991): 54-84.

Gibson, Ginger, and Jason Klinck. "Canada's Resilient North: The Impact of Mining on Aboriginal Communities." *Pimatisiwin: A*

Journal of Aboriginal and Indigenous Community Health 3, no. 1 (2005): 116–39.

Gibson, Robert B. "Sustainability Assessment and Conflict Resolution: Reaching Agreement to Proceed with the Voisey's Bay Nickel Mine." *Journal of Cleaner Production* 14, no. 3–4 (2006): 334–48, doi:10.1016/j. jclepro.2004.07.007.

Glenday, Daniel. "Dependency, Class Relations and Politics in Rouyn-Noranda, Québec." PhD Thesis. Carleton University, 1981.

———. "Le domain colonial: Class Formation in a Natural Resource Enclave." *Canadian Journal of Sociology / Cahiers canadiens de sociologie* (1984): 159–177.

Godkin, David. "Tough Slogging for BC Coal Miners." *Canadian Mining Journal* (January 1, 2015). www.canadianminingjournal. com/features/tough-slugging-for-bcs-coal-miners/ (accessed 14 April 14th, 2016).

Golder Associates. "Cultural Heritage Evaluation Report: Deloro Mine Site, Township of Marmora and Lake County of Hastings, Ontario." Ontario Ministry of Environment, April 2012.

Goldie, Raymond. *Inco Comes to Labrador.* St. John's, NL: Flanker Press, 2005.

Gordan, Katherine. *The Slocan: Portrait of a Valley.* Winlaw, BC Sononis Press, 2004.

Gordon, Sarah. "Narratives Unearthed, or, How an Abandoned Mine Doesn't Really Abandon You." In Arn Keeling and John Sandlos, eds. *Mining and Communities in Northern Canada: History, Politics and Memory.* Calgary: University of Calgary Press, 61–87.

Government of the Northwest Territories and BHP Diamonds, Inc. Socio-Economic Agreement: BHP Diamonds Project. www.miningnorth.com/wp-content/ uploads/2011/10/EKATI-Socio-Economic-Agreement.pdf.

Graffam, Gray. "Archaeology at the Marmora Iron Works: Results of the 1984 Field Season." *Ontario Archaeology* 43 (1985): 41–53.

Granatstein, J.L. "Arming the Nation: Canada's Industrial War Effort, 1939–45." A Paper for the Canadian Council of Chief Executives, May 27, 2005. www. ceocouncil.ca/wp-content/uploads/archives/ Arming_the_Nation_A_Paper_Prepared_ by_Dr_Granatstein_May_2005.pdf (accessed February 14, 2016).

Gray, John. "We'll Think No More of Inco." *The Globe and Mail Report on Business Magazine.* March 26, 2010. www. theglobeandmail.com/report-on-business/ rob-magazine/well-think-no-more-of-inco/ article1210160/?page=all.

Grinev, Andrei V. "On the Banks of the Copper River: The Ahtna Indians and the Russians." *Arctic Anthropology* 30, no. 1 (1993): 54–66.

Gulig, Anthony G. "'Determined to Burn Off the Entire Country': Prospectors, Caribou, and the Denesuliné in Northern Saskatchewan, 1900–1940." *American Indian Quarterly* 26, no. 3 (2002): 335–59, doi:10.1353/aiq.2003.0039.

Haalboom, Bethany. "Pursuing Openings and Navigating Closures for Aboriginal Knowledges in Environmental Governance of Uranium Mining, Saskatchewan, Canada." The Extractive Industries and Society, 2016, doi.org/10.1016/j. exis.2016.09.002.

Hagar, Albert David. "Ancient Mining on the Shores of Lake Superior." *Atlantic Monthly* 89 (March, 1865): 308–15.

Hall, Rebecca. "Diamond Mining in Canada's Northwest Territories: A Colonial Continuity." *Antipode* 45, no. 2 (2013): 376– 93, doi:10.1111/j.1467-8330.2012.01012.x.

Halpern, Joel. "Use of Minerals by the Copper Eskimo." *Rocks and Minerals* 68 (1952): 21-24.

Hanahan, Fred. Testimony. Proceedings of the Public Inquiry into the Springhill Mining Disaster, 1958. www.mininghistory.ns.ca/ springhill/sp-t-186.htm (accessed 13 May 2016).

Harding, Jim. *Canada's Deadly Secret : Saskatchewan Uranium and the Global Nuclear System.* Black Point, NS: Fernwood Publishing, 2007.

———. *Social Policy and Social Justice : The NDP Government in Saskatchewan during the Blakeney Years.* Waterloo, ON: Wilfrid Laurier University Press, 1995.

Hill, Mark A. "The Benefit of the Gift: Exchange and Social Interaction in the Late Archaic Western Great Lakes." PhD Dissertation. Washington State University, 2009.

———. "Tracing Social Interaction: Perspectives on Archaic Copper Exchange from the Upper Great Lakes." *American Antiquity* 77, no. 2 (2012): 279–92.

Hind, Henry Youle. *Eighty Years' Progress of British North America.* London: Samson Low, Son, & Marston, 1863.

Hinde, John R. *When Coal was King: Ladysmith and the Coal-Mining Industry on Vancouver Island.* Vancouver: UBC Press, 2003.

Hogan, Brian F. *Cobalt: Year of the Strike, 1919.* Cobalt, ON: Highway Book Shop, 1978.

Holmes, William H. "Aboriginal Copper Mines of Isle Royale, Lake Superior." *American Anthropologist* 3, no. 8 (1901): 684–96.

Hoogeveen, Dawn. "Sub-Surface Property, Free-Entry Mineral Staking and Settler Colonialism in Canada." *Antipode* 47, no. 1 (2015): 121–38.

Hornsby, Stephen J. *Nineteenth-Century Cape Breton: A Historical Geography.* Montreal: McGill-Queen's University Press, 1992.

Horvath, Julia. Development and Implementation of a Closure and Remediation Plan: A Case Study of the Faro Mine Closure Project, YT. Queen's University, April 2011. www.queensu.ca/ ensc/sites/webpublish.queensu.ca.enscwww/ files/files/501/Horvath_ENSC501.pdf.

Hovis, Logan, and Jeremy Mouat. "Miners, Engineers, and the Transformation of Work in the Western Mining Industry, 1880-1930," *Technology and Culture* 37:3 (1996): 429-456.

Innes, Larry. "Staking Claims: Innu Rights and Mining Claims at Voisey's Bay." *Cultural Survival Quarterly* 25, no. 1 (2001). https:// www.culturalsurvival.org/publications/ cultural-survival-quarterly/canada/staking-claims-innu-rights-and-mining-claims-voiseys.

Innis, Harold A. *Essays in Canadian Economic History.* Edited by Mary Q. Innis. Toronto: University of Toronto Press, 1962.

———. *Settlement and the Mining Frontier.* Toronto: Macmillan, 1936.

Jenness, Diamond. *The Life of the Copper Eskimos.* Volume XII of the Report of the Canadian Arctic Expedition. New York: Johnson Reprint, 1970 orig. 1946.

Jewiss, Thomas. "The Mining History of the Sudbury Basin." https://uwaterloo.ca/earth-sciences-museum/resources/mining-canada/ mining-history-sudbury-area.

Johnston, Hugh I.M. (ed.) *The Pacific Province: A history of British Columbia.* Vancouver: Douglas & McIntyre, 1996.

Jorgenson, Mica. "'Into that Country to Work': Aboriginal Economic Activities during Barkerville's Gold Rush." *BC Studies* 185 (Spring 2015): 109–136.

Keeling, Arn. "'Born in an Atomic Test Tube': Landscapes of Cyclonic Development at Uranium City, Saskatchewan." *Canadian Geographer* 54, no. 2 (2010): 228–52.

Keeling, Arn, and John Sandlos. "Environmental Justice Goes Underground? Historical Notes

from Canada's Northern Mining Frontier." *Environmental Justice* 2, no. 3 (2009): 117–25.

Keeling, Arn and Patricia Boulter. "From Igloo to Mineshaft: Inuit Labour and Memory at the Rankin Inlet Nickel Mine." In *Mining and Communities in Northern Canada: History, Politics, and Memory,* eds. Arn Keeling and John Sandlos. Calgary: University of Calgary Press, 2015, 35–58.

Kelly, Lindsay. "Remediation Work Paying Off at Former Cobalt Mines." *Northern Ontario Business.* December 8, 2014. http://www. northernontariobusiness.com/Regional-News/Temiskaming-and-Region/2014/08/ Remediation-work-paying-off-at-former-Cobalt-mines.aspx.

Kennedy, Michael. "Fraser River Placer Mining Landscapes." *BC Studies* 160 (Winter 2008/09): 35–66.

Kinnear, John. "Looking Back: A Short History of Coal Mining in the Elk Valley." *Crowsnest Pass Herald,* August 14, 2012. http:// passherald.ca/archives/120814/index5.htm (accessed April 30, 2016).

Kuhlberg, Mark, and Scott Miller. "'Protection to the Sulphur-Smoke Tort-Feasors': The Tragedy of Pollution in Sudbury, Ontario, the World's Nickel Capital, 1884-1927." *Canadian Historical Review* 99, no. 2 (2018): 225–57.

Kulchyski, Peter Keith and Frank J Tester. *Kiumajut (Talking Back): Game Management and Inuit Rights, 1900–70.* Vancouver: UBC Press, 2007.

Kuyek, Joan. "After the Mine: Lynn Lake, Manitoba." MiningWatch Canada Blog, May 27, 2004 http://miningwatch.ca/ blog/2004/5/27/after-mine-lynn-lake-manitoba (accessed June 12, 2016).

Kwong, Y.T.J., S. Beauchemin, M.F. Hossain, and W.D. Gould. "Transformation and Mobilization of Arsenic in the Historic Cobalt Mining Camp, Ontario, Canada." *Journal of Geochemical Exploration* 92, no. 2 (2007): 133–150.

Leacock, Stephen. *My Discovery of the West.* Toronto: T. Allen, 1937.

Leadbeater, David, ed. *Mining Town Crisis: Globalization, Labour, and Resistance in Sudbury.* Toronto: Brunswick Books, 2008.

LeCain, Timothy. *Mass Destruction: The Men and Giant Mines that Wired America and Scarred the Planet.* New Brunswick, NJ: Rutgers University Press, 2009.

———. "The Limits of Eco-Efficiency: Arsenic Pollution and the Cottrell Electrical Precipitator in the US Copper Smelting Industry." *Environmental History* 5, no. 3 (2000): 336–351.

Leddy, Lianne C. "Cold War Colonialism: The Serpent River First Nation and Uranium Mining, 1953–1988." PhD Thesis. Wilfrid Laurier University, 2011.

Levine, Mary Ann. "Determining the Provenance of Native Copper Artifacts from Northeastern North America: Evidence from Instrumental Neutron Activation Analysis." *Journal of Archaeological Science* 34, no. 4 (2007): 572–87.

———. "Native Copper, Hunter-Gatherers and Northeastern Prehistory." PhD Thesis, 1996. University of Amherst, Massachusetts.

———. "Overcoming Disciplinary Solitude: The Archaeology and Geology of Native Copper in Eastern North America." *Geoarchaeology* 22, no. 1 (2007): 49–66.

Leyton, Elliott. *Dying Hard: Industrial Carnage in St. Lawrence, Newfoundland.* Toronto: McClelland & Stewart, 1975.

Lowe, Mick. *Premature Bonanza: Standoff at Voisey's Bay.* Toronto: Between the Lines, 1998.

Lutz, John Sutton. *Makuk: A New History of Aboriginal-White Relations.* Vancouver: UBC Press, 2008.

MacDowell, Laurel Sefton. *Remember Kirkland Lake: The Gold Miners' Strike of 1941–42.* Toronto: Canadian Scholars' Press, 2001.

MacPherson, Alex. "500 Jobs Cut as Cameco Closes Rabbit Lake Uranium Mine." *Saskatoon StarPhoenix* April 21, 2016. http://thestarphoenix.com/business/local-business/cameco-to-shutter-rabbit-lake-curtail-u-s-operations-at-cost-of-585-jobs.

Macpherson, Janet E. "The Pine Point Mine" and "The Cyprus Anvil Mine," in *Northern Transitions*, vol. 1, ed. Everett B. Peterson and Janet B. Wright. Ottawa: Canadian Arctic Resources Committee, 1978, 65–148.

Main, O.W. *The Canadian Nickel Industry.* Toronto: University of Toronto Press, 1955.

Martell, J.S. "Early Coal Mining in Nova Scotia." *Dalhousie Review* 25, no. 2 (1945): 156–172.

Martin, G.L. *Gesener's Dream: The Trials and Triumphs of Early Mining in New Brunswick.* Fredericton, NB: Canadian Institute of Mining, Metallurgy and Petroleum-New Brunswick Branch, 2003.

Martin, John R. *The Fluorspar Mines of Newfoundland: Their History and the Epidemic of Radiation Lung Cancer.* Montreal: McGill-Queen's University Press, 2012.

Martin, Susan R. *Wonderful Power: The Story of Ancient Copper Working in the Lake Superior Basin.* Detroit: Wayne State University Press, 1999.

Martin, Wendy. *Once Upon a Mine: The Story of Pre-Confederation Mines on the Island of Newfoundland.* Canadian Institute of Mining and Metallurgy special vol. 26, 1983. Available via http://www.heritage.nf.ca/articles/environment/once-upon-a-mine.pdf.

McAllister, Mary Louise and Cynthia Jacqueline Alexander. *A Stake in the Future: Redefining the Canadian Mineral Industry.* Vancouver: UBC Press, 1997.

McCord Museum. *Lethbridge: Coal City in the Wheat Country.* www.mccord-museum.qc.ca/scripts/projects/CH/animCH.php

McDonald, Kenneth. *Port Morien: Pages from the Past.* Sydney: University College of Cape Breton Press, 1995.

McDowell, Laurel Sefton. "The Elliot Lake Uranium Miners' Battle to Gain Occupational Health and Safety Improvements, 1950-1980." *Labour/Le Travail* 69 (Spring 2012): 91–118.

McGhee, Robert. *Arctic Voyages of Martin Frobisher: An Elizabethan Adventure.* Vol. 28 of McGill-Queen's Native and Northern Series, edited by Sarah Carter and Arthur J. Ray. Montreal: McGill-Queen's University Press, 2001.

———. *Copper Eskimo Prehistory.* Ottawa: National Museum of Man, 1972.

———. *The Last Imaginary Place: A Human History of the Arctic World.* New York: Oxford University Press, 2005.

McKay, Ian. "The Realm of Uncertainty: The Experience of Work in the Cumberland Coal Mines, 1873–1927." *Acadiensis* 16, no. 1 (1986): 3–57.

———. "Industry, Work, and Community in the Cumberland Coalfields, 1848–1927." PhD Dissertation, Dalhousie University, 1983.

McKenna, Cara, "Red Chris Mine Failure would Eclipse Mount Polley Damage: Report." CBC News, November 19, 2014. www.cbc.ca/news/canada/british-columbia/red-chris-mine-failure-would-eclipse-mount-polley-damage-report-1.2841126.

McMahon, Gary, et al. *Large Mines and the Community: Socioeconomic and Environmental Effects in Latin America, Canada, and Spain.* Washington, DC: World Bank, 2001, www.idrc.ca/en/book/large-mines-and-community-socioeconomic-and-environmental-effects-latin-america-canada-and.

McNish, Jacquie. *The Big Score: Robert Friedland, Inco, and the Voisey's Bay Hustle.* Toronto: Doubleday Canada, 1998.

McPherson, Robert. *New Owners in Their Own Land: Minerals and Inuit Land Claims.* Calgary: University of Calgary Press, 2003.

Mesec, Dan. "On the Scene at Blockade of Mount Polley's Sister Mine Red Chris." *The Tyee*, August 11, 2014. http://thetyee.ca/News/2014/08/11/First-Nations-Blockade-Red-Chris.

Midgely, Scott. "Contesting Closure: Science, Politics, and Community Responses to Closing Nanisivik Mine, Nunavut." In *Mining and Communities in Northern Canada: History, Politics, and Memory*, eds. John Sandlos and Arn Keeling. Calgary: University of Calgary Press, 2015, 293–314.

Millward, Hugh. "The Development, Decline, and Revival of Mining on the Sydney Coalfield." *The Canadian Geographer* 28, no. 2 (1984): 180–85.

Mining Association of Canada (MAC). *Facts and Figures of the Canadian Mining Industry, 2015.* http://mining.ca/sites/default/files/documents/Facts-and-Figures-2015.pdf.

Mochoruk, Jim. *Formidable Heritage: Manitoba's North and the Cost of Development, 1870 to 1930.* Winnipeg: University of Manitoba Press, 2004.

Moodie, Susanna. "The First Mine in Ontario." *Canada's History* 92, no. 2 (April/May 2012): 12.

Morrison, David A. "Thule and Historic Copper Use in the Copper Inuit Area." *American Antiquity* 52, no. 1 (1987): 3–12.

Morrison, H. and Paul Villeneuve. *Radon-Progeny Exposure and Lung Cancer: A Mortality Study of Newfoundland Fluorspar Miners, 1950–2001.* Ottawa: Epistream Consulting, 2005.

Morrison, H., R. Semenciw, Y. Mao, and D. Wigle. "Cancer Mortality among a Group of Fluorspar Miners Exposed to Radon Progeny." *American Journal of Epidemiology* 128 (1988): 1266–1275.

Morse, Kathryn. *The Nature of Gold: An Environmental History of the Klondike Gold Rush.* Seattle: University of Washington Press, 2003.

Mouat, Jeremy. "The Genesis of Western Exceptionalism: British Columbia's Hard Rock Miners, 1895–1903." *Canadian Historical Review* 71, no. 3 (1990): 317–345.

Mouat, Jeremy. *Roaring Days: Rossland's Mines and the History of British Columbia.* Vancouver: UBC Press, 2011.

Muise, D.A. "Coal Mining in Nova Scotia to 1925," in *Canada's Visual History.* Ottawa: National Film Board of Canada and Canadian Museum of Civilization, 1994.

Muise, Delphin A. and Robert G. McIntosh. "Coal Mining in Canada: A Historical and Comparative Overview." National Museum of Science and Technology, 1996.

Munro, A. (1913). An Era of Progression: The Draining of Cobalt Lake and its Effect on the Town. CIHM/ICMH microfiche series no. 81099. North Bay, ON: Daily Nugget Press.

Nelles, Henry Vivian. *Politics of Development: Forests, Mines, and Hydro-Electric Power in Ontario, 1849–1941.* Carleton Library Series vol. 200. Montreal: McGill-Queen's University Press, 2005.

Neufeld, David. "Dredging the Goldfields: Corporate gold mining in the Yukon Territory." *Journal of the West* 43:1 (Winter 2004): 30–38.

Newell, Dianne. *Technology on the Frontier: Mining in Old Ontario.* Vancouver: UBC Press, 1986.

Newsome, Eric. *The Coal Coast: The History of Coal Mining in BC, 1835–1900.* Victoria: Orca Book Publishers, 1989.

"The Nickel Question." *The Canadian Mining Review* 18, no. 5 (May 1899), 130–31.

Noble, B.F. and J.E. Bronson. "Integrating Human Health into Environmental Impact Assessment: Case Studies of Canada's Northern Mining Resource Sector." *Arctic* 58, no. 4 (2005): 395–405.

Noble, Bram and Keith Storey. "Towards Increasing the Utility of Follow-Up in Canadian EIA." Environmental Impact Assessment Review 25, no. 2 (2005): 163–80, doi:10.1016/j.eiar.2004.06.009.

Nolin, Catherine and Jaqui Stephens. "'We Have to Protect the Investors': Development and Canadian Mining Companies in Guatemala." *Journal of Rural and Community Development* 5, no. 3 (2010): 37–70, journals.brandonu.ca/jrcd/article/view/279/71.

Norrie, Kenneth, Doug Owram, and John Emery. *A History of the Canadian Economy.* Scarborough, ON: Nelson, 2002.

Nova Scotia Archives. *Men in the Mines: A History of Mining Activity in Nova Scotia, 1720–1992.* https://novascotia.ca/archives/meninmines/default.asp.

Nunavummiut Makitagunarningit. Website and blog, https://makitanunavut.wordpress.com.

O'Faircheallaigh, Ciaran. *Negotiations in the Indigenous World: Aboriginal Peoples and the Extractive Industry in Australia and Canada.* New York: Routledge, 2016.

Office of the Auditor General of Canada. Decommissioning of the Cluff Lake Uranium Mine in Saskatchewan, Petition No. 120. June 25, 2004. www.oag-bvg.gc.ca/internet/English/pet_120_e_28843.html.

Ontario Ministry of Northern Development and Mines. *Harvest From the Rock: A History of Mining in Ontario.* Toronto: Macmillan, 1986.

Pearkes, Eileen Delehanty. *The Geography of Memory: Recovering Stories of a Landscape's First People.* Nelson, BC: Kutenai House Press, 2002.

Penrose, Beris. "'So Now They Have Some Human Guinea Pigs': Aluminium Therapy and Occupational Silicosis." *Health and History* 9, No. 1 (2007), 56–79.

Percival, J.B., C.G. Dumaresq, Y.T.J. Kwong, K.B. Hendry, and F.A. Michel. "Arsenic in Surface Waters, Cobalt, Ontario." Current Research 100, Geological Survey of Canada (1996): 137–146.

Phillips, Alan "Our Wild Atomic City," originally published in *Maclean's*, May 25, 1957. www.metalsnews.com/Metals+News/RoM/Republic+of+Mining/BLOG230855/Elliot+Lake+Uranium+Mining+History++Our+Wild+Atomic+City++by+Alan+Phillips+ (Originally+Published+in+Macleans+Mag.htm (last accessed June 15, 2016).

Pompeani, David P., Mark B. Abbott, Byron A. Steinman, and Daniel J. Bain. "Lake Sediments Record Prehistoric Lead Pollution Related to Early Copper Production in North America." *Environmental Science and Technology* 47, no. 11 (2013): 5545–52.

Pompeani, David P, Mark B. Abbott, Daniel J. Bain, and Matthew S. Finkenbinder. "Copper Mining on Isle Royale 6500–5400 Years Ago Identified Using Sediment Geochemistry from McCargoe Cove, Lake Superior." *The Holocene* 25, no. 2 (2015): 253–62.

Porsild, Charlene. *Gamblers and Dreamers: Women, Men, and Community in the Klondike.* Vancouver: UBC Press, 1998.

Pratt, Kenneth L. "Copper, Trade, and Tradition among the Lower Ahtna of the Chitina River Basin: The Nicolai Era, 1884–1900." *Arctic Anthropology* 35, no. 2 (1998): 77–98.

Prebble, Peter and Ann Coxworth. "The Government of Canada's Legacy of Contamination in Northern Saskatchewan Watersheds." Saskatchewan Notes. Centre for Policy Alternatives (July 2013). http://environmentalsociety.ca/wp-content/uploads/2014/08/Beaverlodge-Legacy-of-Contamination.pdf (accessed September 28, 2016).

Prins, Megan Katherine. "Seasons of Gold: An Environmental History of the Cariboo Gold Rush." MA Thesis, Simon Fraser University, 2007.

Proctor, Jason. "De Beers Puts Shuttered Snap Lake Diamond Mine up for Sale." CBC News, July 22, 2016. www.cbc.ca/news/canada/north/de-beers-snap-lake-sale-1.3691716.

———. "Environmentalists Win Defamation Court Battle with Taseko Mines." CBC News, January 27, 2016. www.cbc.ca/news/canada/british-columbia/environmentalists-win-defamation-court-battle-with-taseko-mines-1.3422475.

Rennie, Richard. "The Copper Mining Communities of Notre Dame Bay, 1845–1945: A Case Study in Industrialization, Sustainability and the Political Economy of Resource Development." Paper presented in Department of History Seminar Series, Memorial University. Memorial University Library.

———. *The Dirt: Industrial Disease and Conflict at St. Lawrence, Newfoundland.* Black Point, NS: Fernwood, 2008.

Rhatigan, James. "Mining Meaning: Telling Spatial Histories of the Britannia Mine." *Journal of Historical Geography* 67, no 1 (2020): 36–47.

Rodon, Thierry, and Francis Lévesque. "Understanding the Social and Economic Impacts of Mining Development in Inuit Communities: Experiences with Past and Present Mines in Inuit Nunangat." *Northern Review* 41 (2015): 1–27.

Roy, Patricia E., and John Herd Thompson. *British Columbia: Land of Promises.* Don Mills, ON: Oxford University Press, 2005.

Russell, Edmund. *War and Nature: Fighting Humans and Insects with Chemicals from World War I to Silent Spring.* Cambridge: Cambridge University Press, 2001.

Saarinen, Oiva W. *Between a Rock and a Hard Place: A Historical Geography of the Finns in the Sudbury Area.* Waterloo, ON: Wilfrid Laurier University Press, 1999.

———. *From Meteorite Impact to Constellation City: A Historical Geography of Greater Sudbury.* Waterloo, ON: Wilfrid Laurier University Press, 2013.

Samson, Daniel. "Industrial Colonization: The Colonial Context of the General Mining Association, Nova Scotia, 1825–1842," *Acadiensis* 24,1 (Autumn 1999): 3–28.

Sandlos, John "A Mix of the Good and the Bad: Community Memory and the Pine Point Mine." In Arn Keeling and John Sandlos, eds. *Mining and Communities in Northern Canada: History, Politics and Memory.* Calgary: University of Calgary Press, 2015, 137–65.

Sandlos, John, and Arn Keeling. "Claiming the New North: Development and Colonialism at the Pine Point Mine, Northwest Territories, Canada." *Environment and History* 18, no.1 (2012): 5–34.

Sandlos, John, and Arn Keeling. "Toxic Legacies, Slow Violence, and Environmental Injustice at Giant Mine, Northwest Territories." *Northern Review* 42 (2016): 7–21.

Saskatoon StarPhoenix. "Mining Companies, Northern Communities Renew Uranium Development Partnership." June 22, 2016. http://thestarphoenix.com/business/mining/mining-companies-northern-communities-renew-uranium-development-partnership.

Scobie, Willow and Kathleen Rodgers. "Contestations of Resource Extraction Projects via Digital Media in Two Nunavut Communities." *Études/Inuit/Studies* 37, no. 2 (2013): 83–101, doi:10.7202/1025711ar.

Selleck, Lee and Francis Thompson. *Dying for Gold: The True Story of the Giant Mine Murders*. Toronto: HarperCollins, 1997.

Smith, Philip. *Harvest from the Rock: A History of Mining in Ontario*. Toronto: Macmillan, 1986.

Statistics Canada, Historical Statistics of Canada, Section P: Mining. www.statcan.gc.ca/pub/11-516-x/pdf/5220017-eng.pdf.

Statistics Canada, Historical Statistics of Canada, Section Q: Energy and Electric Power. www.statcan.gc.ca/pub/11-516-x/pdf/5220018-eng.pdf.

Streisel, Luke "The Miners Strike Out: The Lethbridge Coal Miners' Strike of 1906." *Alberta History* 54, no. 4 (2004): 2–7.

Studnicki-Gizbert, Daviken. "Canadian Mining in Latin America (1990 to Present): A Provisional History." *Canadian Journal of Latin American and Caribbean Studies* 41, no. 1 (2016): 95–113, doi:10.1080/08263663.2015.1134498.

Stueck, Wendy and Justine Hunter. "Taseko Brushes Off Ottawa's Rejection of BC Gold-Mine Proposal." *The Globe and Mail*, February 27, 2014. www.theglobeandmail.com/news/british-columbia/despite-rejection-taseko-promises-to-pursue-new-prosperity-mine-project/article17141295.

Sudbury Area Risk Assessment Group. Sudbury Area Risk Assessment. www.sudburysoilsstudy.com/EN/indexE.htm.

Surtees, Robert J. *Treaty Research Report: The Robinson Treaties (1850)*. Treaties and Historical Research Centre, Indian and Northern Affairs Canada, 1986.

Swift, Jamie. *The Big Nickel: Inco at Home and Abroad*. Toronto: Between the Lines, 1977.

Tataryn, Lloyd. *Dying for a Living*. Ottawa: Deneau and Greenberg, 1979.

Taylor, G.W. *The History of Mining in British Columbia*. Saanichton, BC: Hancock House, 1978.

Tester, Frank James, Drummond E.J. Lambert, and Tee Wirn Lim. "Wistful Thinking: Making Inuit Labour and the Nanisivik Mine near Ikpiarjuk (Arctic Bay), Northern Baffin Island." *Études/Inuit/Studies* 37, no. 2 (2013): 15–36.

Thistle, John, and Nancy Langston. "Entangled Histories: Iron Ore Mining in Canada and the United States." *The Extractive Industries and Society* 3, no. 2 (2016): 269–277.

Thistle, John. "Forging Full Value? Iron Ore Mining in Newfoundland and Labrador, 1954–2014." *The Extractive Industries and Society* 3, no. 1 (2016): 103–116.

Toledano, Michael. "Dene People in Northern Saskatchewan Are Resisting Uranium and Tar Sands Mining." *Vice*, February 11, 2015. www.vice.com/en_ca/read/a-dene-alliance-formed-to-resist-uranium-and-tar-sands-mining-in-saskatchewan-892.

Tough, Frank. *As Their Natural Resources Fail: Native Peoples and the Economic History of Northern Manitoba, 1870–1930*. Vancouver: UBC Press, 1997.

Trudeau, Pierre, ed. *The Asbestos Strike*. Trans. James Boake. Toronto: James Lewis and Samuel, 1970.

Tucker, Albert. *Steam into Wilderness: Ontario Northland Railway, 1902–1962*. Toronto: Fitzhenry & Whiteside, 1978.

United Nations. Reports of International Arbitral Awards: Trail Smelter Case (Canada and United States), vol. 3 (April 16, 1938 and March 11, 1941): 1905–1982. http://legal.un.org/riaa/cases/vol_III/1905-1982.pdf

University of British Columbia Allard Law School. Case Study Files. "Windy Craggy," www.allard.ubc.ca/sites/www.allard.ubc.ca/files/uploads/enlaw/pdfs/windycraggy_05_15_09.pdf.

Urangesellschaft. Press Release, July 4, 1990. https://makitanunavut.files.wordpress.com/2012/04/18.pdf.

Van Horssen, Jessica. *A Town Called Asbestos: Environmental Contamination, Health, and Resilience in a Resource Community*. Vancouver: UBC Press, 2016.

Van Wyck, Peter. *Highway of the Atom*. Montreal: McGill-Queen's University Press, 2010.

Villeneuve, Paul J., Howard I. Morrison, and Rachel Lane. "Radon and Lung Cancer Risk: An Extension of the Mortality Follow-up of the Newfoundland Fluorspar Cohort." *Health Physics* 92, no. 2 (2007): 157–169.

Wallace, Carl Murray. *Sudbury: Rail town to Regional Capital*. Toronto: Dundurn, 1996.

Warnock, John W. *Exploiting Saskatchewan's Potash: Who Benefits*. Regina: Canadian Centre for Policy Alternatives, Saskatchewan Office, 2011. https://www.policyalternatives.ca/sites/default/files/uploads/publications/Saskatchewan%20Office/2011/01/Exploiting%20SK%20Potash%2001-25-11.pdf.

Wayman, M.L., R.R. Smith, C.G. Hickey, and M.J.M. Duke. "The Analysis of Copper Artifacts of the Copper Inuit." *Journal of Archaeological Science* 12 (1985): 367–75.

Westray Mine Public Inquiry (N.S.) and K. Peter Richard. *The Westray Story: A Predictable Path to Disaster*. Report of the Westray Mine Public Inquiry, 1997.

Weyler, Rex. "Back from Extinction: BC's Forgotten Sinixt Nation Reoccupies its Homeland. A Tale of Tenacity and Joyous Rebirth." *The Tyee*, June 30, 2008. http://thetyee.ca/News/2008/06/30/BackFromExtinction.

White, Daryl. "The Great Nickel Scandal." *Canada's History* 93, no. 6 (December 2013/January 2014): 40–45.

Whittlesey, Charles. *Ancient Mining on the Shores of Lake Superior*. Vol. 155 of Smithsonian Contributions to Knowledge. Washington, D.C.: Smithsonian Institution, 1863.

Wightman, Nancy M. and W. Robert. "The Mica Bay Affair: Conflict on the Upper-Lakes Mining Frontier." *Ontario History* 83, no. 3 (1991): 193–208.

Wiles, Anne, et al. "Use of Traditional Ecological Knowledge in Environmental Assessment of Uranium Mining in the Athabasca Saskatchewan." Impact Assessment and Project Appraisal 18, no. 2 (1999): 107–14, doi:10.3152/147154699781767864.

Winton, Alexandra and Joella Hogan. "'It's Just Natural': First Nation Family History and the Keno Hill Silver Mine." In Arn Keeling and John Sandlos, eds. *Mining and Communities in Northern Canada: History, Politics and Memory*. Calgary: University of Calgary Press, 89–118.

Wirth, John D. *Smelter Smoke in North America: The Politics of Transborder Pollution*. Lawrence: University Press of Kansas, 2000.

Woywitka, A.B. "The Drumheller Strike of 1919." *Alberta Historical Review* 27, no. 3 (1973): 1–7.

Wright, Richard. *Barkerville and the Cariboo Goldfields*. Vancouver: Heritage House Publishing, 2013.

Wynn, Graeme. *Canada and Arctic North America: An Environmental History*. Santa Barbara: ABC-Clio, 2007.

Yellowknives Dene. Yellowknives Dene: Impact of the Giant Mine on the Yellowknives Dene. Dettah: Yellowknives Dene First Nation Council, 2015. http://www.mvlwb.ca/Boards/mv/Registry/2007/MV2007L8-0031/remediationplan/GiantSupportingDocs/SD_A_Environmental%20Conditions/SD%20A1_Giant%20Mine%20TK%20Report%20YKDFN.pdf.

Zahalan, R.G. Mining in Manitoba. Educational Series ES80-3. Winnipeg: Department of Energy and Mines, 1980.

Zaslow, Morris. *Reading the Rocks: The Story of the Geological Survey of Canada, 1842–1872*. Toronto: Macmillan, 1975.

Zeller, Suzanne. *Inventing Canada: Early Victorian Science and the Idea of a Transcontinental Nation*. Toronto: University of Toronto Press, 1987.

ACKNOWLEDGEMENTS

In addition to our own studies of mining communities across Northern Canada, this work builds on the considerable scholarship and writing of a great many students of mining history before us, many of whose works are noted in the references. We particularly note the substantial work of Jeremy Mouat, the dean of Canadian mining history, whose mining bibliography and published work is the first stop for anyone seeking to understand the industry's past. We have also drawn extensively on the many excellent case studies of mines and communities by graduate students at universities across the country — especially our own, where students under our supervision have completed a number of excellent theses on places from Buchans, Newfoundland, to Keno Hill, Yukon. The rotating membership of our "Northern Mining Research Group" at Memorial University provided feedback on a couple of chapters and many insightful discussions of mining-related questions. Finally, our work draws on a large number of local community history books, articles, and web pages, the vast range of which testify to the enduring popular appeal of mining history and the enthusiasm of local historians, curators, and archivists.

We are grateful for the generous funding received from the Social Sciences and Humanities Research Council (SSHRC) and ArcticNet that has sustained fourteen years (and counting) of research on mining history in northern Canada. We are also appreciative of the research assistance support we received through the Memorial Undergraduate Career Enhancement Program (MUCEP).

This book was itself several years in the making and featured a considerable supporting cast. Our early efforts to identify and prepare a database of images was supported by the able research assistance of Jeanette Carney, Howard Butler, Kayla Hollett, Sarah Stirling and Miranda Burrage-Goodwin. At Lorimer, we worked closely with a series of able (and patient) editorial assistants and editors, including most recently Robin Studniberg, Laura Cook, Sara D'Agostino, Ashley Bernicky, David Gray-Donald and Cecilia Stuart. James Lorimer, who first approached us about writing a history of mining in Canada, provided guidance and supportive feedback, especially at the project's early stages.

VISUAL CREDITS

Alan Sorum: page 200

Alberta Culture and Tourism: page 119 (top)

Arn Keeling: page 133 (top)

Avataq Cultural Institute, photo by Pierre M. Desrosiers: page 13

BC Archives: page 57 (A-03178), 61 (D-06815), 64 (I-55094), 107 (bottom, B-05286), 110 (D-08521), 118 (top, E-01194), 119 (bottom right, F-05339)

Bibliothèque nationale: page 101, 102, 103 (all), 104, 105 (all)

British Museum: page 29 (top)

Canadian Museum of History: page 28 (top, S99-5425; bottom, S99-5424), 29 (bottom, S2002-8329)

Canship, photo by Tim Keane: page 189

City of Victoria Archives: page 58 (top right, 197911-01)

Coal in Our Blood: 200 Years of Mining in Nova Scotia's Pictou County: page 179, 180, 181

Columbia Basin Institute of Regional History (CBIRH) and Kimberley District Heritage Society: page 109

Cumberland Museum: page 41

Dangerous Women Project: page 100

Estate of A.Y. Jackson/SOCAN: page 127

Flickr: page 31 (Graeme Churchard), 44 (Dennis Jarvis), 58 (bottom left, Walt Stoneburner), 59 (top left, Jonathan Miske; top right and bottom, Reed Probus), 65 (all, Mike), 75 (bottom right, Adam Jones), 85 (Jason Woodhead), 86 (all, Jason Woodhead), 112–113 (Murray Foubister), 157 (Susan Drury), 164 (bottom right, Tim Beckett), 193, 194 (Jeremy Board), 201 (bottom, Glen Belbeck), 203 (left, The Tedster), 205 (Tim Beckett)

Fortunes in the Ground: Cobalt, Porcupine & Kirkland Lake: page 80, 83 (right), 84, 92 (all), 93 (bottom), 94, 95, 96 (right), 97, 98, 99 (top left, bottom right)

Glenbow Museum: page 20 (bottom right), 27

The Hillcrest Mining Disaster: page 117 (all)

The History of Mining in British Columbia: page 63

iStock: page 6–7, 91 (all), 106–107, 207

Jason Pineau: page 185

John Sandlos: page 208

Library and Archives Canada: page 23 (PA-099933), 24 (left, R999-94-3-E; right, C-086091), 25 (top, PA-101252; bottom, C-070250), 33 (C-004356), 36 (PA-016944), 38 (1958-037, C-003062), 39 (left, 2266910; right, C-005142), 42 (PA-029182), 45 (PA-02918), 48 (1991-31-2), 51 (PA-137858), 56, 67 (PA-022511), 70 (top, PA-022512), 71 (C-004490), 72 (PA-013413), 73 (C-005389), 79 (PA-015636), 81 (PA-015279), 86 (PA-037575), 87 (PA-014179), 96 (left, PA-017605), 125 (2264976), 128 (C-023983), 134 (PA-205815), 137 (left, WRM 4712; right, PA-196740), 138 (left, PA-196741; right, PA-196749), 139 (top left, PA-196742; bottom right, PA-128762), 146 (top right, 4314201), 154 (1987-078), 155 (1987-078), 162 (4086000), 163 (right, 4948461)

McCord Museum: page 49

Memorial University of Newfoundland Digital Archives: page 141, 142, 143

National Resources Canada: page 12, 168, 169

Northern BC Archives and Special Collections: page 196

Northwest Territories Archives: page 9 (N-1987-021: 0008), 129 (N-1979-052-4877), 131 (N-2002-002-0551), 133 (bottom, N-1987-021: 0006), 146 (top right, N-1999-015: 0034), 146 (bottom left, N-1979-052-2723), 147 (N-2001-014: 0288), 148 (right, N-1988-035-0030), 149 (N-1979-052), 150 (N-1979-052-7798), 153 (G-1979-023: 0017), 156 (C&C/G-1989-007), 171 (G-1995-001: 0533), 173 (top left, G-1995-001: 1514; bottom right, G-1995-001: 2845), 174 (G-1995-001: 1490), 187 (G-1995-001: 8606)

Nova Scotia Archives: page 37 (B41 1895), 40 (N-862), 43 (N-5195), 46 (1997-233 no. 8), 47, 135 (1305-26), 136 (13.14)

Nunavut Archives: page 152 (N-1979-051: 2316S)

Ontario Archives: page 78 (F 1335-1-0-1-29),

87 (RG 2-71, VM-24), 90 (RG 2-71, CNC-19), 93 (top, C 7-3, 682), 99 (top right, C 320-1-0-8-5)

Provincial Archives of Alberta: page 116 (all)

Provincial Archives of Saskatchewan: page 161 (top left), 163 (left), 164 (top left)

Royal BC Museum and Archives: page 60, 111 (I-28329), 118 (bottom, E-02631), 170 (I-15096)

Shingwauk Residential Schools Centre, Algoma University: page 53

Shutterstock: page 4, 123 (bottom), 198, 203 (right), 210, 212

Thunder Bay Museum: page 52, 54

Toronto Reference Library: page 130, 164 (*Toronto Star* Photo Archive, TS-2-125-GO-048), 166

Trek Ohio: page 20 (top left)

University of Michigan Museum of Anthropological Archaeology: page 13 (right), 16 (top), 18, 19, 21 (all)

University of Saskatchewan Archives: page 159, 161 (bottom right)

University of Washington Libraries: page 67, 68 (top), 69, 70 (bottom), 74–75 (top)

Vancouver Archives: page 82–82 (top), 114–115 (top and bottom)

Ville de Val-d'Or: page 201 (top)

Wikimedia: page 13 (left, Gordon E. Robertson), 22 (Joe Mabel), 26 (Gordon E. Robertson), 34 (Fralambert), 74–75 (bottom, gillfoto), 76 (Diego Delso), 77 (Diego Delso), 176–77 (Turgan), 182 (Planet Labs)

Wisconsin Historical Society: page 16 (bottom)

Yellowknife Historical Society: page 126, 148 (left)

Yukon Archives: page 68 (bottom), 121, 122, 123 (top)

INDEX